Land of the Hart

Land of the Hart ISRAELIS, ARABS,

THE TERRITORIES, AND

A VISION OF THE FUTURE

Arie Lova Eliav

Translated from the Hebrew by Judith Yalon

The Jewish Publication Society of America

Philadelphia

Said Rabbi Judah in the name of Rabbi Assi: "Sixty times ten thousand townships had King Jannai on Har Hamelekh, and [the inhabitants] in each of them were as they who came out of Egypt." . . . Said Ulla: "I have seen that place and it cannot contain even sixty times ten thousand reeds." Said a Zadoki to Rabbi Hanina: "You lie!" Said Rabbi Hanina: "It is called 'Land of the Hart': just as the skin of the hart cannot hold its flesh, so the Land of Israel when it is inhabited can provide space for everyone, but when it is not inhabited it contracts."
—Gittin 57a

CONTENTS

Land of the Hart

AUTHOR'S NOTE

This book first appeared in Hebrew in 1972. It has been updated for this English edition and in light of the Yom Kippur War.

A. L. E.

PROLOGUE

In the years immediately preceding the Yom Kippur War, we in Israel were in the throes of a process in which crass pragmatism stifled ideology and momentary joys were preferred to permanent values. Pragmatism itself became an ideology. We reasoned as follows. The world is in a state of confusion; sometimes it appears to be quite lunatic. The struggle between us and the Arabs seems interminable, and our domestic problems appear incapable of being resolved.

As a result, we adopted a "saving" pragmatism that urged us to live from hand to mouth, to eat and drink, and to let the future take care of the future.

This pragmatism continues to exist even today, after the Yom Kippur War. And it is leading Israel to an extreme materialism that is coming to dominate our lives.

Zionism—the liberation and renaissance movement of the Jewish people—was the negation not only of the Jewish fatalism which put its faith in a messianic era and in miracles, but also of the materialism of the Diaspora. The first Zionist visionaries set themselves long-term goals in the light of their assessment of contemporary Jewry. They knew that those goals would be reached only through self-denial and self-sacrifice.

Zionism has fully achieved only one of its goals: the founding of the State of Israel. But the founding of the state was to have been only a means toward the fulfillment of the higher purposes that Zionism set itself: the gathering of the majority of the Jewish people in the Land of Israel and the creation of a new Jewish society based on justice, equality, and human freedom.

Two of these goals have yet to be achieved. With great effort there has gathered in Israel only about one-fifth of the Jewish people. And our society is still far from being a just one.

In the process of creating the Jewish state, and as a result of the blood feud with the Arabs into which it stumbled, Zionism set itself a third goal: peace with the Arabs. But this too eludes our grasp.

Despair over the struggle for these goals is bringing Israel to ideological, political, and social darkness. Relinquishing one of these goals, or preferring one to another, distorts the face of Zionism. Merely to assemble the Jewish people in Israel without indicating how a distinctive and just society is to arise there, or to postpone the hour of peace with the Arabs to some distant future, is to give the lie to Zionist doctrine, either knowingly or unknowingly.

It is for us a matter of life and death to learn how we might best achieve these combined goals, even if in the reality of our lives they seem often to be mutually contradictory. In laying down a scale of priorities for the achievement of these goals, we must make peace with the Arabs our chief concern. Peace must not exclude the other goals. It can be accomplished together with them, and must not be separated from them.

Peace with the Arabs is indeed a goal of first importance. But at the same time it should be emphasized that the preservation of our existence and the concern for our national security which guide our deliberations in matters pertaining to our lives and future must guide us in deciding on the best ways to achieve it.

If we were an island in a tranquil ocean, then a discussion of our future would not have the ominous dimensions it has today. But that is not our reality. If we should for any reason lose hold of our instinct for self-preservation, then we are liable to be consumed in the fire of Arab hatred.

All through the years of our independence as a nation, what has enabled us to dream of peace with the Arabs, and to work for it, has been our strength. This strength deters the Arabs from perpetrating their designs upon us. The wishes of their more extreme leaders have always been perfectly clear: were it in their power they would wipe us off the face of the earth. Our deterrent strength is not only physical. It is nourished by faith in the justice of our enterprise; it rests on a sound economic and social base and on our achievements in science and technology; but it consists chiefly in the strength of the Israeli armed forces. Any crack in that rampart will seem to the Arabs to be a weakness, and will tempt them to try once more to breach it.

If we deny the great aims of Zionism, if the flow of immigration is reduced, if our ties with the Jewish people are weakened, if our economy should collapse, if severe rifts should cut through our society, if chasms of ethnic, religious, or class differences should yawn, if there should occur a real or apparent weakening of the strength of our armed forces—if any significant combination of these events should occur, then the Arabs will once again try their luck in a war of vengeance. Only a socially, economically, and militarily strong Israel can afford to seek paths to peace, unconventional paths, which will take into account the situation of the Arabs in general and of the Palestinian Arabs in particular, which will indeed mean compromise with the Arabs, but not at the expense of our existence.

Both we and the Arabs have stumbled into a trap of fears, dreads, and psychological complexes. The Arabs, who have yet to be reconciled to the fact of our existence, live in fear of "Israel's limitless expansionism," on the one hand, and the "crusader theory" regarding their numerical superiority (a hundred million versus three million!) on the other. We for our part live in dread of holocaust, the horror of the "destruction of the

Third Temple," and with an inferiority complex regarding our size. We live—and who can blame us after two thousand years of exile—enslaved by an "all the world is against us" complex.

Only yesterday our people were murdered by the Nazis, who regarded the crematoriums of Auschwitz as the "final solution," while the Christian world raised not a finger to rescue us; only yesterday we fought a bloody war with British soldiers for the right of our remnants to reach safety in the Land of Israel; only yesterday hundreds of millions of Christians believed that we crucified their Messiah. Can all that be forgotten?

What object lesson shall we learn from the world in which we live—the world of Biafra, Vietnam, Bangladesh, Ireland, the world in which one people catches another by the throat, the world of the impotent United Nations—unless it be that if we love life we must rely on our own strength.

Complex for complex, dread for dread—this, then, is our web of relations with the Arab world. Neither we nor the Arabs will be able, all at once, to overcome this dread and liberate ourselves from our mutual complexes and suspicions. For the foreseeable future, then, there is hardly a chance of either side disarming.

In this situation both we and the Arabs—if we both want to live and not shed the last drop of one another's blood—must very carefully, step by step, like sappers in a minefield, begin to defuse the complexes, the suspicion and the dread. In one of our wars I was a sapper. I taught our soldiers how to dismantle mines and bombs. I hope in this book to do a sapper's work in the fields of our life.

Our prophets, seeking to describe the Land of Israel, chose the hart as a symbol of the beauty and glory of the land. In subsequent Jewish thought this image took on a unique significance, in which the good and perfect qualities of the land were likened to the special qualities of that lovely and noble animal. Can we, in the closing decades of the twentieth century, after a hundred years of the return to Zion and twenty-five years of the existence of the State of Israel—can we so hope and act that our land will indeed be a Land of the Hart?

We are treading a narrow and tortuous path up a mountainside. Abysses yawn all around. Does our path lead to a land of life, and will our country be a "hart to all the lands"?

This book will attempt to deal with these questions.

Arie Lova Eliav

1

THE JEWS AND THE
LAND OF ISRAEL

BEGINNINGS

As sons of the Jewish people and of our homeland—the State of Israel—we often ask ourselves: What is the meaning of our existence, from where have we come, where do we find ourselves today, and where are we going? Our reply must be first of all to ourselves, and then to the world around us.

We have always been a peculiar people. The seal of the "people that dwelleth alone" is one we bear by the nature of our being. In fact, at the beginning of our journey, from the times of the forefathers until we became a people, we were to outward appearances not essentially different from the many tribes that, from the dawn of history, wandered in search of a land and a home. It was only when we settled the Land of Israel and established our kingdom that the difference, the distinctiveness, became conspicuous.

It was not our form of government that set us apart—many greater peoples than we had judges and kings. Nor was it any special style of architecture or art; on the contrary, we by no means distinguished ourselves in those fields, and there arose in the ancient world great cities that far surpassed the towns of Israel. And in size of population and territory Israel could certainly boast no superiority. Always, even in the ancient Middle East, we were a small state; even during the reigns of David and Solomon, at the height of Israel's greatness, we were a small people compared to contemporary empires.

For centuries, in a pagan world (parts of which attained heights of technological, scientific, philosophical, and artistic development far beyond our own) our sole asset was our faith in the one God. In all other areas of life we were distinguished neither for good nor for bad: tyranny, treachery, jealousy, hatred, relations between man and man, between family and family, tribe and tribe, between one class and another—in all these we resembled other nations. We loved our land; we fought over it and for it, but no more and no less than did other peoples who have vanished. We developed a language and culture which were not, at the time, of a higher or lower level than those of the peoples around us.

Our faith—the belief in one God, Creator of heaven and earth—distinguished us from the outset. Monotheism, which had its birth at the time of the patriarchs and flourished and reached its zenith in the era of the prophets, set us apart in the ancient world and made us exceptional, both as individuals and as a people for whom the zealous faith in the one God that our ancestors had tenaciously held had become a law of life. Consequently, we appeared foreign and strange, different and eccentric in the eyes of the other peoples of the ancient world.

When our Temple was destroyed and we were exiled from our land and scattered among the nations of the world, our uniqueness grew. We carried our God and our culture with us when we departed into exile. Our faith in one God and many other elements of our culture were bequeathed by us, through Christianity and Islam, to hundreds of millions of people throughout the world.

Moreover, as we went into exile there were added to our adherence to our faith and its basic precepts the oddity and the distinction of our desire to return once more to our land. Zionism was not born with Theodor Herzl, it was born with the exiles of Babylon. Many peoples have been exiled from their lands, and there is nothing more natural than that the first generation of exiles should pine for the homeland they have left behind. But this combination of a belief peculiar to ourselves and our longing and strong desire, which grew stronger with the passing generations, made the wandering Jew, as an individual and a people, something different, totally incomprehensible, and therefore hated and persecuted.

Always we have had to explain ourselves, our right to exist, as a scattered and divided people. We have had to explain, first of all to ourselves, father to son, master to pupils, and leaders of the exiled to their communities, that this right was purchased through the affliction, persecution, slaughter, suppression, and relentless hatred that fell to our lot. Hence the vital need for education to the faith and Jewish tradition, and the longings for the messianic era.

But we also had to explain our raison d'être and the meaning of our existence to the nations among whom we wandered and lived: who we were and what our faith was, why we did not assimilate among them, what "demon" so ceaselessly pursued us, what it was that bound us together in the various lands of the exile, and why we preserved our religion and its customs with such zeal.

Generations upon generations of life in exile passed by. On the foundations of its faith and the longing for Zion, which in the popular consciousness had been elevated to a Zion on High, the Jewish people created cultural and spiritual assets to guard independent Jewish existence, to erect around itself as many fences as possible, to fortify the Jew's spirit, his faith in God, and his longing for Zion. These cultural and religious values heightened the distinctiveness of the Jewish people and its pride in that distinctiveness.

The most characteristic Jewish trait during the thousands of years of exile was that of pride in uniqueness. Contrary to popular belief, Diaspora Jews were the proudest of men. To die for the sanctification of the Name, to suffer execution rather than transgress certain laws, to tread the long path of Jewish martyrdom when in many cases the way lay open to them to abandon Judaism—this demanded a great measure of Jewish and human pride.

As a result of the rise of modern nationalism in Europe, where the great majority of the Jewish people were centered, hatred of the Jews rose too. If for many generations the Jews had been hated because of their religious uniqueness, they were now faced with questions of "Sons of what nation are you?," "To what people are you loyal?," and "Do not your longings for Zion conflict with your loyalty to the people in whose midst you dwell?"

With the heightening of hatred and persecution in the nineteenth century, some Jews tried—as happened over the whole course of Jewish history—to escape from Judaism by assimilating with the peoples among whom they lived. Many others fled Europe to other parts of the world, while a few revived the Zionist idea that had always potentially existed. If we define Zionism as the aspiration to return to the Land of Israel, one may say that Judaism is monotheism plus Zionism, and that the whole history of the Jews in the Diaspora is the history of Zionism.

Modern Zionism advanced a simple slogan: the establishment of a safe refuge in the Land of Israel for every Jew who wishes or is forced to return there. Its leaders could no longer endure the sufferings of the people, and raised their voices in favor of the return of the Jews to their land. They regarded this as the sole solution to the anguish of the Jewish people.

To the question "Where did we come from?" we shall therefore reply that we came from here, from the Land of Israel, and that we are the direct descendants of our ancestors born in this land. Two thousand years is a very long time, but we are still able to make this reply with absolute clarity and pride, because for a hundred generations we have preserved our uniqueness as a people and our bonds with this land. We have not assimilated, we have not merged, and others have hardly been absorbed among us.

By way of retort to the vicious arguments of anti-Semitic propagandists, especially of the Soviet and Arab camps, that we are nothing but the shadow of a people, having nothing whatever to do with our ancestors in the Land of Israel, we may ask: How many contemporary peoples can say of themselves that they are the direct descendants of their forefathers of two thousand years ago? Can the English, for example, confidently claim that they are the children's children of the Britannic tribes that fought the Roman invaders, when so many peoples have become part of them since—Romans, Anglo-Saxons, Danes, Norwegians, Swedes, Normans, and French? Are the Belgians of today the descendants of the Belgae who fought Julius Caesar? Are they not a mixture of Flemings and Walloons, themselves an amalgam of other peoples? And the Iranians—are they the descendants of the sons of Cyrus, or a mixture of Persians, Kurds, Azerbaijanis, Turkish and Afghan peoples, and Arab tribes? And the Greeks—are they really the descendants of the ancient Hellenes? The same questions could be put to most of the peoples of the world, great and small, with no intent to detract from the value of any people or hold it up to contempt, but merely to underline that the Jews are the direct descendants of their forefathers in the Land of Israel, and that their genealogy was never severed, from the time of the destruction of the Temple to this very day.

We have, it is true, been exiled from our land and we have wandered over the entire face of the globe; we have lived in climates and landscapes as different from one another as the equator (reached in their wanderings by the Jews of India) is from the North Pole (near which, in Siberia and Canada, Jews also live). We have wandered and lived for thousands of years among peoples differing from each other—among Portuguese and Yemenites, among the pioneers of the United States and the Berbers of the Atlas Mountains, among the Scots and among the Kurds—and we have had to adapt to sun and light, to heat and cold. During the thousands of years of wandering the color of our skin has changed: in the ancient Land of Israel, as Egyptian colored reliefs bear witness, it was that of the almond, the barley, and the ripe wheat of our land. On returning to our country we brought with us pigments from all the countries of the Diaspora: the mahogany black of the Cochin Jews, the burnished copper of the Jews of Yemen, and the white skin of the Jews of Ashkenaz (Germany) and the north.

It is also true that during our thousands of years of exile we became fluent in many tongues, and even carved out for ourselves here and there a lingua franca from the languages of the peoples among whom we lived—Yiddish with its dozens of dialects; the Ladino of those originating in Spain; the peculiar Arab dialect of the Jews of Yemen; the Tati language of the Jews of Daghestan; the Targum of the Jews of Kurdistan; the Moroccan-Berber of the Jews of the Atlas.

We have indeed been influenced by cultures, customs, and ways of life of the many peoples among whom we have lived. But we are nonetheless the sons of a single people, offspring of the Jews of the ancient Land of Israel. And this people, which one hundred years ago began to return to its country, is the very same one that was exiled.

"DESTINED TO RETURN"

The *Yalkut Shimoni* states: "Just as this hart repairs to the world's end and returns to his place, so Israel, although scattered over the whole world, is destined to return."

Efraim Abrahamshvili (in Georgian, "the son of Abraham"), who recently returned to Israel from the Soviet Union, was born thirty years ago in Kutaisi, Georgia. He is a son of the Jewish community in Kutaisi, which has existed for a thousand years and more, and is a descendant of the Jews who arrived in Georgia in the days of Rostawili and Queen Tamara, from the mountains of Armenia, to which they came (in the reign of King Tigranes) from Babylon, where they had been exiled during the reign of King Zedekiah.

Berl Katznelson, who immigrated to this land about sixty years ago and founded a kibbutz on the banks of the Jordan River, was born in Bobruisk, Byelorussia. His ancestors lived for hundreds of years in little townlets in the Pale of Settlement in Russia and Poland, and their ancestors, offspring of priests of justice (*kohanei tzedek*—"katz") migrated in the Middle Ages to Poland from Ashkenaz, where they had lived for hundreds of years. Many of them were slaughtered by the crusaders, and a small number fled eastward. These *kohanei tzedek* went to the Rhineland, to Worms and Magenta, from Italy, having been banished to Rome with the exiles of Titus and Hadrian.

Dr. Joseph Cohen Maguri, justice of the peace at the Tel Aviv Magistrates' Court, was born in Cairo, to which his father had come from San'a in Yemen to buy up provisions, en route for the Land of Israel. The family came to Jerusalem on the eve of World War I. During the war it went into exile in Egypt, to return immediately afterwards.

Joseph attended the Tahkemoni School in Jerusalem and graduated in law at the University of Cannes, in France. His ancestors had lived in San'a for many generations. The *Remnants of Yemen*, a book by Abraham, son of the learned Rabbi Haim Alendaf, notes that one of Joseph's early ancestors, the Honorable Rabbi Pinhas Ben Yahya Hacohen Majari, of blessed memory, wrote the important book *Light of the Torah*. "And we have in our hands a confirmation that this family is of the seed of Jehojarib, the high priest, and they had a genealogical tree, and the name Jehojarib is in the Arab language Majari."

Lester Abrahamson, who works as an expert in a large and modern electronics plant, was born in Los Angeles in the United States. His ancestors, pursued by the fury of the pogrom, had arrived from the Ukraine in a small, much-buffeted vessel.

There, in America, they worked themselves to exhaustion as tailors. He himself volunteered in the days of illegal immigration to serve as a seaman aboard a dilapidated immigrant ship bringing Jewish fugitives from Nazism to the shores of this country. His forefathers, the Abramowicis—sons of Abraham— lived and earned their support as peddlers, innkeepers, and petty merchants among the Polish aristocrats and the Ukrainian people. Many of them were killed and butchered and their womenfolk raped in the pogroms of 1648 and 1649. Their forebears went to the Ukraine from Galicia, to which they had fled from the Holy Roman Empire, having arrived from Italy, where they had been sent with the exiles of Judea Capta in the year 70 C.E.

Abraham Abraham, who immigrated to Israel in the early 1950s, during the great waves of immigration, and built his home in the moshav Nevatim in the Negev, and now grows roses and gladioli and exports them to Europe, was born in Ernakulam in Cochin on the southern edge of the Indian subcontinent. His forebears were peddlers, merchants, and small artisans in that provincial town, where they lived for hundreds of years, handing down a tradition that they were the descendants of sailors in the merchant fleet of King Solomon who set sail to the land of Ophir to seek ivories and parrots and gold and bring them to Jerusalem. During the reign of King Solomon they founded in Cochin a sailors' and merchants' colony, where they lived a long time until the bad news reached them of the destruction of the First Temple at the hands of the Babylonians, who razed the Temple and exiled the king, the priests, and the people. The sailors remained in Cochin and obtained permission to live there, until the reign of the House of David is restored. For two thousand years the Jews of Cochin sang: "How goodly on the mountains are the feet of the herald of good tidings." They returned to Israel with their wives and children in 1954, the seventh year after the founding of the State of Israel.

Tania Zvi (the word *zvi* means "hart") immigrated to the

Land of Israel in the spring of 1947 aboard the illegal immigrant ship *Haim Arlosoroff*. Tania came from a detention camp in Cyprus after she and two thousand of her shipmates, women and men, had fought on deck against the British Royal Navy, which barred their passage at sea; many were fired upon and wounded. Tania came to the Land of Israel from Sweden, where at the end of World War II she had found a haven, after having been incarcerated in the death camps of Nazi Germany. Her parents and her younger sisters were shot to death before her very eyes in the forests of Estonia, by the Gestapo. Tania was born in Kaunas, Lithuania. Her father, Moshe, was a timber merchant and numbered among his forebears both rabbis and merchants. His ancestors arrived in Lithuania from Poland, having fled from France, where their ancestors had built a Jewish exiles settlement in Massilia during the Roman Empire under the caesars, after they had been exiled from Eretz Yisrael —Land of the Hart.

Mas'ud Yifrah, who immigrated to Israel at the time of the founding of the state and built his home in the Lakhish region, was born in the village of Varzazat south of the Atlas Mountains in Morocco. His forebears were cobblers and leather workers in their village, which was a center of crafts and trade for the Berber tribes. From his home, ringed around with date palms, he could see the eternal snows on the noble Atlas Mountains. His forefathers arrived at the fringe of the Sahara many generations before from Marrakech, from Tetuan and from Fez, to which they had come from Egypt, via the long desert road across North Africa. They had fled the Roman sword after the Bar Kokhba uprisings, roving westward, and continued to wander to the south until they settled among the Berbers.

David Shaaltiel arrived in the Land of Israel in the 1920s as a young pioneer from Germany. Here he organized Jews to defend their lives and in the War of Independence commanded the defenders of Jerusalem. He was born in Hamburg to a prominent family of bankers and merchants who had lived generation upon generation in that great port and commercial town, which they reached in their flight from Christian vengeance in Portugal, to which they had fled from the dread Inquisition in Spain. His ancestors lived for many generations in Spain, contributing to the commercial, cultural, and spiritual life of Muslim Spain. They had come to Spain from Babylon, in the wake of the Arab jihad horsemen, and they had lived in Babylon ever since Nebuchadnezzar had exiled the sons of Shaaltiel from Jerusalem the capital.

Yehezkel Zakkai, who built his home in the village of Orah in the hills of Jerusalem, immigrated to Israel after the establishment of the state. He was born in the mountains of Kurdistan among the Barazani tribes. His forebears who lived among the proud free warrior Kurds were tillers of the soil, shepherds, and, intermittently, artisans. They spoke with the Kurds in their language, while among themselves they spoke in Targum, the ancient Aramaic known many, many generations before to their ancestors in the north of the land of Babylon, ever since the days of the prophet Yehezkel. When they remembered Zion they swore, "If I forget thee, O Jerusalem, let my right hand forget its cunning." They indeed remembered Jerusalem, and came there to redeem and revive her bare mountains.

Yosef Zinati of Peki'in in Galilee did not immigrate to the Land of Israel because he is a descendant of the few who never left this country. His ancestors were born in Peki'in and so were their ancestors, who lived for generations upon generations among the Arabs of Peki'in and watched as the Turks and the Mamelukes, the horsemen of Timor, the crusaders, the Byzantines, the Persians, and the Parthians and the Romans came and went. His early ancestors fought and fell with other zealots in the strongholds of Galilee, and were also among those who heard the sermons, the preaching, and the admonitions of a young Galilean Jew of Nazareth, whose name in Israel at that time was Yeshu son of Yosef the carpenter.

Reuven Sadeh immigrated to Israel at the time of the founding of the state and lived for a few years with his parents in an immigrant village in Samaria. When he came of age he enlisted with a paratrooper reconnaissance unit. He was born in Madrid, Spain, where he and his parents found a temporary haven in their flight from the Nazis. He was a young man of handsome appearance, good-hearted, devoted, industrious, innocent, and enthusiastic; his hands possessed great dexterity. He had acquired no civilian trade, but whatever he did, he did well, with all his heart and soul. He had one "trade": he was a paratroop section commander. In 1961, on being demobilized, he married his girl, Dinah, and became the first settler in the little town of Arad, which was then growing upon the rocks of the Judean desert between Massada and Sodom. There he built his home and established a family.

With the first reserve call-up, on the eve of the Six-Day War, he went to his paratroop battalion and with it breached the lines of the Arab Legion. With the combatants he climbed up to the hills over against the Temple Mount from the east; he fell opposite Lions' Gate, at the foot of the Temple wall, upon the highway along which his ancestors walked into exile.

Reuven Sadeh wrote a few days before his death:

Somewhere in Israel, evening of 25.5.67. Army number 349528 Corporal Sadeh Reuven, Military Post 2623.

Dear Lova,

For two days now I have been here with my unit. There are some fellows here who, like me, have served in this unit for many years. Some veteran and more experienced and some younger. Anyway, we are all of us well trained and as fit as the regular soldier.

I do not know how this is going to end. Perhaps we shall return home soon, and everything will be settled peacefully. But if not, I want you to know that not one of us has failed to grasp how grave the situation is. As for me, when I immigrated to Israel at the time of the founding of the state, I found everything here, everything I had never had, and that much I owe this country and I hope to discharge my debt in my own way, through work and development.

Some of my friends have come here, who had transferred to other, easier units a long time ago on account of their health. One came with his leg in a cast. Some of the boys begged to be allowed to rejoin. Being an emotional type I am deeply affected by these things, and I know myself that I would not act differently. In short, you can rely on us.

Yours,

Reuven

The Zionist doctrine is contained in this simple testament. Only here in Israel did this exiled and wandering Jewish youth find "everything I had never had," and to this land he owed everything. Reuven Sadeh discharged his debt—with his blood and with his life.

OUR RAISON D'ETRE

The dream we had dreamed and fought for—the founding of a Jewish state—came to be realized on May 15, 1948; but the state is still beset by many dangers, and its war of existence has not ceased even to this very day. Our main target now is to insure the state's survival, lest it be wiped off the face of the earth, and that it, along with the other nations of the world, may merit reaching the threshold of the twenty-first century, and perhaps make a greater contribution than is expected of a small nation to the solution of the problems facing humanity.

But anyone who does not understand the sense of uniqueness in which Jews in the young State of Israel live cannot fathom the workings of our minds or grasp the motives that guide us and govern our present and future actions.

The Jewish state arose through constant struggle over this land with its Arab neighbors, and it is now populated by nearly three million Jews, who are a mere one-fifth of the world Jewish population. The Jews of Israel regard themselves as an integral part of the Jewish people and aspire to realize the principal goal of Zionism: creating a safe refuge for every Jew who wishes or is forced to immigrate to the Jewish state. There are many Jews in the world who so desire at present and will so desire in the future, and Israel is and will be their only hope.

Israel is the only state in the world to arouse its neighbors' wrath not because of its form of regime or the size of its territory, but by the mere fact of its existence. Our existence here and our aspirations of absorbing many more Jews in this land are as a gauntlet thrown down before the Arabs, and many of them keenly desire to end our existence. Anyone who does not comprehend the continual trauma this causes us will not understand a single one of our acts.

Our raison d'être is our very life, and defending it. Only one who can grasp and sense the depth of feeling, the tremendous mental and spiritual energy that for two thousand years was pent up without outlet in the Jew, and which brought about the establishment of the state, and the physically and spiritually superhuman efforts which were invested by us in its establishment—only he can understand our tremendous pride at having achieved our objective. Only he can comprehend the constant fear and misgivings that gnaw at our hearts and sometimes craze us—that all the sacrifices and the toil, all the spiritual and material assets, and all that we have here created and accumulated, all that has flourished and grown in our land may be destroyed and brought to ruin as though it had never existed.

This fear, under whose shadow we live, governs what we do and refrain from doing in this country; it dictates our psychological reactions, which appear so incomprehensible and sometimes irrational to our enemies and friends. One can understand neither us nor our past, neither our present nor our hopes for the future, unless one can grasp the fact that, for us, the right to live here, to raise children, to work, to build, to create, to love, to engage in every sphere of human activity is axiomatic, that we are not to be liquidated, and that we shall fight by every conventional and nonconventional means against those who want to destroy us. Since the founding of our state, our desire to live as a state on equal terms with others is the strongest motive directing our lives. Only when this dreadful fear—the fear of liquidation, which in all the world has no parallel—is lifted from us shall we be able to live as a rational society and state.

THE BEGINNING OF THE RETURN

How and when did we return to our land? It is true that ever since we were exiled and dispersed among the nations of the world there was always a small Jewish presence here, and Jewish communities have existed for hundreds of years in Jerusalem, Hebron, Safed, and Tiberias, as well as in Acre and some other towns and villages. But until a hundred years ago the members of these communities were by way of being exiles in their own country. Tens of thousands of Jews came to this country in the course of generations to weep for the destruction of the Temple or to die and be buried in the holy soil. But their way of life, their sources of livelihood, and their hopes were in the main no different from those of the Diaspora Jews.

What was unique and marvelous in Judaism was not these small communities in the Land of Israel, but the force of religious national longings of all Diaspora Jewry, upon which Zionism was nourished, and the desire of Jews to return someday to the Land of Israel and raise it up once more as a Jewish state.

The turning point, from a Zionism of longings to the Zionism of deeds designed to fulfill the messianic aspiration of our people, occurred about one hundred years ago. As a result of intensified Jewish persecution and the growth of the modern nationalist movement, Jews—small groups at first—decided that they would no longer wait for the coming of the Messiah and that they would hasten the denouement by rational methods and means.

The first aim was to return to the tilling of the soil in the Land of Israel. Farming, which in the mid-nineteenth century was still the principal source of livelihood, was foreign to Diaspora

Jewry. Agriculture and farming thus became a main objective, symbolizing the will of the Jews to return to their land. These Jews, who dwelt in the great cities, towns, and townships of the Diaspora, regarded the return to soil cultivation as something more than a mere change of trade. They regarded it as the road of the return to Zion.

Over a hundred years ago the Zionists, even before they were known by that name, implemented the beginnings of this revolution when they founded the Mikweh Yisrael Agricultural School and ploughed the first furrows in the soil of Petah Tiqva. Their achievement in no way resembles the conquests of colonialist settlers throughout the course of human history. Those who settled in other parts of the world usually came in the wake of the soldiers of an occupying force; or reached an uninhabited country, saw nothing remarkable about the farming which had always been their trade in the society from which they had come, and continued to pursue it in the new land.

In the Palestine of the 1870s the early Zionists conquered no lands at all; indeed, even if they had wanted to it would have been beyond them, for they were isolated and weak. With the best part of their resources they bought some tracts of the Arabs' land, generally against the will of the Turkish rulers of the country. These were usually impoverished areas that the Arabs were unable or unwilling to cultivate.

These Jews conquered not the soil but themselves. They "conquered" farming, in the clear recognition that only in this way, and through tremendous exertion, could they ever in the distant future create the basis for their return to their homeland. Since Mikweh Yisrael and Petah Tiqva, agriculture and the tilling of the soil have become a magnetic force and the test for the modern Jewish revolution—from the abstract Zionism of longing to the Zionism of realization.

There is no need to tell again the tale of the founding of the first Jewish villages—the Bilu settlements, the settlements of the various Hovevei Zion societies, the Baron Rothschild colonies, the *kevutzot* and the kibbutzim and the first cooperative farms, or of the pangs of the conquest of work by students and tenderfoot town dwellers—for it is etched in our memory. We must, however, again remind ourselves and our Arab neighbors of a decisive fact in the complex of our relations with them: that from the commencement of Jewish settlement in Palestine until the founding of the state, during which time we faced the danger of utter extinction, we did not conquer from them the terrain upon which our settlements were founded.

When the first Jewish settlers came to Palestine about one hundred years ago, they did not find an uninhabited land. About three hundred thousand persons, most of them Arabs, were living here at the time, and, as we have stated, the settlers bought their lands at the full price. Among the Jewish purchasers of land were private persons and agents. As agents will, they purchased the land from its owners or from Arab agents and then sold it to others. In the course of time groups of Jews organized to buy the land, using money from contributions raised in the Diaspora. Baron Rothschild, too, bought tracts of land which he colonized with Jewish settlers, as did the Jewish National Fund, which had been founded by the Zionist movement at its inception. The JNF began buying land for Jewish settlement wherever it was available, from the pennies slipped into the blue and white boxes that were to be found in thousands of Jewish homes throughout the Diaspora.

However, the purchase of land was only a part, and not always the most difficult part, of the process of Jewish settlement on the land. This country was thinly populated; large areas of it were desert, swamp, and quicksand. The Jews who settled on the purchased lands were men who had arrived here by unconventional routes, in a thin and intermittent trickle, individually or in small groups of several dozen persons at the most. The young Jewish students who came to the Land of Israel over a hundred years ago, particularly from East Europe, unfurled the banner of "Beit Yaakov Lechu Venelcha" (Bilu, the acronym for

"House of Jacob Let Us Arise and Go"). They knew, perhaps by instinct rather than from any comprehensive ideology, that their desperate struggle would begin only after they had come to Palestine. They fought against everything and everyone, and first against themselves: their bodies and their flabby muscles, quite unaccustomed to the labor of farming, their sacrifice of their urban way of life and the temptation to return home to their parents, to a familiar environment, to an easier life. They struggled with a harsh climate they were unaccustomed to, with diseases they had never known (foremost among them malaria), and with the difficulty of mastering a new language. For these young revolutionaries decided to adopt the ancient language of their people, which had not been used as a spoken language since the beginning of the exile. They struggled with the Turkish regime, whose favors they had to purchase through bribery and flattery, by ruse and by obsequiousness. Once they had driven their first stakes into the soil they also had a twofold struggle with the Arab inhabitants of Palestine: first, to understand the Arabs and their language so as to be able to speak with them, to gain their assistance, trade with them, and live among them; second, to defend their property and lives from theft, plunder, and occasional murder at the hands of their Arab neighbors.

Theft and robbery were at that time a matter of course in the disintegrating Turkish empire. While pasturing their sheep the wandering bedouin tribes would also turn a hand to plunder. The Arabs too—fellahin and town dwellers—lived in fear of theft, robbery, and plunder. It is true that blood revenge was an enshrined custom among many Muslim Arabs, but it is not true that the Arabs who attacked the first settlers and their colonies were bent solely on theft and robbery. These were their principal motives, but it is also a fact that no sooner had the Zionist enterprise in the country begun than some of the local Arabs, who were later to call themselves Palestinian Arabs, forcibly opposed the Jews' return to the country and their attempts to settle it. The motives of those Arabs is one of great importance, for it is essential that we realize that the Arab-Jewish conflict had begun even then—a hundred years ago.

The Palestinian Arabs of those days had as yet no ideology to counter Zionism, which itself was still not fully developed. They, too, acted intuitively at first. But even then their reactions were unquestionably natural: they were rejecting a foreign body that had come to dwell in their midst.

The struggle with their environment almost exhausted the early Jewish settlers. There were very many who could not meet the test, whose physical strength was not enough to sustain them, who had not enough obstinacy, faith, and persistence to go on, and they returned to the Diaspora. Others died an untimely death brought on by disease, especially malaria. A generation later, at the close of the nineteenth century and the start of the twentieth, the Jewish attempt to settle Palestine faced the danger of both physical and spiritual collapse and was nearly recorded in our chronicles as one more abortive attempt in the long history of the Jewish people to bring an end to the exile.

And here it should be repeated that the Jewish settlers arriving in Palestine not only bought every dunam of land legally, but they bought the very worst tracts, the uncultivatable land —not because they wanted it, but because generally speaking this was the only type of land the Arabs would sell.

For centuries Arab farmers had clustered in the region of the Judean Hills, Samaria, and Galilee. The ruin and desolation that waves of conquerors left in their wake had despoiled the countryside and forced the fellahin away from the plains, the valleys, and coastline, to the mountains. Through no fault of their own, but as a result of wars and later as a result of the distribution of lands by the Turks to the great effendis, they found themselves concentrating on hill farming.

The semiquicksands along the coast which were purchased by the Jews were, at the time, the most impoverished of soils.

The land of Hadera was muddy, disease-ridden, and malaria-infested, and the lands of the Jezreel Valley were marshy, undrained, and difficult to cultivate. This, with few exceptions, was the situation in all the early settlements. In the land along the coast, in the plains, and in the valleys, soil has now become so rich and has brought forth such bounteous crops that it is difficult for us, and will be even more difficult for future generations, to believe that it was not always so, but was made so through a human agent—the Jewish settler.

As we have said, many settlers died of disease, many fell prey to the sword, and many of those who remained paid a further price. As a result of their wish and need to mix with the local Arabs, to learn their language and customs, some of the settlers began employing Arab laborers on their farms and on the lands they had purchased. Under the conditions then prevailing, nothing could have been more natural. These settlers became "colonialists" in the classic sense of the word: European settlers coming to a country and using the natives as cheap labor. Thus a "cooperation in living" came about between the first Jewish settlers and the Arab population, which had become reconciled to this influx of foreigners, just as in the past over the course of many generations Arabs had grown used to foreign enclaves in their midst. This Jewish-Arab "cooperation in living" contributed to the weakening of the early Jewish settlement enterprise.

During those years of crisis, salvation came to the Jewish farming villages from a man whose contribution to the Zionist cause can perhaps be more accurately gauged now than it could at the time. At the end of the nineteenth century Baron Edmond de Rothschild began to channel capital to Palestine and to accustom the settlers to modern methods of agriculture and administration. Today there can be no doubt about it: without the baron's help in capital and instruction, the men of the first wave of immigration could not have held out.

THE ZIONIST ENTERPRISE
AT THE TURN OF THE CENTURY

With the advent of Theodor Herzl and the inception of the political Zionist movement at the beginning of the present century, and with the setting up of its political tools (the Zionist Congress) and economic instruments (Jewish Colonial Trust, Jewish National Fund), the return to Zion took on a new dimension. It became an all-Jewish political movement with the clearly defined purpose of founding a safe refuge for the Jewish people in the Land of Israel, or, more simply and clearly—and Herzl never concealed this aim—of establishing a Jewish state in the Land of Israel.

The argument now being voiced that the Arabs and the nations of the world were unaware of the purpose of Zionism in the Land of Israel is simply untrue: it has been known since 1896, when Herzl published his treatise *The Jewish State*. There could be no mistake about it. Indeed, the governments of Turkey, Great Britain, Germany, and other countries, to whom Herzl applied for help at various times, very clearly understood the ambition of this man who had founded a universal political movement, and what it was he wanted of them: to found a Jewish state in Palestine, or in part of it.

The Arab nationalist movement too, which during the same years when political Zionism was being born was coming into this world in Damascus and other places, grasped the fundamentals of the Zionist doctrine and began to develop ideological and political antibodies to counter it.

It was the very breadth of Herzl's vision, conceived long before conditions were ripe for its realization, that gave rise to severe crises and frustrations at the beginning of the twentieth century and almost brought the Zionist movement to a very low ebb in the last years of his life.

Herzl received negative answers from the world's statesmen. His movement and its objectives appeared to world policymakers to be idle dreams. Although many Jewish people were enthusiastic about his doctrine, some became sworn enemies of Zionism. The extreme Orthodox saw it as a heresy, a new and dangerous false messianism, while the early Jewish socialists regarded it as a flight from the "true" problems of oppressed Jewish society. In practice most Diaspora Jews rejected Zionism, both those who remained immovably in their countries of domicile and the millions who fled Europe for the New World —America.

At this juncture—with a weak Jewish settlement enterprise in Palestine, under the Turkish yoke, a deep crisis in political Zionism, and mass Jewish migration from East Europe to America—the first pioneers of the Second Aliya arrived at the port of Jaffa. These young men and women tried to establish a comprehensive Zionist ideological doctrine. They adopted the political-Zionist goal of the return of the Jews to their land and the founding of a safe refuge for the Jewish people. They also set themselves another aim: the creation of a new Jewish society based on universal values of justice, equality, and human freedom, which would derive its strength from the socialist doctrine. They gave Zionism a new dimension, and, along with the idea of national renaissance upon which it was founded, they saw it as a movement for social revolution.

True, the first Jewish settlers in the 1870s and 1880s also wanted social changes—as indicated by the fact that they turned to the tilling of the soil and became farmers. Moreover, they and the first Zionist ideologists wanted to establish in their ancestral land a Jewish society that would be different from the one they had lived in previously; but their ideas were rather amorphous. Some of them aspired to found here an ideal, beautiful, primitive, biblical society; others imagined a Jewish society such as the one that had existed in the days of the Great Sanhedrin in the early period of the Talmud.

Herzl too, of course, had regarded the founding of a Jewish state not only as a political but also as a social enterprise. Heart and soul, he hoped that the Jewish state would not be like all other states, but rather a beautiful, just, and tolerant state in which Jews and non-Jews could live in equality, through mutual understanding and even mutual affection. But Herzl believed that his vision would be materialized at a stroke through the Jewish genius. His book *Altneuland* pictured a marvelous utopia, but gave no formula as to how it was to be brought into existence.

The thinkers of the Second Aliya created a blend of Zionist and socialist doctrines. It was this merging of two revolutionary philosophies that lent these few people, the creators of the labor movement, power out of all proportion to their numbers, enabling them to overcome countless difficulties and obstacles. These young people understood that it was not enough merely to preach utopia and set oneself sublime objectives, but that to achieve their Zionist-socialist aims they must practice in person what they preached.

The pangs of their acclimatization were no less severe than those of the Bilu. Even though they did find a few dozen Jewish settlements with Jewish tillers of the soil and the beginnings of Jewish towns or suburbs, for them as socialists all this was sadly tainted. They found in this country Jewish landowners, farmers, and merchants who looked to them like kulaks, feudalists, and bourgeoisie of the type they had known in the Diaspora. As socialists it was their duty to oppose them, but as Jews and Zionists they had to cooperate with them in the long journey toward the building of a Jewish society and state. The pioneers of the Second Aliya had to cope not only with the vagaries of the climate and a poor and scanty diet, but also with the difficulties arising from their split personality.

The answer the Second Aliya pioneers gave themselves was that they not only had to settle the country and become tillers of the soil, but they also had to become a proletariat. They inured themselves to manual labor: to the hoe and the mattock, to quarrying and stonecutting and every other form of hard work. They hoped in this way to be true to themselves, both as Zionists coming to transform the deserts of their country into flourishing farmland and as socialist laborers ready to turn their callused hands to any work. Deliberately and consciously they made themselves the base of the economic pyramid, for their socialist doctrine instructed them that only in this way could a new and just society, one not founded on *Luftgeschaeften,* be established.

The members of the Second Aliya were perhaps even less well prepared than their predecessors to adapt to the conditions of this country. Nursing such great expectations, they could not but be impatient, wanting to achieve their goal by leaps and bounds. Many of them—some say the majority—returned embittered to the Diaspora. But those who remained and held out began to build Zionism by forging new tools which at the time appeared anomalous not only to Turkish-ruled Palestine, but also to that period of history. Only now can we perceive how great was the vision they nurtured. They laid the first foundations of the consumer and producer cooperative movement, of the trade union, of the Sick Fund, and of building and industrial workers' societies. The crowning glory of their achievement was the founding of the kibbutz (collective village) and the moshav (cooperative village) as a way of life for Jewish workers in the Land of Israel, and as the most efficient and complete tool ever devised for realizing their Zionist-socialist yearnings.

The men of the Second Aliya added a new dimension to their ideology: the vital need to form a Jewish armed force to defend Jewish settlements and Jews in general in the Land of Israel. In the Diaspora, Jews and weapons had been two mutually exclusive notions. During the long course of Jewish Diaspora history there had been Jews who had borne weapons (for example, Jewish warrior tribes in Yemen), and Jews had also fought in various armies, especially in recent times when they had begun to be accorded civil rights. There had also been instances in which Jews were press-ganged into the army, as in the days of Nikolai I in czarist Russia. But all these had been exceptions. Jews were generally the victims of persecution and the doormat on which regular armies or irregular combatants in their countries of domicile wiped their feet. Their lives were always precarious possessions and their property was there for the plundering. Whenever possible they saved their lives and their property in the only ways open to Diaspora Jewry: payment of ransom or flight in search of a new haven.

Before the modern Zionist era, the fate of the few Jews in Palestine was no different from that of Diaspora Jewry. Some of the harbingers of Zionism, such as Rabbi Alkalai, did dream of a Jewish army. The settlers of the first villages, who upon arrival in Israel at once encountered the need to defend their lives and property, at first chose the method accepted in the Diaspora and in the Middle East: they "purchased" protection and defense by engaging Arab guards or by paying ransom and protection money to robbers. True, there were then the beginnings of a Jewish guard organization and also armed Jews who guarded the villages; but on the whole these were exceptions. And the guards themselves, such as Abraham Shapiro of Petah Tiqva, "father of the guards," were unique, renowned in their day, and their names are still surrounded by an aura of legend.

Herzl too dreamed of founding an army in the Jewish state. But as he believed the state would be established with the consent of the great powers and by virtue of international law, he deluded himself by believing that its establishment would not be accompanied by a prolonged bloody struggle. The army in his utopian state was to be mainly a symbol of political independence and not a fighting army. As for "muscle Jewry" and the new Maccabees—these he pictured as sportsmen rather than warriors.

The early settlers of the Second Aliya were unable to reconcile themselves to the situation of "protected Jews" in their own land, since this phenomenon was one of the reasons they had left the Diaspora. Their view of the structure of Jewish society in the Land of Israel, whose principal components (as in any normal people) would be farmers and laborers, was incompatable with a situation in which these farmers and laborers failed to defend themselves from their aggressors (as would any healthy people).

They had no intention of establishing an army to fight the Turkish rulers of the country. They wanted to forge an armed force suited to the conditions then prevailing in the country—a force of armed guards who would defend themselves against armed brigands, in the accepted style of the wild Middle East of those days. What was not so customary was that these armed guards were to be Jews. It is hardly surprising that these first guards started out by imitating Arab customs, modes of combat, style of horsemanship, and guard rules and procedures, learning from them the ethics of the warfare then being waged between the Jewish settlers and their Arab attackers.

THE PEOPLE OF THE LAND

In the first decade of the twentieth century, as the Turkish Empire disintegrated and the tide of nationalism swelled, an Arab nationalist movement began to emerge, especially in Syria.

This young movement began viewing the Jewish exploits with ever-growing suspicion. The Arabs might have been able to put up with the existence of the isolated Jewish farming villages founded at the end of the nineteenth century, but the activities of the Second Aliya people aroused increasing alarm among the founders of the Arab nationalist movement. They were seeing new Jews bent on the strangest new pursuits—Jews enthusiastically engaging in all forms of difficult and menial work and rising to defend themselves alone and unaided. From the outset the attitude of the first Zionists to Arabs in general and to the Arabs of Palestine in particular was both ambivalent

and indefinite. They could not ignore the fact that the homeland to which they were returning had been populated by an
Arab community for many generations, and that they had to
come up with some formula as to how they were to live in it
together.

The first Zionists, few and isolated as they were, attempted
to live a life of daily cooperation with their Arab neighbors, the
"people of the land." The Arabs who lived in Turkish Palestine
at the beginning of the Zionist immigration were scattered all
over the country. Most lived in the towns and villages of the
mountainous regions, and the remainder along the coastal plain
and in the valleys.

The first Zionists, versed in the lore of Bible and Aggada,
Mishnah and Talmud, and romantic Hebrew literature *(Love of
Zion, The Guilt of Samaria)*, believed that in the olden days the
land, flowing with milk and honey, had had a population of from
three to five million, that every desolate *tel* (artificial mound or
hillock) had once been a living town, that all the mountains and
hills were once covered by forest, woodland, and orchard, and
that the mountains had dripped with sweet juice. They knew
that Jerusalem had once been a great capital, had had a population of tens of thousands, and had contained temples and palaces. What then was more natural—they naively thought—than
that room should be found in this land for millions of people
living together, Jews and Arabs, every man under his vine and
his fig tree? Though the road to the fulfillment of the dream was
very long, and day-to-day living was very hard, and though the
"people of the land" would from time to time rise up to attack
them, they took comfort in the thought that they would "be the
first," saying one to another: "We shall be among the builders,
we shall pull taut the string and stretch the plumb line."

And what of the future, what of relations with the Turkish
overlords and the Arabs? In answer to these questions they
explained that while they were not free to desist from the task,
neither was it theirs to complete. Thus they lived and worked,

filled with a wondrous innocence. It is entirely likely that any "realistic" thinking would have brought them to despair and cause them to leave the country.

Among the first ideologists of Zionism were some more hard-headed types, like Ahad Ha-am, who from the very outset perceived the Arab problem in all its gravity. They were convinced that in the future there would be no avoiding a clash between the Jews and "the people of the land," and they tried, in their own way, to find a solution that would be compatible with the Jews' desire to return to their land and would also solve the problem of the Arab inhabitants.

Nor did Herzl ignore the problem of the country's Arab population. But he believed that in the progressive world he dreamed of, technology and mechanization would proceed apace, peace and progress would reign, and the Middle East too would be a part of this process. It would become an international crossroads for commerce and industry; there would be room in it for a Jewish state, inhabited by Jews and Arabs, side by side, in cordial, neighborly relations. This state would bring progress, happiness, and prosperity not only to its Arab inhabitants but also to the neighboring Arab states.

In a certain sense Herzl—as was only natural to the man and his times—regarded the homecoming Jews as "the bearers of the white man's burden": it was their responsibility to impart to the backward East some of the fruits of Western culture and civilization, thereby activating a system of give and take with the Eastern civilization and engendering mutual relations in all spheres of life. As Herzl looked around him and saw the great colonialist empires—Britain, France, Germany, and others—sending the flower of their youth to bring what appeared to him to be progress to Asia and Africa, it occurred to him that the Jewish people too, whose homeland was in the East and who had been forcibly banished and had imbibed the noblest values and qualities of the peoples of the West, could be a model bearer of progress and peace, especially since, unlike other

Europeans, the Jews were not coming to a strange country but returning by right to their homeland.

In Herzl's utopia there was no room for world wars, for bloody socialist revolutions, for an extreme Arab nationalist movement that, justifiably in its own eyes, would not want to give any other people a place in the state or in any of the new Arab states that were to arise and restore to the Arabs the majesty and pomp of their glorious past. In his utopian Jewish state there was no place for the man whose impulses were evil from his youth, or for slogans such as "In blood and fire did Judea fall, in blood and fire shall Judea arise," or "The judgment of Muhammad is by the sword."

The members of the Second Aliya were unlike those of the First Aliya, who did not have an orderly ideology but had a doctrine that was simple and basically naive; and they were unlike Herzl, who gave the Arab problem a utopian answer. Because they wanted to found their enterprise on the truths of the Zionist-socialist doctrine, they had to grapple with the problem of the Arabs of Palestine and provide an answer to it. The answer was not easy to find. They struggled with the problem without arriving at a clear-cut solution. The doctrine of Berl Katznelson, David Ben-Gurion, and their comrades regarding the Arabs of Palestine is somewhat vague and contains many question marks. Some, not unnaturally, wanted to ignore the problem and leave it to future generations (this desire to ignore the problem of the Arabs of Palestine has been a leitmotif in our lives ever since). They could not, of course, ignore the day-to-day repercussions of the problem—they were simply not allowed to—and they encountered it at every turn: in dealings with land, work, defense, and guerrilla warfare. They tried to lull their disquiet with the hopeful thought that the issue would somehow resolve itself and disappear of its own accord. (Incidentally, a similar although more exaggerated tendency attended the beginnings of the Arab nationalists' treatment of the issue of the Jews. They too nursed the unrealistic hope that the

Jews would somehow disappear from the Middle East, and they paid an even greater price for their lack of realism than we did.)

Some Second Aliya people hoped that the Arabs would leave here of their own free will and go to other countries, and that the problem would thereby be solved. Others thought that a Jewish Zionist-socialist state could be established only by "blood and fire." To the greatest and best thinkers of Zionist-socialism it became apparent that if they wanted to be honest with themselves and with their doctrine, it was incumbent upon them to find a solution within the boundaries of a socialist Jewish state for the Palestinian Arabs too. These motives led a few of the philosophers of Zionist-socialism, at its outset, to devote considerable place in their doctrine to the fate of the Arab fellah and laborer, whom they saw in their abasement and degeneracy. Some of them began to weave vague ideas of a socialist state and society in which Jewish farmers and laborers would live alongside Arab farmers and laborers, and would in the final analysis become a binational state.

The conflict between the fierce and burning desire to better the lot of their people and found a just Jewish society in the Land of Israel for an exiled and persecuted people, whose only place was here, and the need to deal justly with the Arabs of this country and not take possession of the land at their expense, dogged the Zionist labor movement and its founders from the beginning. To this very day it has given them no respite.

HISTORIC RIGHTS AND THE LAND OF THE TWELVE TRIBES

Another issue that arose at the inception of Zionism, one that is of vital significance to the understanding of the how and the why of our lives in Israel today, was what constituted, in terms of area and boundaries, the Land of Israel that the original Zionists aspired to. Bound up with this question is the intricate problem of "historic rights," which even today is a source of deep perplexity and a bone of contention among ourselves, and between us and our Arab neighbors.

Without attempting to penetrate the shrouds of mysticism enfolding the divine promise to Abraham and his seed, to bequeath them the land stretching from the Euphrates River to the River of Egypt (assuming, for argument's sake, that the reference was to one of the tributaries of the Nile), suffice it to say that in all the long history of Israel and its land, the Jewish people never inhabited the area thus demarcated, and the history and culture of the Jewish people did not develop within those boundaries.

On the other hand, the Land of the Twelve Tribes may indeed be said to be the historic Land of Israel, where the Jewish people came into being, where its destiny was shaped, its spiritual works were devised, its kings reigned, and its prophets prophesied, over which it constantly fought and from whence it was exiled. The borders of the Land of the Twelve Tribes are as clear as they could be, considering the surging, war-bedeviled history of the Jews in their land: from the slopes of the Lebanon and Hermon mountains in the north to the Red Sea and the Gulf of Eilat and Etzion-Geber in the south; from the Great Sea—the Mediterranean—to the eastern frontier of the inheritances of the tribes of Reuben, Gad, and half the tribe of Manasseh (that is, as far as the heights of Golan, Gilead, and Bashan inclusively). This area more or less coincides with the border of western Palestine and eastern Transjordan of the British Mandatory era. Nor was it idly included by the British in their mandate, for they also more or less envisaged the boundaries of the Land of Israel of the Twelve Tribes. Of course this land too had been torn, in almost every generation, by wars and invaders from north and south; Philistines, Ammonites, Moabites, Edomites, and others had struck into the interior and fought the Jews almost unremittingly, and Jewish dominion extended to parts of the country more continuously than to the whole. It is true that dissension among the Jews led to the founding of separate kingdoms that fought one another cruelly. Despite all that, this is the land the Jews always dreamed of in exile and swore to return to and rebuild, for they carried their country's geography in their hearts for two thousand years. Her mountains, valleys, streams, rivers, and seas they had come to know from the pages of the Book of Books. Their towns, palaces, villages, and fields lived among its fading pages, the images of their judges and prophets, kings and captains gazed upon them from between its lines, and the cadences of the psalms sang in their hearts as they read its words. All these came into being and were established in the Land of the Twelve Tribes where Jewish history had had its beginnings, where the Jewish people was born, where it lived, where it wallowed in its own blood, and from whence it was banished.

In this land, the Land of the Twelve Tribes, lived the patriarchs; from here they went down into Egypt; to this place Moses led the people; over this land Joshua fought; here lived Yiftah and Shimshon and Gideon and Ehud; here Saul was anointed; David fled to its wilderness and founded his capital in Jerusalem; here Solomon reigned; this land was torn apart by Jereboam; here Isaiah prophesied, and Amos and Hosea and Jeremiah. From here the ten tribes went into exile; here Ezra and Nehemia returned. Here was established the House of the Hasmoneans; in its expanses Herod raised palaces and castles. Over its districts and towns the Zealots fought a desperate war; from it the Romans led away columns of exiles; here the Bible —Pentateuch, Prophets, and Hagiographa—was completed and the Mishnah—the oral law—was created; and in its houses of study the Jerusalem Talmud was pored over by scholars.

These are the chronicles of a land and a people closely bound up with one another. Not even two thousand years of physical severance could erase the profound mark they left on one another or the everlasting covenant they had mutually contracted.

When Jews prayed, "Restore our judges as of yore," they

referred to the judges of the Land of the Twelve Tribes; and when they cried, "Renew our days as of old," their "old" meant in the days of the Land of the Twelve Tribes.

When the first Zionists began to return to the country about a hundred years ago, the question of its borders simply never arose. In their mind's eye they beheld the whole of the ancient land, the whole Land of the Twelve Tribes, and they were prepared to settle on any part of it that the Turks would permit them to and the Arabs would sell.

It was in the nature of things that, on arriving in Palestine by sea, the first settlers purchased some of the sandy tracts of soil on the Plain of Sharon, settled it, and called their first communities Petah Tiqva and Rishon-le-Zion (Gateway to Hope and First of Zion). They also bought stony soil in the hills of the Galilee and called the settlements they founded there Yesod Hamaale (Hilltop Foundation) and Rosh Pina (Cornerstone). They also bought lands east of the Jordan and wanted to settle them, but did not succeed.

And Herzl? What state did he aspire to, in terms of area and boundaries? His principal motive was the distress of the Jews and the almost prophetic feeling that unless they made haste to assemble in a state of their own, they were in for a holocaust. This feeling led to desperate attempts to advance the founding of the state through shortcuts, for which neither the Jewish people nor his contemporary world were ready. Having despaired of the help of the Turkish Empire, he tried to bypass it and obtain from the British—the then rulers of Egypt—a concession for Jewish settlement in an area to the south of Palestine, in El Arish. Biblical geography was important to him too, but not enough to let the fact that El Arish lay a hundred kilometers south of the Land of the Twelve Tribes put him off his great objective: the founding of a Jewish state. When this plan fell through he was prepared, by way of an interim solution, to establish a Jewish state in Uganda, Africa. But he encountered tremendous opposition from the majority of the

Zionists, proving how closely Zionism was linked to Zion; there was and could be no substitute for the Land of Israel in the people's consciousness. He sensed that it alone could serve as the focus for the tremendous energy required to perpetrate the Jewish nationalist revolution.

In *Altneuland* Herzl envisaged the establishment of a Jewish state in a Palestine of no accurately delineated boundaries, although he presumably also saw the Land of the Twelve Tribes as the geographic basis for this state. Herzl stressed the concentration of Jewish genius and modern technology in the Land of Israel, and its transformation into a highly modern state, whose many towns and villages would lie contiguous to one another and whose standard would be that of any small, densely populated, highly developed European state.

The men of the Second Aliya sensed with every fiber of their being that there were no shortcuts to the Jewish state, and that they would attain it only by faits accomplis such as another kibbutz, another moshav, more agriculture and manufacture, a proliferation of Jewish laborers and defenders. They did not reject political Zionism; they well understood its value. But they felt that it could derive its strength only from the land, only from the field of daily work in the Land of Israel. Men of the Second Aliya, like their predecessors of the Bilu, saw the Land of the Twelve Tribes as their country; they, too, staked out claims in the Galilee and the Emeq, in mountain and plain; they too tried their luck and failed in Horan, in Bashan, in the Golan and the Gilead.

WORLD WAR I

On the eve of World War I less than a hundred thousand Jews lived in Palestine, about half of them members of the old community—Jews whose presence there antedated political Zionism—and Jewish villages did not exceed fifty in number.

The basic characteristics of the Zionist enterprise found expression in the first forty-five years of Zionism (1870–1914). The few Jews who had so far gathered in the land already had an ideology, or, more precisely, several ideologies; they had an objective and a path; they had created the initial set of tools; and, most important, they were imbued with the mighty strength of the seed of a sapling. Any keen and penetrating observer of this minuscule Zionist phenomenon at the time of the onset of World War I would have discerned the tremendous dynamic force contained within it.

The small Jewish colony in Palestine was regarded with admiration by thousands of young Jews throughout the Diaspora. They were quite prepared to immigrate to join the new builders of the country. And it was with gratitude, too, that the world Zionist movement gazed upon the Yishuv, the Jewish community in Palestine. Zionist leaders such as Nahum Sokolov and Chaim Weizmann understood that only by virtue of the strength of these hundred thousand people and the realities they had established in the country could they knock at the world's doors and demand the country for their people. At the same time, the leaders of the Arab nationalist movement began to look fearfully and with hatred upon this living thing which some of them felt was capable of becoming a predatory monster in the course of time. Out of general interest and curiosity, the politicians and strategists of a number of states who had a stake in the Middle Eastern geopolitical region began to observe this phenomenon.

Almost from the beginning of World War I, the Turks saw the new Jewish immigrants and settlers as a small but malignant thorn in one side of their crumbling empire. They began to banish and exile them from the country and almost doomed the young Jewish enterprise in the Land of Israel.

As the war began, some Zionist leaders in Palestine and others in the Diaspora went to work to win support for their cause among the Turks and Germans. Their main effort, however, was directed at the Allies: the British, French, Americans, and, to a certain extent, the Russians. Weizmann, Jabotinsky, and other leaders quickly understood that the Allies would sooner or later occupy the region and become its masters, and that negotiations must be entered into with them as soon as possible.

The Jews of Palestine, many of whom were exiled by the Turks and found refuge in Egypt, took a bold step forward. Led by Yosef Trumpeldor, a one-armed former officer in the Russian army, a few hundred of them volunteered to fight the war alongside Britain. They were organized into a mule drivers' battalion which fought in the battle of Gallipoli against the Turks. Even though these men belonged only to a service branch, it was an omen of things to come. The members of this battalion wore the uniform of the British army and fought under a British flag, but they had an emblem and a Jewish distinctiveness of their own. (An interesting and fateful historic parallel is that in the same year that the Jewish mule drivers' battalion was established, Lawrence of Arabia began to organize the first Arab rebels against the Turks.) Soon, Zionist leaders in both Palestine and in the Western Diaspora began to press for the establishment of a Jewish fighting force in the British army, which would enter Palestine when the British army conquered it from the Turks. There arose in Palestine a movement of Jewish volunteers for the British army, which, despite the bitter argument it provoked, encompassed the best of the youth and the pioneers. Moreover, part of the Jewish community founded an underground in Palestine, which engaged in intelligence and espionage on behalf of the British.

Thus it was that Weizmann, Jabotinsky, Berl Katznelson, Golomb, and Ben-Zvi founded the Jewish Battalions, while Aharonson and his comrades formed the underground Nili (Netzah Yisrael Lo Yeshaker—The Eternity of Israel Will Not Lie). The Jews had a definite feeling that on the day the British entered Palestine they must be with them; and that in any political decision touching upon the future of Palestine, the Jewish force, which had fought over the country and was among its occupiers, must be a factor. Zionist aspirations took shape in the Jewish Battalions and in Nili. The best of the moshavot members and the Second Aliya pioneers came flocking to their banners.

The Balfour Declaration of November 2, 1917, was electrifying to world Jewry, who heard in it an echo of the footfalls of the Messiah. Its implementation was the pinnacle of the Zionist movement's political effort under Weizmann's leadership. Jews were too amazed and delighted to worry about the niceties of the paper's vague wording, which in the course of time became a matter of heated contention between the British and the Jews, the British and the Arabs, and the Arabs and the Jews.

While the Jews rejoiced and were glad and proud of the Balfour Declaration, the Arabs behind the Turkish lines continued blowing up the bridges over the railroad to Hejaz, and organized themselves into a semiregular fighting force on the side of the British. Their kings and leaders, meanwhile, received written and verbal promises from the British which by no means accorded with the content of the Balfour Declaration, and were given without the assent of those who formulated and signed it.

Thus it came about that at the time of the British conquest, and the entry of Allenby's force into Transjordan, Arab armed forces entered with them, confident that the British would pay their debts and keep their promises to grant the Arabs national independence in those parts of the Turkish Empire that had fallen into their hands. Jewish troops, on the other hand, carrying the emblem of the seven-branched candlestick and the blue and white flag, put their trust in the Balfour Declaration and hoped that the Land of Israel would be for the Jews.

THE BEGINNING OF BRITISH RULE

The story of the thirty years of British rule, from 1918 until 1948, which had an ill-starred beginning of conflicting promises made to Jews and Arabs, is one of hopes and disappointments, expectations and frustrations, confrontations and ceaseless struggles among the three sides of the triangle: the British, who were governing the country and trying to maintain a precarious balance between the Jews and Arabs; the Jews, who were forcibly entering and building the country, sometimes against the will of the authorities, and were fighting both the British and the Arabs; and the Arabs, who opposed Jewish entry into Palestine and resisted both the British and the Jews by every possible means.

The Jewish hopes that the Balfour Declaration would be succeeded by the messianic era were quickly dashed against the rock of hard day-to-day reality. The world was in the throes of a postwar revolution. The Bolshevik Revolution in Russia plucked out from the body of the people millions of Jews, among them thousands and thousands of youths who, captivated by its ignis fatuus, believed it to be the solution to all the problems of the Jewish people. Jews from other countries made no move to immigrate to Palestine. Post-World War I immigration was a thin trickle.

It began to become apparent that the British, particularly the military government personnel and the Colonial Office administration, had no intention whatever of becoming a "tool in the hands of Zionism." On the contrary, they began looking askance at Jews bursting in on them waving the Balfour Declaration, and they began to display a measure of obtuseness and even hostility toward the Jewish cause.

Furthermore, beginning with the 1920 riots, the Arabs began better-organized attacks on the young Jewish colonies than had taken place under the Turks. For the first time the small Jewish community faced the violent opposition of nationalist Arabs who could not bear that Zionism should even exist and were dead set against a Jewish national home—which to them was tantamount to a Jewish state—being founded under Jewish auspices in what they thought was their Palestine.

Another heavy disappointment was in store for the Jews in

1922 when, quite arbitrarily and for entirely different purposes, the British removed east Transjordan from Palestine, severing it at a stroke from the realm of the mandate granted them by the League of Nations, and established there a Hashemite kingdom. Half of the promised land was thus suddenly torn from its body, and the Jews, with their feeble forces, had to reconcile themselves to this first partition of the Land of the Twelve Tribes.

Within the borders of western Palestine—then Mandatory Palestine—they indefatigably forged ahead, in the teeth of political frustrations and bloody riots, with the upbuilding and strengthening of the Jewish community. Some tens of thousands of Jews immigrated to Palestine in the first postwar decade, among them thousands of young and enthusiastic pioneers. These Jews of the Third and Fourth Aliya turned their energies to agriculture and small manufacture and even laid the foundations of industry. They made impressive progress in the building of towns, and founded new points of settlement on land that they continued to buy from the Arabs. The new British overlords took even greater pains than had the Turks to insure that any purchase of land by Jews was transacted legally and at full price.

In the 1920s the Jews in Palestine, with the assistance of the Jewish people, began forging the first tools for an emerging Jewish state. They founded the Jewish Agency for Palestine as a worldwide Jewish political and economic instrument; and they also founded the Va'ad Le'umi (National Committee) as a semiautonomous domestic administration. They also established the General Jewish Workers Federation (the Histadrut) as a body incorporating the trade unions and serving as a workers' instrument for medical insurance, producer and consumer cooperation, settlement, construction, industry, and educational, cultural, and artistic enterprise.

Behind the backs of the British authorities the Jews also founded an armed underground force for defense of their lives and settlements. This force—the Hagana—deriving from and nourished by the Hashomer (an armed guard organization during Turkish rule in Palestine) and the Jewish Battalions of the First World War, began to be transformed into a countrywide instrument. Jews began stockpiling weapons—now a revolver, now a rifle—and secretly training their youth.

The Palestinian Arabs also increased in strength and number during that first decade of the British Mandate. Subject, like the Jews, to British rule, they enjoyed a relatively high standard of education and health. Infant mortality declined while the birthrate shot up. Moreover, the modern, effervescent Jewish community, with which they were locked in national struggle and to which they could not reconcile themselves, exerted a mighty influence upon them, despite their reluctance. The Jews not only channeled large amounts of capital into the hands of Arab landowners, they also began employing thousands of Arab workers.

The Jewish-Arab involvement affected the Palestinian Arabs in a thousand and one ways. Though this was neither their object nor intent, the Jews became a major catalyst in the lives of the Arabs of Palestine.

The Arab national awakening, as well as the direct and indirect influence of the Jewish national home and the modernization instituted by the British colonial rule, brought in their wake a mighty and rapid change in the political, economic, and social structure of the Palestinian Arab community. The Arabs of Mandatory Palestine began to come to life, sloughing off the torpor and backwardness that had been their lot for hundreds of years under the rule of the Ottoman Empire. They began, in their own way, to found institutions and to develop a partially armed resistance movement, with the aim of extirpating the Zionist enterprise before it made any headway.

THE 1929 AND 1936 RIOTS

About ten years after the mandate began, the Arabs attacked the Jews throughout the whole country, murdering men, women, and children in towns, villages, and isolated settlements.

The 1929 riots aroused Jewish armed resistance on a scope and with a force never before known. The two antagonists faced each other with weapons at the ready. This was the beginning of an armed struggle between two nationalist movements with fundamentally conflicting aspirations. Anyone who sees these events as a clash between pitiful Jews fighting for their lives and gangs of Arab plunderers is being false to both Jews and Arabs. There were, of course, defenseless Jews who were cruelly murdered, and the pogrom-bent Arabs did not hesitate to plunder and ravage. Most of the Jews knew what was coming, however, and counterattacked. Many of the Arabs were fighting the Jews not only for the sake of murder and bloodshed but also as one fights against an enemy who has come to conquer what he considers to be his land.

The British overlords of the country were faced with the spearheads of two national movements. The British had at their disposal a military force far in excess of the strength that both camps together could muster. Somewhat belatedly, they restored law and order. A relative quiet of about seven years' duration prevailed in the land.

During those years, until 1936, the Jews continued to immigrate to Palestine in greater numbers than before, and to build and strengthen it day by day. Moreover, the Jews began to see black clouds gathering on the horizon, drawing nearer and fast covering the skies of all the world. The general rise of Fascism in Europe; the particular brand of Nazi Fascism, which flew the flag of hatred toward the Jews; the first pogroms against the Jews of Germany—all these implanted in the hearts of farseeing Jews a sense of fear for the danger threatening the lives of large segments of their people. The need to establish a "safe refuge" for the Jewish people became most urgent.

For their part, the Palestinian Arabs also began to gaze with growing wrath, indeed almost with dread, on the Jewish national home, which, in spite of all their protests, violent outbursts, and importuning of the British, was swelling and spreading before their eyes in both quantity and quality. Like their counterparts in nationalist movements in other Arab countries, many of them began to regard the black clouds now covering the international horizon as a glimmer of hope for their cause. Mussolini declared himself to be the "defender of Islam." What could have better suited the anti-Jewish and anti-Zionist aspirations of the Arabs than the slogans of the Nazis?

Bloody riots broke out in mid-1936. They lasted three years and brought with them a wave of violence among Arabs, Jews, and British. The Arab nationalist leaders tried—with no little success, despite their own conflicts—to mobilize the great majority of the Arab community to passive resistance and active warfare against the Jews and the Zionist enterprise. The Arab combatants were organized in gangs. But we might employ a different terminology, one more pertinent to our own time, and say that they were participants in a popular uprising which had all the characteristic manifestations: a protracted general strike, preparedness for sacrifice, and guerrilla warfare. One may, of course, regard Sheik Kassem and others as merely leaders of robber gangs; but at this juncture there is no need for us to make light of the fighting spirit of those Arabs. They perpetrated cruel slaughter and we fought back. We defended ourselves with marvelous heroism, and we did not allow them, in those cruel, awe-inspiring, and glorious years, to wipe out a single settlement.

By 1936 the Jewish community was better prepared for battle than it had ever been in the past. It was also better armed for self-defense and could now indeed give as good as it got. During the years of relative quiet that preceded the events of

1936, the Hagana was organized and grew into a popular underground force. The British, who saw that the Arab insurgence in Palestine was threatening their authority and their hold in that part of the world, which in light of the danger of a new world war had gained in importance, began deploying greater combat forces for its suppression. It should be stressed that the British attached far greater importance to the needs of the British Empire than to the protection of the Zionist enterprise, toward which they displayed increasing disregard.

At the end of those three years (1936–39) the Arab insurgence was put down with an iron hand. In the Middle East as a whole and in Palestine in particular, the British had begun to concentrate ever-increasing forces. The Jewish force had been toughened. Construction and settlement projects had continued steadily, even when the rioting had been at its height. Jews continued to arrive in Palestine, some of them illegally and in defiance of the British.

Although the military force of the Palestine Arabs had been suppressed by the British, the Arabs did not come to terms with the situation, and their hostility grew. Both camps, the Jewish and the Arab, buried their dead and swore to go on with the struggle. Any Arabs who had believed that the Jews in Palestine would always be a minority and could be treated with tolerance by their potential rulers now clearly understood that the Jews would now neither rest nor peace until they attained their objective: a state of their own.

Likewise, any Jewish leaders who may have once thought that it would be possible to come to terms with the Arabs now knew in their hearts that on the way to their goal—a Jewish state—they were in for an uncompromising and bloody conflict with the Palestinian Arabs and with the Arab peoples. Some of the leaders of the local Jewish community, as well as Zionist leaders, began to try to reach a solution which would lead to Jewish independence without further shedding of Jewish or Arab blood.

Palestinian Arabs were no longer regarded merely as "hewers of wood and drawers of water." Jewish leaders correctly understood that they were dealing with an Arab nationalist movement as legitimate as their own, with a people that wanted to attain, in the very same country, both national independence and a state of its own. They also began to view the Arab nationalist movement and its attendant historical processes as a whole, and realized that in the future the Jewish state they had dreamed of and fought for would not repose within the bosom of the British Mandate but would be surrounded by independent Arab states, with whom it would struggle—and eventually live. They also sensed that a day would soon come when a dreadful disaster would break about the heads of the Jewish people in the Diaspora and that it was essential that the Jews themselves hold the key that would unlock the gates of Jewish immigration to all or part of Palestine, so that the land might serve as a haven for the victims of the oncoming holocaust. British leaders too, or at least some of them, despaired of finding a solution that would satisfy the Arab wolf, whose teeth they had felt on their own flesh, and at the same time insure that the Jewish lamb, who before their eyes was metamorphosing into a butting ram, would not be devoured alive.

THE PARTITION PLAN

As a result of the 1936 riots and the circumstances they engendered, a plan of partition came into existence, by recommendation of the Peel Commission, whereby western Palestine would be divided in two: the Galilee and the central coastal plain would become a Jewish state, the rest of Palestine would be established as an Arab state, and Jerusalem would be an international city under the British aegis.

Jewish leaders were divided in their reactions to this plan. Some of them, headed by Weizmann and Ben-Gurion, accepted the principle of partition without giving their support to the boundaries and the maps proposed by the Peel Commission. They did so in acknowledgment of the fact that this prize, this land to which both Arabs and Jews laid exclusive claim, must be shared.

These leaders understood, no less clearly than their opponents, how vast a waiver this would constitute of the Jewish people's historic rights to the entire country, the inheritance of the twelve tribes. They no less than the others bore an emotional affinity for the east bank of the Jordan, the portion of the descendants of Reuben, Gad, and half the tribe of Manasseh, which was torn away during the 1920s, and to the Judean and Samarian mountains. But they were prepared to concede them in return for the founding of an independent Jewish state and on condition that the Arab nationalist movement consent to that state's existence. They were prepared to waive, not the historic rights of their people, but the fulfillment of part of those rights in portions of the promised and destined land where the Jewish people had found an Arab population demanding its rights.

Those who supported the partition plan had another motive, perhaps no less important: with the founding of the state the Jews would possess the key to the gates of immigration. To open the gates of the country to millions of Jews was at that time far more important than any other principle, including that of the fulfillment of all their just historic rights over the land.

Their opponents among the Jews regarded the partition as a disaster—not only because in their opinion anyone who agreed to the principle of partition would consent, under pressure of harsh reality, to an even worse partition and finally to a mere Jewish ghetto on the shores of the Mediterranean, but also because they considered the boundaries of the proposed Jewish state in part of western Palestine to be indefensible. Their starting point was that the Arabs would not agree even to a small Jewish state in part of Palestine; sooner or later they would attempt to destroy it, and a state so poor in territory and devoid

of strategic depth would be unable to defend itself. They regarded the supporters of the partition plan as impatient souls
who might well bring disaster upon the Zionist enterprise.

The reaction of Palestinian Arab leaders and the Arab states
to the partition plan was negative and unambiguous. The Arabs,
as stated, were never misled by words and phrases such as
"Jewish national home" and always understood the true significance of the Zionist aim. Thus the day when the words "Jewish
state" appeared in an official British document, the Peel Commission report, was for them a bitter and fateful one. They
wanted to have no part of any principle of partition or equal
rights for two peoples and two national movements. The idea
of partition was one that they rejected outright, on the grounds
that "Palestine is our home; it is being overrun by invaders who
act as if it belonged to them; no Jewish people exists, and certainly no Jewish people having any rights whatever to this country. The invaders' place is in the sea."

The Arabs' reaction, the absence of any willingness on their
part to compromise, gained the plan's opponents greater support among the Jews, who claimed, "There is no one to talk to!"
The British government, too, which from the outset had regarded the conclusions of the Peel Commission simply as
recommendations or a sort of trial balloon, gave them no firm
backing. The Arabs' total opposition and the Jewish controversy
made the British all the more reluctant to accept the partition
plan, and they washed their hands of it.

It is now more than thirty years since this controversy first
raged in Zionist circles, and even today it still reverberates—
under completely different conditions and circumstances, of
course. The argument is about the principle of partition. No
one, at least among Jews, disputes the historic right of the Jewish people to the Land of the Twelve Tribes. What is at issue is
whether one should be prepared to waive fulfillment of part of
those historic rights for the sake of the neighboring Palestinian
Arab people, in order to establish two states, for two peoples,
within the same stretch of territory.

This argument is being pursued, mainly among ourselves, to this very day. On the day that an open and frank discussion of this kind commences among Palestinian Arab leaders too, and some of them stand up and say, candidly and courageously, that they are prepared to waive fulfillment of part of their rights in favor of the neighboring Jewish people in order to establish two states for two peoples within the same stretch of territory, then one of the first steps will have been taken toward true dialogue between the two peoples.

WORLD WAR II

As World War II approached, the British sought to win the Arabs back to their side in the Middle East. They knew that one of the most tempting baits for the Arabs would be to give expression to a policy that would hamper the Zionist enterprise. Therefore they published the White Paper of 1939, which in essence closed the gates of Palestine in the face of Jewish immigrants and also drastically restricted the land-purchasing potential of Jews.

To a certain extent the White Paper did serve as a sop to the Arabs; but it did not transform them into friends of the British. At the same time, it roused the ire of the Jews, making them the sworn foes of the British authorities in Palestine. The Jews began to regard the British and not the Arabs as the main obstacle to the progress of their enterprise and as the ones who were barring the gates of Jewish immigration and foreclosing any possibility of delivering the Diaspora from certain destruction.

With the outbreak of World War II, the British took their stand in the vanguard of those fighting against Nazi Germany and Fascist Italy. The Jewish community in Palestine rallied to the banner and entered the war, which was also a war for the survival of the Jewish people. The small Jewish Yishuv, about half a million in number, mustered thirty thousand volunteer soldiers for the war effort. They fought in the ranks of the

British army on the fronts of the Middle East, in the Western
Desert, and in Europe.

As war raged, the great holocaust descended upon the Jewish
people, and one-third of its number—some six million persons
—lost their lives.

About twenty-five years have passed since then, and in the
Land of Israel there has arisen a generation to whom the holocaust is known from documents, books, the trial of Adolf Eich-
mann, and stories of survivors. But anyone who does not understand the full force of the shock the Jewish people sustained and
sustains to this very day as a result of the holocaust, and the
reactions it still arouses in us, will fail to understand not only
what happened afterward—the violent struggle, the rebellion
against the British, the illegal immigration, the founding of the
State of Israel—but also the reactions of the Jewish people in the
State of Israel and the rest of the world to contemporary events.

It should not be forgotten that those who now lead the State
of Israel and the Jewish people are still members of the generation of the holocaust. Some underwent it in person; others
fought and tried to rescue their doomed brothers but could not;
others stood helpless, cried out, and tried to recruit the aid of
"enlightened" humanity, but to no avail.

Nor should this be forgotten: in every other home in Israel
and the Diaspora, there still lives the memory of fathers and
mothers, brothers and sisters, sons, daughters, relatives who
died in the holocaust. The fact that we continue to live our daily
lives and give birth to daughters and sons would seem to indicate that the wound has healed and is no longer bleeding; but
in the heart of the Jewish people the terrible aftermath of the
holocaust still remains. Not only corpses were consumed by fire
in the ovens and gas chambers, but also a faith in humanity and
its values. If this was what people could do to us, if they could
become rampaging beasts of prey, if they could wreak this upon
us in the middle of the twentieth century, in an age that has
pretensions to universal values, if they were capable of doing

this to defenseless, helpless people, one can only conclude that man's worst enemy is man, that there is no conscience and no civilization.

The Jews who were rescued from the holocaust have become embittered, have lost their faith in the human race and its values, and have learned their lesson: "Woe to the weak!" The lesson that the inmates of the death camps learned upon their persons has become a warning signal to the Jewish people: "None will help him who does not help himself! Be strong and thou shalt live!"

If the Jewish cup of affliction was not filled to overflowing after the holocaust, if there remained in Jewish hearts a spark of faith and hope that the victory over the Nazis would bring Jews life and redemption not only as individuals but also as a people, the postwar years came along and added insult to injury. Those who survived and remained in Eastern Europe found themselves in the "black years" of Stalin, and those who fled westward to Palestine found the gates of the country slammed in their faces by the British.

In the years 1945–47, the Jews of Palestine, together with the remnants of the holocaust, helped by world Jewry, mustered what remaining strength they had for the fight against the British. The Yishuv's armed struggle, the flight and the illegal immigration to Palestine, by untrodden paths, through the desert, and over the sea, was a desperate one. The fighting Jews placed the British, who had defeated the Nazis, in a position of having to permit Jewish immigration to Palestine or to imitate Nazi methods—to beat and kill Jews. In 1947 the British government decided to get out of Palestine and leave the decision as to the fate of the country in the hands of the newly established United Nations.

Out of motives that arose partly from political and world power calculations and partly from the stricken conscience of nations that had stood aside while the Jewish people was being destroyed, on November 29, 1947, the United Nations decided to partition western Palestine into a Jewish and an Arab state and to make Jerusalem an international city.

The great majority of Jews in Palestine, as well as the Jews in the British concentration camps on Cyprus and elsewhere, and the Jews in the Diaspora accepted this solution joyfully. It was the joy of the poor, of warriors weary of the slaughter and yielding to the world's decision to grant them reparations and allot them a small piece of land of their own in ancient Palestine where they could live, produce, lick their wounds, erect memorials to their dead, and raise their children.

The Palestinian Arabs, along with other Arab nations, who had hardly fought in the world war and who had gained in power and strength, opposed the UN resolution. The Arabs, who in many countries now stood on the threshold of liberation and independence, their oil-rich states now a geopolitical and economic factor of the first degree, retorted with an unambiguous "No!" to the Palestine partition plan. They fondly imagined that even if the UN decided on partition, it would never come about and that they would throw the Jewish "invaders" into the sea.

The Arab nationalist movement was at the time in high gear. The war-weary English and French were prepared to grant the Arabs, in the foreseeable future, national and political independence in most of their lands. The Arabs had never experienced the sufferings that had fallen to the lot of the Jewish people, and up to that time had sustained the destruction of not a single Arab village in Palestine; nor had a single Arab gone into exile or become a refugee. They did not understand, perhaps could not understand, and certainly did not want to understand what the Jews had borne in the past, particularly during the holocaust. They did not understand the Jews, this people-that-was-not-a-people, these destitute refugees, persecuted and hated by all; they could not perceive the tremendous force that was latent in Jewish postwar despair. They certainly could not understand how six hundred thousand Jews would defend themselves against a great and very powerful Arab world, and how they would be capable of implementing the partition on their own. They were confident, as they had every reason to be, that no people, certainly not the British, who were now leaving the country, would come to the aid of the Jews. What they did not reckon with was the Jews' lack of alternative. Since all the Jews of Palestine and the survivors of the camps took the resounding Arab "No" and the "Throw them into the sea" slogan literally, they saw themselves once more threatened with a holocaust.

THE WAR OF INDEPENDENCE AND THE FOUNDING OF THE STATE

In late 1947 the Jews and Arabs embarked on a cruel, bitter, and bloody struggle that rapidly became an all-out war. When the British Mandate ended on May 15, 1948, this war was already well under way in all parts of the country, from the Galilee through Jerusalem to the Negev. Almost every Jewish and Arab point of settlement became a front line. So intertwined in the geographic sense were the Jewish and Arab communities that no village, neighborhood, suburb, or town was far from the front.

The nearer the date of British departure drew, the more cruel the war became. The Jews understood that the moment was fast approaching when they would remain face to face not only with the Palestinian Arabs, but also with the regular armies of five, six, or seven independent Arab states, which were mobilizing their armed forces and placing them in a state of readiness for the day when the British left the country. The Jews knew that the Arab armies would enter Palestine with the clear intention of "throwing the Jews into the sea" and "liberating" the land from the Zionist enterprise, which they would utterly wipe out.

The Jews started a race against time, trying to consolidate their position in an unbroken area along the coastal plain, so as to have a port in which to unload the arms arriving from overseas. It should not be forgotten that at that time, while facing the very real danger of intervention by regular Arab armies equipped with armor and artillery and possessing a navy and an air force, the Jews, whose army had just begun to emerge from its underground status, had only a few thousand rifles and revolvers, and some hundreds of machine guns and light homemade mortars. That race against time and the fearsome initial imbalance of arms became deeply etched in the psychology of our generation.

In the fateful months of early 1948 the Jews put all their resourcefulness, ability to improvise, and financial know-how into procuring and shipping arms. In April and May 1948 the area of Palestine began to experience the cruel onslaughts of the Arabs against Jewish urban and rural areas of settlement. Arabs seized Jewish land. The Jews defended themselves, fought back, and seized Arab lands. A Jewish and Arab refugee problem was created.

Throughout the seventy-eight years of the Zionist enterprise and the dispute between Jews and Arabs, from 1870 to 1948, not one inch of land had been taken from the Arabs by force and not one single Arab became a refugee. However, when the War of Independence broke out, we faced a heartrending dilemma: either the Arabs would conquer our lands and destroy our settlements, or we would conquer Arab land and Arab villages.

What was liable to befall us at the hands of the Arabs if we did not win this war became clear while the fighting was in its early stages. For the first time in about two thousand years Jewish warriors and civilians were taken captive in their own land—the people of Gush Etzion and the Jewish quarter of the Old City, which had been conquered by the Arab Legion. All Jewish settlements taken by the Arabs were razed: Ataroth, Neveh Yaakov, Revadim, Masuoth Yitschak, and Kfar Etzion, the Jewish quarter of the Old City. Their inhabitants were killed, banished, or expelled. The cruel war brought death, destruction, and refugees to both sides. But soon the Jews gained the upper hand and took more Arab villages than the Arabs did Jewish settlements; and a greater number of Arabs fled for their lives than did Jews.

With the establishment of the state, while the bloody battles still raged, some Jews besought their Arab neighbors in various places to stay and not run away. But one can understand the Arabs for not heeding such advances and for fleeing their villages in fear of the Jewish sword above their heads. Arab leaders encouraged their flight, confident that after May 15 the Arab armies would sweep away the "Zionist gangs," and that then whoever had run away would return in the wake of the victorious Arab armies and help make a final settling of accounts with the Jews. But one should not ignore the fact that the Arabs, with their women and children, fled from the raging flames of war, as refugees take flight in every war. What the Arabs could not grasp was that the Jews had nowhere to run. Moreover, the Jews had firmly resolved never to become fugitives again and to die rather than let such a thing happen. This resolve was not understood by the Palestinian Arabs, or indeed by the leaders of the Arab states and the commanders of their armed forces. On May 15, 1948, a concerted attack was launched on the State of Israel. Arab armies came from the north, the east, and the south, tens of thousands of regulars, with their Bren-gun carriers, their tanks, and their artillery. At the same time, Arabs began bombing Israel from the air and shelling her from the sea. For the first time in the history of the dispute between Jews and Arabs over the Land of Israel, the two camps faced one another in direct confrontation.

The establishment of the State of Israel, declared by the leadership of the Yishuv led by Ben-Gurion on May 14, 1948, was the height of achievement of the long chronicle of the Jewish people since it was exiled from its land, a pinnacle that a people reaches only once in its history.

The Israeli army fought a war of about eight months' duration with the armies of the Arab states. When it ended with the victory of the Israeli army in early 1949, armistice agreements were signed between Israel and the Arab states that had attacked her.

In the course of the war the Jews came to know what they could expect from regular Arab armies. The Jewish settlements that stood in the path of the Egyptian army and were occupied by it were utterly wiped out. Only by a supreme effort was the Egyptian army staved off about thirty kilometers south of Tel Aviv. The Jordanian Arab Legion managed to lay siege to about a hundred thousand Jews in Jerusalem. It bombarded them ceaselessly, causing hundreds of casualties, among them women, old men, and children—and almost succeeded in killing off the city's inhabitants by thirst and hunger. The Syrian army, too, which had occupied a number of Jewish settlements in the north of Israel, perpetrated indiscriminate slaughter against both soldiers and civilians.

The price paid by the Arab armies was very heavy, but the price paid by the Arabs of Palestine was greater by sevenfold. Together with the Arab armies that were routed by the army of Israel, hundreds of thousands of Arabs also fled and became refugees.

The war ended. Armistice agreements were signed, and the State of Israel arose within borders which it maintained for the eighteen years preceding the Six-Day War. The territories demarcated by these borders were larger than those recommended by the United Nations Assembly. Whereas under the UN partition plan only part of the Galilee was included in the Jewish state, the whole of the Galilee was now within its borders. The coastal strip was widened in an easterly and southerly direction, and the Negev was almost entirely in Israeli hands. Israel occupied territories and lands which had been in Arab hands and now remained desolate, for their inhabitants had fled and become refugees in neighboring Arab countries.

It should be remembered that the war between the Jews and the Arabs was not over UN borders at all, but over the very existence of the state. Neither the UN nor any other state that voted for the partition plan with the UN boundaries came to Israel's assistance in her war. Even when Jewish Jerusalem, which was supposed to have been part of an international enclave, was about to fall into the hands of the Jordanian Arab Legion, no one lifted a finger to come to its aid. The Jews helped themselves, and succeeded in forcing a corridor into the New (western) City of Jerusalem, while the Arabs managed to hold the Old (eastern) City and to create an unbroken line with the other parts of the West Bank that remained under the Arab Legion's dominance and were annexed to Jordan. Each side retained the territories it had been strong enough to occupy. The 1948 boundaries were carved out by the sword.

The Jews, who had dreamed that their state would be founded peacefully through the purchase of one desolate uninhabited dunam of land after another, through the building, with their own hands and their own money, of villages and towns, who were prepared to seek any mode of peaceful compromise with their neighbors, the Arabs of Palestine, and share the country with them—the Jews had now acquired a state of their own through the terrible means by which most peoples in history had acquired their states: by blood and the sword.

JEWISH REFUGEES AND ARAB REFUGEES

The founding of the State of Israel was therefore an event of decisive importance for both peoples. The Jews did not exult over their victory. Indeed, how could they exult while they wept, not only for their millions of dead in Europe, but also for the thousands who fell in the War of Independence? The Arabs began living their own terrible tragedy, which to this very day pursues them like a nightmare. Thousands, perhaps tens of thousands of them fell in battle; hundreds of thousands of ref-

ugees found themselves wandering, totally destitute, in Arab
countries. But perhaps most painful of all was the realization
that they had been beaten by the Jews, in regard to whom they
had told the world: "Just leave us face to face with them, and
we shall show them the meaning of our strength." This blow to
their dignity and national pride they found to be insufferable.

Once the War of Independence was over, a new set of circumstances had been created. Zionism had gained what it had
set out to achieve. With the founding of the state it could now
set about its main purpose: to become an open and secure
haven for any Jew who wanted or was forced to immigrate to
it. The state was a small one. Its territory did not exceed twenty
thousand square kilometers. Its borders were long and winding,
arbitrary, and full of weak spots. The most vulnerable spot was
the soft and narrow neck of land in the region of the coast,
which in some places was no more than fifteen kilometers wide.
The capital of the new state—Jerusalem—was divided in two,
part in Jordanian and part in Israeli hands. At the time of the
founding of the state, its Jewish population was small, sparse,
and wounded; its coffers were empty and its granaries bare. But
it was firmly resolved to provide immediately for the Jewish
refugees for whose sake the state had been founded.

The partitioned Land of Israel of 1948–49 now had two refugee problems: that of the Arab refugees, who were concentrated under dreadful conditions on the West Bank, which had
been annexed to Jordan by the Hashemites, and in the Egyp-
tian-held Gaza Strip; and that of the Jewish refugees, tens of
thousands of whom were in the detention camps in Cyprus and
in displaced persons camps in Europe, waiting to reach Israel.
And now that the state was established, there were added to
their numbers the tens and hundreds of thousands of potential
refugees among the Jews of the Arab states, who, after the
Jewish victory over the Arabs, found themselves perched as it
were on a volcano and turned their faces toward Israel.

Israel opened wide her gates to the Jewish refugees. Hundreds of thousands of Jewish immigrants, including survivors of the holocaust, living embers snatched from Auschwitz and Bergen-Belsen, from Maidanek and Treblinka, reached the shores of Israel. With them, and also immediately after them, hundreds of thousands of Jews came from the Arab states: fifty thousand Yemenite Jews traveled hundreds of kilometers on foot and in camel caravans until they reached the Aden airfield —from there they were flown to Israel; about a hundred and fifty thousand Iraqi Jews fled to Israel; fifty thousand persecuted Egyptian Jews also arrived in Israel; twenty thousand Jews from Syria and Lebanon and about a quarter of a million Jews from Morocco arrived by roundabout routes over land and sea, as well as fifty thousand Jews from Libya and about fifty thousand from Algeria and Tunisia.

Within a few years the population of Israel had doubled. Before the state had celebrated its first decade of existence, the number of immigrants to Israel totaled about a million, 40 percent of them from Europe, mostly refugees of the holocaust, and about 60 percent totally destitute refugees from the Arab countries.

What took place when Jewish refugees immigrated to Israel after the establishment of the state and Arab refugees fled the country might in effect be described as a population transfer, like others that have occurred in different parts of the world during and after wars, or as part of the settlements reached by the states concerned. For every Palestinian Arab refugee who fled to one of the Arab states, a Jewish refugee arrived from those states. Regarding property, assessments were made of the worth of the property left behind by the Arab refugees in Israel, but no accounting has so far been given of the vast property left behind by Jews who immigrated to Israel from the Arab states, most of which was confiscated by the Arabs.

There are those who have said: "The little State of Israel, with an area of twenty thousand square kilometers, absorbed one and a half million new immigrants, the great majority of whom were refugees, and did so with the help of contributions by world Jewry and with the aid of international capital. Why, then, should not the Arab states, with an area one hundred times that of Israel, and for the most part thinly populated but blessed with some of the greatest natural resources in the world, do the same? If they really wanted to come to the aid of their Palestinian Arab brothers, it should be no hardship for them to allocate the necessary capital and find jobs and homes for about a million Arab refugees and thus rehabilitate them." But the people who propound these arguments do not seem to realize how profound the emotional hurt was, how stunning the force of the blow dealt to Arab national pride, how great was the will for vengeance on the part of the Arabs in general and the Palestinian Arabs in particular; nor have they reckoned with the Arab hope that the small, weak, newly founded State of Israel would sooner or later be defeated in another war, after which the refugees would repossess their former homes.

Thus, Arab leaders and rulers began transforming the Palestinian Arab refugees into a powerful political and psychological weapon in their war against Israel, preserving them in stagnation in compassion-arousing camps around Israel's new borders, and fanning in their hearts the flames of frustration, hatred, and revenge.

During the 1950s Israel began setting up large-scale settlement projects, where the Jewish immigrants were brought to live. Dozens of new towns were built, hundreds of new villages were founded, part on the lands of Arab refugees and part on stony, waste soil and desert tracts never before cultivated. Thousand of boreholes were drilled, tens of thousands of kilometers of water pipes were laid, and hundreds of new industrial enterprises were established. By virtue of immigration and hard work, the State of Israel became in fact a Jewish state. About 15 percent of Israel's population consisted of Palestinian Arabs who had not fled and become refugees. They received Israeli citizenship and gradually, with many ups and downs and much soul-searching and chagrin, began to be integrated into the Jewish state—if not out of love, then out of full or partial acceptance of it and their fate.

When the state was founded, those who stood at the helm were men of the Second and Third Aliyas, headed by David Ben-Gurion. This leadership had indeed realized the Zionist dream in their own lifetimes: a Jewish state open for the absorption of immigrants. Yet these leaders never ceased being pursued by the nightmare, which they bequeathed to our own generation, that this small and tender life could be destroyed at any moment. From their own experience they knew that the continued physical existence of the State of Israel depended on its strength and resourcefulness; and so they plowed the best part of their energy and initiative into fortifying the army and harnessing all the resources of the state and the Jewish people to the supreme task of defense.

The Arabs could not endure the shame of the defeat they had sustained in 1948. They sought to explain how such a thing could have happened and to find a scapegoat. The explanation was invented: tales of "foreign powers" and "imperialist powers" that had allegedly provided the Jews with soldiers, arms, and money. They preferred being "defeated" by mighty empires than by weak Jews. (This skillfully nurtured self-delusion led the Arabs into an error in assessing Israel's own true strength and was one of the causes of their further defeats.) The Arabs had no difficulty finding scapegoats: they settled on the rulers—kings or presidents—of the Arab states that had fought Israel. A few short years after the war saw King Farouk of Egypt deposed, Abdallah murdered, and a series of Syrian presidents either ousted or assassinated. The king of Iraq was murdered. In the mid-1950s the Arabs could say to themselves: "Our former leaders were nothing but traitors. They were corrupt; they failed to prepare the army for the war with the Jews, and instead of purchasing arms they raked in fortunes for themselves. Now that we have ousted them and have new leaders at our helm who were not among the signatories of the armistice agreements with Israel, and who were not responsible for our downfall, we shall prepare with all our strength for the next round. We shall put all our energies into founding a strong, modern army, and when the day comes we shall attack Israel and destroy her." Tension between Israel and her neighbors mounted, and an arms race between them began.

In the refugee camps in Egypt, Jordan, and Syria, Palestinian Arabs, helped by the regular Arab armies, began to establish the fedayeen organizations for the purpose of waging guerrilla warfare against Israel. The members of the fedayeen trained in infiltrating Jewish settlements, murdering civilians, laying mines, and setting ambushes. They tried, with no little success, to undermine the security of life in Israel; in a few areas they actually succeeded in half paralyzing the normal course of life. Israel struck back with reprisal raids, attacking the bases of the fedayeen. Thus began a ghastly vicious circle of "an eye for an eye." The new Egyptian regime headed by Gamal Abdel Nasser closed the Straits of Tiran and blocked the passage of Israeli ships and aircraft to the Red Sea, to Africa, and to Asia. Nasser also joined Egypt to Syria and founded the United Arab Republic. His main purpose was stated clearly: destroy Israel. Israel demanded that Egypt desist from providing cover for the fedayeen and reopen the Straits of Tiran. But the fedayeen attacks intensified and the Straits of Tiran remained closed to Israeli shipping.

FROM THE SINAI CAMPAIGN TO THE SIX-DAY WAR

In 1956 the Israeli government decided to initiate military action to liquidate the fedayeen bases in the Gaza Strip and Sinai, and at the same time to deal the Egyptian army a telling blow. The British, and more particularly the French, who at that time wanted to force Nasser to repeal the nationalization of the Suez Canal, began coordinating and planning a combined action with Israel. The Sinai Campaign, which started in October 1956, ended in a brilliant military victory. The Israeli army swept over the Sinai Peninsula and almost reached the Suez Canal.

The British-French "Mosquito" operation, aimed at taking the canal, ended in a shameful failure. The opposition of the Americans, who had not been consulted about the operation, and the threats of the Soviets, who now perceived an excellent opportunity for penetrating the Middle East, resulted in the British being frightened off, and nipped the operation in the bud. The British-French effort quickly crumbled, their forces retreated from Port Said, and the UN forces reached the canal.

Israel was subjected to tremendous American, Russian, and international pressure, and she agreed to retreat from Sinai and the Gaza Strip in return for vague international promises that the Straits of Tiran would always remain open to her shipping and that a UN force would be stationed at Sharm el Sheik, Sinai, and the Gaza Strip, as a buffer between her and her enemies.

By representing the Israeli operation as part of the British and French military action, Nasser cunningly and very skillfully succeeded in converting the military defeat he had sustained at the hands of Israel in Sinai into a psychological victory. He could now strut before his own people and the Arab world as the man who had succeeded in overcoming two mighty imperialist powers and the State of Israel combined.

The effects on the Arabs of Nasser's psychological victory lasted for ten years; their national pride was not damaged as a result of the Sinai Campaign. Nasser and his supporters began to believe that they really had routed everyone, including the Israelis, and that, if strengthened, their army would be able to enter a third and decisive round in which "they would throw the Jews into the sea."

Moreover, the Sinai Campaign provided the Arabs with "proof" that Israel was seeking expansion and further conquests of Arab territory. The assertion that Israel is an expansionist state with a boundless appetite for encroachment had always found a willing ear among the Arabs. The fact that the Jews had twice agreed to the partition of the country was in their eyes a mere stratagem behind which lay concealed the "true aim" of the Jews: the conquest of as much Arab territory as possible. Arab leaders also made use of the slogans of Israeli political parties of extremist ideology to show that the Jews aimed to conquer the whole of western Palestine and Transjordan and were directing their gaze at the banks of the Euphrates and the Nile. Among the masses they spread the tale of a map hung in the Knesset building, showing the borders of a gigantic future Jewish empire.

Israeli contentions that Israel was prepared to content herself permanently with the 1949 armistice boundaries as final borders, on the sole condition that they be recognized by the Arab states and that peace treaties accordingly be signed between the Arab states and Israel, were of no avail.

Israel's persistence in going ahead with her agricultural and urban development projects, and with the absorption of hundreds of thousands of new immigrants after the 1956 war, were in Arab eyes further proof that little Israel was filling up with masses of Jews, who sooner or later "would burst out and overrun additional territories." In vain Israel reiterated that to import millions of Jews she had no need of even one more dunam of land, since half of her territory was completely uninhabited, and that she would absorb the immigration by modern technology and methods entailing no added terrain.

By the mid-1960s, when Israel had become a state of two and a half million inhabitants, the hostility of the Arab peoples and their leaders had not diminished. Their desire for revenge had not abated, nor had their suspicion regarding Israel's expansionist intentions been allayed. On the contrary, the hostility, the will to revenge, and the suspicion had been fanned to even greater intensity by a new generation of leaders, sprung from the Palestinian Arabs, who saw the destruction of Israel as a state to be the sole and final solution to their problem.

Israel had not plumbed the full depth of these feelings of the Arabs in general and the Palestinian Arabs in particular. A few years of relative quiet on the border, from the late 1950s until mid–1967, had led to a slackening of tension inside Israel and to a swift rise in the standard of living. Israel had allowed herself to slide into grave political wrangles and factionalism, and was devoting herself to devising measures to slow down the economy, which resulted in severe unemployment.

The renewal of fedayeen and Fatah activities on the borders and in the interior, in the mid-1960s, came as a surprise. Israel had also failed to assess accurately the depth of Soviet penetration into the Arab states.

The first arms deals between Egypt and the Soviet Union had been made in the mid-1950s, and in the 1956 Sinai Campaign, part of the Egyptian army was equipped with modern Soviet weaponry. It was inevitable that the Soviet Union should try to penetrate the vacuum created when the British and French left the Middle East, and that the Soviets should try to exploit the Arab-Israeli dispute to their own ends by appearing as the defenders of the Arab cause. Nevertheless, it might have been supposed that with her realistic knowledge of the true balance of forces between the Arab states and Israel, the Soviet Union would also serve as a restraining factor, and would not advise the Arab states to enter into a decisive military confrontation with Israel. The Soviets, one would imagine, were bound to have seen that if the Arabs lost this campaign, their own prestige would be severely damaged. But if the Arabs won and liquidated the State of Israel with the help of Soviet weapons, the Soviet Union as well as the Arabs would stand accused of genocide.

In 1967 Israel felt that the Arab states, headed by Egypt, were not yet ready to engage in total war. Egypt had become involved in an ill-starred war in Yemen, which should have proved to her leaders that their army was not yet capable of grappling even with nonregular troops equipped with primitive weapons. Israel also believed that Nasser himself knew the truth of the drubbing his army had taken in Sinai in 1956 and that he at least was not intoxicated by the propaganda that had transformed that defeat into a victory.

But Israel had not reckoned with the Palestinian Arab factor. She had not fathomed the depth of ferment that had arisen among the younger generation of Palestinian refugees, who under the tutelage of the Arab states had become an explosive element in the Middle East. These Palestinian Arabs saw that by means of terrorism and guerrilla warfare both Arab and other "liberation movements" were going from strength to strength and succeeding in liberating their countries. They watched the victory of the Algerian Liberation Front (without understanding that it had fought against an army sent from a dissent-torn and war-weary home country). They reveled in the victory of Castro (without noticing that in Cuba what had taken place was an internal social revolution, not the war of one people against another). They were deeply impressed by the modes of combat and the success of the Viet Cong (ignoring the fact that in Vietnam the struggle was between two social systems and two powers, each exploiting one half of the very same people).

The Palestinian Arabs climbed aboard this careering bandwagon and founded the Fatah and other "liberation movements" along the lines of models then existing in various parts of the world. The purpose of their organization was to destroy Israel and found on her ruins an Arab Palestine. They would do so by waging ever-increasing terror within Israel and also by drawing the Arab states into the struggle with Israel. Well aware that Israel would react to any military action on the part of the Arab states, they hoped and believed that in the final analysis the armed frontier clashes would lead to total confrontation between the Arab armies and Israel.

These young Palestinian Arabs regarded the founding of a guerrilla movement, which would relentlessly and mercilessly fight Israel, as the only way of achieving a "return" to their homeland and the eradication of the Jewish state. They began to implement their program in the mid-1960s, and they succeeded in intensifying terrorist activities on Israel's borders and in her interior. They managed to draw extremist Syria into constantly mounting military activity. Their calculation that Israeli reprisals would escalate the conflict was correct.

THE SIX-DAY WAR

As though by an irresistible force, the Egyptians were swept into the maelstrom set in motion by the Palestinian Arabs. Thus without planning or forethought on the part of any factor other than the Fatah, an unbearable tension came to prevail in May 1967 between the Arab states and Israel. The danger of a military confrontation between them grew. Within a few days the great Arab armies and the Israeli army faced one another in battle array. Nasser managed to have the UN force sent from Sinai and moved most of his army up to the Israeli border. Intoxicated by this slight "victory," he again closed the Straits of Tiran. When this operation (which involved nothing but the expulsion of a few hundred UN soldiers from Sharm el Sheik) also went over easily, he declared an approaching "Day of Reckoning" and the imminent destruction of Israel. A mighty wave of excitement engulfed the Arabs. Jordan and her king were caught up in the whirlwind of war and Syria felt herself to be the chief dervish in this dance of death that had begun to spin around Israel. The other Arab states too, to a greater or lesser degree, became inflamed at the thought that the day of vengeance and requital was at hand.

In this explosive state of affairs, the Soviets did not exercise their restraining influence. On the contrary, overtly and secretly they planted in Arab hearts the hope that this time the Soviet Union would back the Arabs to the hilt. The states of the West, the Americans and the others, wrung their hands and expressed sympathy and regret. Israel was left alone to face the Arab armies.

The Arabs did not understand (and this was not the first time their lack of understanding had led to their defeat) the reaction of Jews in Israel and the world to their threats. The Jews took the Arab threats very seriously, crediting them with the full weight of their terrible meaning. The Arabs did not understand the degree of emotional turbulence into which their threats had plunged the entire Jewish people, which not long since had undergone the holocaust. Nor did the Arabs fully grasp the fact that the two and a half million Jews living in Israel clung to their land and loved it, as any other people loves its homeland, and were prepared to defend it and die for it.

It is quite possible that the divisiveness, the quarrels, the mutual recriminations, and the sharp criticism leveled by the press at certain aspects of life in Israel, and the open and frank public discussion of them, appeared to the Arabs (and possibly to the Soviets too) as signs of internal weakness in the country. And they could not gauge how great was the strength of Israel's army, and of the large and modern—even by universal stand-ards—reserve force which Israel could cast into the battle arena at a few hours' notice.

Who except Israel's nearest Arab neighbors could, on the face of it, have been expected to understand some of these basic facts from past experience, and correctly estimate the power of the coiled steel spring they were up against? But the bitter lessons of 1948 and 1956 were suddenly forgotten in May 1967, and the Arabs, almost without exception, were seized with a frenzy of vengeance upon Israel. There was not a power in the world that could have cooled their ardor and prevented the war.

On June 5, 1967, as Israel felt the noose drawing tighter, she released the coiled spring and the Israeli army hurtled into the fray with tremendous force, overwhelming the armies of Egypt, Jordan, and Syria, which stood blocking their path. Within six days she conquered the whole of Sinai as far as the Suez Canal, the West Bank along the whole length of the Jordan River, and the Golan Heights.

When the smoke of battle cleared, a stunned silence fell upon conquered and conquerors alike. The former were dumb-founded at the magnitude of the defeat and the latter at the scope of the victory. The whole world was stupefied. Even those who had believed in Israel's strength had had no inkling of how great the victory would be; and those, like the Soviets and others, who had believed in the power of the Arabs, could not grasp how great was the defeat they had sustained. After the cease-fire was declared, and the Jews and Arabs had buried their dead, both sides were faced by a completely new situation, a new map of the Middle East. Moreover, from now on the Arab-Israeli dispute had become a true focal point of international tension and a danger to world peace.

First of all—and perhaps here lies the key to an understanding of the new situation—each side was convinced that the worst of its fears and suspicions had been amply borne out. If the Jews had been in need of decisive proof that the Arabs meant to destroy them, the Arabs had provided such proof in the most convincing manner. Volumes could be filled with the unambiguous declarations voiced by the Arabs regarding their intention of liquidating Israel. The overt statements, the fire-and-brimstone speeches of the Arab leaders, the hysterical reaction of the inflamed and bloodthirsty masses seen on television and movie screens in Israel and the rest of the world—all these will take the Jews of Israel a very long time to forget.

The dread foreboding of those days was also deeply etched into the consciousness of world Jewry. While most of the Jews of Israel knew their own true strength and were imbued with the force of their will to victory, many of the Jews of the Diaspora went about in fear that one day they would hear the dread tidings of the liquidation of the State of Israel and the slaughter or exile of its Jews. The memory of the holocaust reared its head and cast its shadow upon world Jewry, and resulted in the unqualified identification with Israel that came from the whole of world Jewry: Zionists and anti-Zionists, Orthodox and secular,

those steeped in national consciousness and those bent on assimilation. All were vividly aware, even more than during the
War of Independence, that the Arab threat to destroy Israel was
a direct threat against the whole Jewish people and against
every individual member of it.

For the Arabs, the brilliant victory of the Israeli army, which
conquered territories three times the size of Israel, supplied the
"proof" that their constant suspicion of Israel's expansionist
ambition was warranted. In vain Israel argued that this had
been both a preemptive and a defensive war, and that had her
forces not carried the war into the enemy's camp, the latter
would, within hours or days, have crossed her exposed and
vulnerable borders and tried to destroy her. And to no avail
were Israel's explanations that on June 5, the day the war
against Egypt broke out, Israel had asked the king of Jordan not
to open fire on the eastern front and had promised that his
kingdom would come to no harm.

It was all in vain. The Arabs had to have some pretext for the
magnitude of their defeat. They tried to convince themselves
that in fact they had intended no harm, that their armies had
not intended to attack Israel at all, that the maneuvers they had
engaged in had been a mere "demonstration of strength," that
all their talk had been mere inflamed rhetoric and verbal fire-
works. They tried to convince themselves that it was Israel that
had taken advantage of the situation and unleashed a surprise
attack for the purposes of conquest and expansion. Only by
offering themselves such explanations could the Arabs achieve
some psychological veneer, thin though it might be, to conceal
the naked truth.

This time the defeated Arabs could not claim, as they had
done in 1956 (and to some extent in 1948 too), that foreign
forces had fought at the side of the "cowardly Jews." This time
the war had been that of a people that had of its own accord
decided to take up arms, without consulting its friends and
without asking anyone to send even a single soldier to its aid.

TERRORIST ACTIVITIES AND THE
WAR OF ATTRITION

The first Arabs to recover from the defeat were those in the Palestinian Arab armed organizations. They were able to explain the situation to themselves more easily than were the others, since it was they who had propelled the Arab states toward the military confrontation. Their explanation focused upon the accusation of Israeli expansionism. The Israelis would not rest, they claimed, until they reached the Euphrates and the Nile and from there dictated peace terms to the Arab world.

Moreover, the leaders of the Palestinian Arab organizations believed that now, strangely enough, they had stumbled upon an opportunity to conduct a true guerrilla war against Israel and destroy her from within. They hoped that they would be able to organize a classic war of the defeated against their conquerors. They would establish an armed underground based within and leaning upon an Arab population ruled by a foreign power, which would also be helped by thousands of Israeli Arabs situated in Israel's very heartland. They were convinced that, together with the Israeli Arabs and a million Palestinian Arabs who were now under Israeli occupation, and with the help of the Arab states, they would be able to wage guerrilla and commando warfare against Israel, give her no rest, make life unbearable for her citizens, and deter immigrants and tourists from coming to the country. And, furthermore, the Palestinian Arab organizations now saw themselves as combatants against Jews everywhere, since the Jews themselves had proved to them that all were potential and actual Zionists; it was therefore necessary to strike terror into Jews everywhere in the world: in Zionist organizations and Israeli embassies and institutions abroad, in the air and on land and sea.

In the first three years after the Six-Day War, the Palestinian Arab organizations, headed by the Fatah, went through a period of tremendous reinvigoration and growth. They mobilized tens of thousands of Arab Palestinian youngsters and received large-scale assistance in money and weapons from the Arab states. They were able to convince large sectors of world public opinion that they were a "liberation movement" and that they did not want to destroy the Jews of Israel, but merely to found there a multinational, democratic, Palestinian state in which Jews and Arabs would live side by side. They also managed to step up terrorist activities among the Jewish population: to blow up markets and restaurants; to attack air transport; to harass border settlements by means of ambushes, mine-sowing, and attacks by Katyushas (Russian-made rockets); and, at very heavy cost to themselves, to inflict hundreds of casualties, many of them fatal, among the inhabitants of Israel. By dint of these activities they became in Arab eyes stouthearted avengers, brave warriors who were restoring to the Arabs their national pride. For a brief moment, they believed their terrorist exploits had brought them to the point of accomplishing their aims.

It did not take long, a little more than a year, for the Arab states to begin to recover and hammer out a doctrine of combat against Israel. They crystallized the Khartoum Doctrine, that of the three No's: no negotiations, no recognition, and no peace with Israel. Merely by giving vent to these resounding "No's" the Arab states found some relief. They claimed: It is true that we lost the battle, but we have not lost the war, and we shall yet arise and defeat the Jews and restore not only our lands but also our honor.

Nasser's Egypt was the first to emerge with a new method of combat adapted to the new circumstances—the method of the war of attrition. The principle of this method was: "All that was taken by force shall be regained by force." But since the Arabs were still not strong enough to regain territories and to liberate them from the occupying force, they imagined that they would hit the Israeli army in its most vulnerable spot and where their own positions were the strongest: on the Suez Canal. There they would be able to concentrate a mighty static force, mainly of artillery and mortars, which would batter the few Israeli soldiers encamped on the canal, sap their strength by means of incessant bombardment, destroy their thinly spaced positions, uproot them from the canal, and in this way win a first-class strategic and psychological victory. On the strength of this they would go forward until they accomplished their final objective.

The Egyptians therefore launched a war of attrition and did in fact manage, at very heavy cost to themselves, to attack the Israeli army positions on the canal. For a brief moment it seemed to Nasser that this time he had indeed chosen the right mode of combat. Syria and Jordan, noting that the Palestinian Arab armed organizations were succeeding and that the Egyptians had opened fire, began to take more vigorous action, to shell Israeli army positions and the border settlements, and to extend their aid to the Palestinian Arab organizations.

The Soviet Union arrived at a new situation assessment immediately after the war, and did her best, with no small success, to turn the Arab overthrow and Nasser's defeat to her own advantage. She converted Arab weakness into a source of strength for herself and thereby came to dominate the Arab world. She stepped up her anti-Israel propaganda and appeared on every available rostrum as the great protector of the Arabs. She penetrated Egypt and Syria with more experts and military personnel and restocked them with new military matériel and sophisticated weapons, so as to raise Arab morale—while, of course, also increasing their dependence on the Soviets. Within three to four years the Soviet Union succeeded beyond her own expectations in her new mission. By one means or another she harnessed seven out of fourteen Arab states to her chariot. Egypt and Syria were more dependent on her than the others. With the help of the Israeli-Arab dispute and the Arab defeat, the Soviet Union realized the age-old dream of the Russian czars to reach the warm waters of the Mediterranean Sea and convert the Middle East into a springboard to Africa and the Indian Ocean.

*   *   *

During the first years after the Six-Day War, Israel had to face a terrorist war in her midst and in the territories held by her, and a static war of attrition on her cease-fire lines. These modes of combat were new to Israel. She had, of course, adjusted to murder, terror, and sabotage in her territory from the day she was founded (indeed, such activities were the lot of Jewish settlers in Palestine from the beginning of the Jewish-Arab dispute a hundred years ago). After the Six-Day War, more modern and more effective methods of terror were employed.

Leaving aside for the moment the issue of the territories and the Palestinian Arabs, there is a consensus among the Jews in Israel as to the absolute necessity of fighting the terrorist movements by all means and with all tools, and with all the strength that a war of this kind demands.

This cruel form of warfare was dictated by the terrorist leaders themselves: in this war the terrorists balk at nothing and do not distinguish between civilians and military personnel. On the contrary, they refrain from direct and overt contact with the military and choose to strike at civilians. They mingle with the citizenry; they operate without uniform under cover of darkness; they hit and run; they want to instill perpetual and pervasive fear. For them there is no front and no border.

The Palestinian Arab terrorists had certain advantages vouchsafed to few guerrilla movements. They had bases in all the states surrounding the enemy country, to which it was possible to escape at any time and from which they could sortie at any time. They received tremendous assistance in money, equipment, and arms of all types, and also instruction and advice, from the Arab peoples, from the Communist states, from Arab guerrilla and commando experts, from a variety of "revolutionaries," and from mercenaries.

Against this mode of combat Israel developed methods of her own, some of them tried over the decades in the struggle with Arab gangs and some new and highly modern.

The Palestinian Arab terrorists, who might have been expected to know the Israeli Jew better than other Arabs, made a fatal mistake in copying the exact pattern of guerrilla methods used in other countries under totally different conditions. The Arabs forgot that the Israeli Jew was in effect a seasoned guerrilla fighter himself, with a great deal of experience in underground combat, accumulated over many decades in Palestine and the entire world. They forgot that up until a few years before, guerrilla weapons had been the classic arms of Jewish combatants, who until the founding of the State of Israel had always been the few facing the many—and that Hashomer had fought the Turks and the Arabs, and the Hagana, the Irgun (Irgun Zvai Leumi—National Military Organization), and Lehi (Lohamei Herut Yisrael—Israel Freedom Fighters) had also fought typical guerrilla warfare against the Arabs and the British.

The Jews, moreover, had not long ago fought a desperate guerrilla war in the Diaspora and had formed armed undergrounds and resistance movements against the Germans. What were the ghetto uprisings and the Jewish partisans' warfare if not guerrilla warfare? What were the flight from post-World War II Europe and the illegal immigration into Palestine if not underground activities on an international scale? Furthermore, the 1948 war itself had more than a few of the traits of guerrilla war, and the reprisals by Israeli commando units after the founding of the state were also based on guerrilla warfare in the enemy hinterland.

Generally speaking, Israel's situation as a small state in opposition to the hostile Arab world surrounding it and threatening to swallow it up, might be said to dictate to it a guerrilla way of life. And if that is defined as the thorough utilization of resourcefulness, improvisation, cunning, and surprise deployed by a few against many, we shall understand how great the Israeli army's experience in this type of warfare was.

The Palestinian Arab armed organizations also ignored the

fact that the Israelis were not Americans or Europeans ruling a foreign and remote land, the customs of whose local population they did not know, whose language and idioms they did not understand. When these organizations, headed by the Fatah, embarked on sabotage and terrorist activities, Israel sent against them her army, her police, and her diverse security forces. She developed a method of antiguerrilla warfare which consisted basically of cracking the sabotage cells in the early stages of their development, isolating the Arab population in the Israel-held territories from these cells by making it clear, sometimes heavy-handedly, that the Israelis would not stand for any Arab village or town serving as a hideout or base for terrorists.

By hunting down sabotage cells through the use of all rapid means of transport and communication, including helicopters; by commando counterattacks across the borders and massive assaults on saboteur bases deep in their hinterland; by sowing fear among the terrorists that the long arm of Israeli antiguerrilla fighters would reach them everywhere; by exposing terrorist cells abroad, throttling them before they got well under way; by planting agents inside sabotage organizations; by sealing (through electronic and other devices) the borders, to prevent the passage of Arab saboteurs; by studying the internal communications and pecking order of various echelons of the Palestinian organizations; by using all kinds of psychological warfare; by all these and many other means—some very secret—Israel fought on this cruel front.

Moreover, Israel warned the Arab states, from which the Palestinian Arab squads used to sortie, that she held them responsible for these activities. When the warnings proved ineffectual, her army several times crossed the cease-fire borders and heavily attacked the saboteur bases in the neighboring countries.

The Israeli effort succeeded, although not completely, in attaining its main objective: in antiterror actions a very great number of Palestinian Arab terrorists were killed, the Palestinian Arab population in the occupied territories was isolated almost completely from the saboteurs, and instead of armed Arabs making the Israelis' lives unbearable, their own lives became almost unendurable.

The reaction of the Palestinian armed organization leaders to this failure was to aim arrows of wrath at the rulers of certain Arab states, notably Jordan, where they tried to create enclaves similar to the "Fatahland" in Lebanon.

Their energy, cheated of its prey in Israel, was now turned inward—in an inter-Arab internecine war. In Jordan, where their activities had centered, the Palestinian Arabs earned the wrath of the rulers and the army, which dealt them many a hard, cruel blow. In other Arab states, too, the authorities refused to allow them to raise their heads and kept them under surveillance. Notwithstanding the lip service paid it by the whole Arab world, the armed Palestinian Arab movement found itself badly broken down after five years of combat.

The answers given by Israel to the war of attrition on the canal were also unconventional: counteractions in depth, cross-border raids and assaults on Egyptian bases, deep entrenchment on the borders, use of the air force as airborne artillery against the enemy guns—all these "attritioned the attritionists."

In August 1970 both Egyptians and Israelis grasped at the American initiative and established a cease-fire along the canal. Thus in the military arena Israel had given answers of her own to the new challenges put to her by the Arabs, and still remained firmly entrenched on the post-Six-Day War cease-fire lines.

What took place in the political arena? During the first months after the Six-Day War, Israel was in a state of delirium. The swift and sudden change from fear of annihilation to brilliant victory, combined with the searing pain over the hundreds who fell in battle; the encounter with new landscapes: the Old

City of Jerusalem, Judea, Samaria, the Golan Heights, Gaza, Sinai; the sight-seeing tours and excursions into the new territories and the encounters with their inhabitants—all conspired to throw Israel and its leaders into bewilderment regarding the future. The feeling was that at any moment there would be a telephone call from the defeated Arab leaders, we would sit down with them at the conference table, and everything would "work itself out." It seemed as though the Arabs who had fallen into our hands would quickly become loving cousins. And why not?—the conquest had been "quick and clean," and now Arab bazaars were full of Jewish customers from all over the country. Why shouldn't the Arabs fall in love with us, the beautiful Israelis?

But it did not happen. Our lack of understanding and preparation for a meeting with the inhabitants of the territories that had fallen into our hands was almost absolute. We were not ready, either psychologically or practically, for a situation in which we suddenly found ourselves in possession of new territories and a new population of about a million Palestinian Arabs, including most of the refugees of the 1948 war. It took us some time to realize that their fate was now in our hands and that we were responsible for their day-to-day lives and their future. The military government in the territories was quickly organized, with the Israeli army's usual flair for first-class improvisation. Within a short time the army had set up an administration and services system, and instituted a system of law and order in the administered territories, while the government adopted an open-bridges policy between the Gaza Strip, the West Bank, and east Jordan.

Terror and the war of attrition jerked Israel back to harsh, cold reality. She began to understand that the Six-Day War had brought no miraculous solution to the dispute; that Arab reactions would remain intransigent and irrational and were proportionate to the severity of the beating they had taken; that the Arabs would not reconcile themselves to what Israel had done to them but would thirst for vengeance.

AFTER THE SIX-DAY WAR

The outcome of the Six-Day War brought Israel to a moral, ideological, and political crossroads. Israel had to face the issue of her size: Were the boundaries of the Jewish state to be determined by the War of Independence borders and by certain additional strategic territories needed for security, or did the country stretch over areas far greater than those encompassed by it at the close of the War of Independence? To this day Israel has not given herself, the Arabs, or the world a clear answer to this question.

The problem had to do not only with the new territories as geographical acquisitions, but also with the Arab population residing in them. It related to our existence as a *Jewish* state and also to our historic rights over the territories.

The resultant new situation brought with it many answers— some based on principle and some on pragmatism—and various contrasting philosophies. For all the years of the existence of the State of Israel there had been a consensus on the part of its political leadership and the great majority of its political parties to the effect that if the Arabs would come to terms with her on the basis of the borders of the 1949 armistice agreements, Israel would declare that she neither had nor would have in the future any further territorial objectives. This is not to say that in peace negotiations Israel would not have demanded changes in her boundaries, such as access to the Western Wall, the Jewish quarter of the Old City of Jerusalem, Mount Scopus, and so forth. She would have demanded that its citizens be given the right of free and unhampered access to the West and East Banks, and that a definite and binding formula be found which would insure that the Straits of Tiran would not be closed to her ships and that the Suez Canal would be open as well. In principle Israel was prepared to declare that, implausible though her borders might be, they would suffice.

During all the years of the state's existence prior to the Six-Day War, even political parties such as Herut, on whose banner was engraved the slogan "The Jordan has two banks; this one is ours and so is that," never urged in their platforms that territorial expansion be a declared and overt aim of Israel. Never did such parties call upon the people to occupy forcibly additional territories.

But after the Six-Day War our attitude underwent a radical change. Frankly and openly displayed to public view, to ourselves, the Arabs, and the world at large—as should be the case in a democratic state—were the vast differences in our answers to this crucial question, answers that were often diametrically opposed to one another.

There was a tiny extremist fringe group who claimed (some on the basis of the promise given to the patriarch Abraham in the age-old covenant, some on the basis of Israel's security needs, and some on the basis of both) that the State of Israel should in the future stretch from the Euphrates River to the Nile. In their opinion peace would come only if Israeli troops stood on these borders, for only then would the Arabs concede that they did not and were not likely to possess the strength to fight so mighty a nation; and in this way the divine promise too would be kept. The supporters of this doctrine were not prepared, at any price, to concede even one inch of the territories occupied during the Six-Day War, which in their opinion constituted only part of the Land of Israel of the covenant. They did not explain exactly how these large additional territories— the whole of east Jordan, large parts of Syria, and additional parts of Egypt—were to be joined to the Land of Israel. They were certainly prepared for these areas to be annexed peacefully; but some say outright that as a result of future wars with the Arabs, the Israeli army will reach the Euphrates and the Nile. Nor do these people give any precise answer as to what is to be done with the millions of Arabs living within those boundaries, except to drop hints about "population exchanges" and "moves."

The fact that this ideology was supported by only a very small number of Jews in Israel and the world does not exempt us from presenting it here as one opinion among many, not only because it is well known among the Arabs and in the world, but also because, however extreme, it is clear and "final." It is not evasive, and although for most of us it may be the height of absurdity, it appears to its few present-day advocates to be the height of justice for the Jewish people and the height of security for the state. This opinion was not espoused by any party in the then existing Knesset, nor was it given any form of parliamentary expression. But its existence on the outer edges of the spectrum of varying opinions must be indicated if the picture presented here is to be a clear one.

Another opinion, which *was* given parliamentary and political expression prior to the Yom Kippur War, was that of the advocates of the "Greater Land of Israel" policy. This was advocated by the Herut party and also by elements of other parties (the Orthodox, the Liberals, and a faction of the Labor party). This view had two components: the first was a national-religious one. It held that Israel should not yield a single inch of Judea and Samaria, which are the historic cradle and backbone of the people of Israel, or the Golan Heights, which were Jewish in the past, or the Gaza Strip and Sinai, over which we have, according to them, greater historic rights than the Arabs.

The second component was a security one: since this school of thought was convinced that in the future, just as in the past, the Arabs would want to destroy Israel and would settle for nothing less than that, the borders on which Israel's forces then stood were strategically the best and the safest. Thus there could be no substitute for them. Any retreat from those borders and the restoration of any territories whatever, even in return for peace treaties and agreements, appeared to them to be a fatal mistake, in both national-religious and security terms. Advocates of this view were persuaded that only if and when we annexed all the territories to the State of Israel and made them an integral part of it would the Arabs understand that we were firmly resolved not to retreat at any price. Out of this recognition and for lack of alternatives, the Arabs, they argued, would come to understand that they had no choice but to make peace with a strong Israel.

Those who followed this school of thought did not explicitly state their attitude regarding the historic relationship of Israel to the lands east of the Jordan (Reuben, Gad, and half the tribe of Manasseh); but it may be assumed that most of them would have been prepared to waive further territorial ambitions. As to the reaction of the great powers and world public opinion, the argument was that when Israel annexed all the territories, everyone would grow accustomed to the new state of affairs, to borders from which there would be no retreating and for which Israel would be prepared to fight to the end. Once these facts were established, they believed, even Israel's enemies would accord her greater consideration and respect and would be reconciled with her. It goes without saying that the advocates of this position were in favor of rapid and large-scale Jewish settlement in all the new territories. They wanted to see Jewish towns or Jewish urban housing developments near or within every Arab town and the construction of as many Jewish settlements as possible.

With regard to the future status of the Arabs of the territories in the "Greater Land of Israel," there were various approaches. Some said that upon annexation they should be given full rights of citizenship, like the Arab minority in Israel. Others said that the Arabs of the territories should be accorded their full citizenship rights gradually, and only when peace was established. Some believed that if and when all the territories were annexed to Israel, many Arabs would "one way or another" emigrate to the Arab states and the problem would "solve itself."

At the other end of the spectrum of opinions there were the doctrines of Rakah (Reshima Kommunistit Hadasha—New Communist List) and the other extreme left-wing groups, which advocated not only Israel's full retreat to the 1948 boundaries, but also the return of all or most of the Palestinian Arab refugees of 1948 to their previous places of domicile in Israel. Only after these steps were taken, they argued, would there be grounds for the Arabs to recognize Israel's existence and make peace with her. Rakah, which took its stand in accordance with instructions from Moscow, did not always acquiesce even to the 1949 cease-fire borders. It continues to obey its Kremlin masters even today in the aftermath of the Yom Kippur War.

In opposition to these extreme views, the average Israeli took roughly the following position after the Six-Day War: it is certainly wonderful that we have reached new and more secure borders, and have dispelled the threat of physical annihilation that hung over us. We are attached to the new territories, the lovely landscapes, and the historic sites. We understand the economic importance of the territories, their raw materials, their settlement possibilities, and their potential for the development of tourism. Had the territories been empty or had their Arab inhabitants vanished as a result of the war, we would undoubtedly annex, settle, and develop them.

But the average Israeli knew and understood very well that the status of these territories did not resemble that of the territories of his State of Israel, which he was and is prepared to defend anywhere and at any time. The average Israeli was prepared, in principle, to restore territories in return for peace, and he was prepared to regard the retention of those territories as a surety for the peace that would someday be established with the Arabs. At the same time, he did not believe that the Arabs—any of them: Palestinians, Jordanians, Egyptians, Syrians, or others—were prepared to come to terms with him and the fact of his state's very existence. He therefore suspected that the restoration of territories, even in return for the formal signing of a peace agreement, would not be the end of the conflict, because even after an agreement was signed, the Arabs were liable to tear it to bits, and then his state would once again be in a vulnerable strategic position, with Arab armies encamped only a few kilometers from its nerve centers, threatening to destroy it.

The Israeli's misgivings did not, however, bring him to the extreme conclusion that the territories had to be annexed. He knew quite well that the annexation of the million Arabs of the territories, even if there were to be a fairly large immigration of Jews to Israel, was liable within a few years to place his state in a situation of economic dependence on a growing national minority of Arabs. The mere thought of it plunged him into nightmarish consternation. He did not want a binational state with a precarious ethnic balance. Not for this had he dreamed of and fought for a Jewish state. Neither did he want forcibly to impose Israeli citizenship upon the Arabs, and create in his state a situation in which their status would be inferior to his. For many generations his forebears had been second-class citizens in the Diaspora, and he well knew how much unfairness and perversion of justice could prevail in such a state.

The average Israeli was thus grappling with difficult questions to which there were no clear-cut answers. He was torn between his fear of annihilation and his strong desire for peace; between the wish to do justice to the minorities in his state and lead a democratic life there, and the recognition that such a democracy could be to his detriment. He naturally tended to push aside the problem, to avoid coming to grips with it, so as not to torment himself and afflict his conscience. He was prepared to find comfort in the magic formula that "time will do the trick," while knowing in his heart that he was simply evading the issue.

The perplexed Israeli had another refuge: "Leave it to the government"; for he told himself: "The government knows better than I." In contrast to other areas of life, such as economic, social, and religious affairs—in which he regarded himself as an expert and criticized everything, neither sparing the government nor relying on it—in these fateful matters, which he designated as "foreign and security affairs," he tended to grant his government almost limitless credit. The Israeli rested secure in the knowledge that his government and its ministers had information and collective experience and intelligence that he himself had not, and that if it reached a decision in these matters, it did so on the basis of full knowledge of the facts. The Israeli has always been sensitive to matters of national security, and he puts them above all else. Israel-Arab relations are in his eyes a matter of security and of preservation of his physical existence, and what could be more natural than for him to rely on the government and allow it to decide what is good and what is vital in the area of security.

In this state of affairs the government in Israel enjoyed very strong backing on the part of the Jewish population. It would have had to make a very grave mistake, or be guilty of palpable failure in security matters, for this confidence to be undermined.

Israeli post-Six-Day War policy was too pragmatic and shortsighted. It was a hand-to-mouth system operating under the slogans: "Time is working in our favor," "Let the future take care of itself," and "We shall cross that bridge when we come to it."

Like the average Israeli, the government was neither willing nor able to annex additional territories "just like that." Like him, it understood the tremendous damage such annexation would cause to its image and its future as a Jewish democracy. On the other hand, the government claimed that there was no one to whom to restore any of the territories, since it was suspicious of every Arab ruler and leader and saw all of them as actual or potential enemies of the Jewish state.

The government announced that after negotiations between the sides it would be prepared, in return for a contractual peace, to concede territories; but it never said which territories. This it left to the future, when the negotiations begin, when there is someone to talk to.

The government handled day-to-day affairs so as to "remain

in business." It had to deal with and make decisions on defense, foreign, economic, and social affairs; it had to solve all urgent problems—and what is not urgent in our country? The government had neither the time nor apparently the willpower, and perhaps did not feel it either necessary or obligatory, to deal with the long-range and fundamental objectives of our life. It felt perhaps that a discussion of these matters was liable to split its collective personality. It comforted itself with the thought that some problems had to be left for the next generation to solve.

THE YOM KIPPUR WAR

On the eve of Yom Kippur in the Jewish year 5734—1973 of the Common Era—Israel was in a lull. Everything seemed quiet. Charismatic Israeli leaders were telling us that there would be no war with the Arabs for ten years, that time was in our favor, that the status quo was working for us.

The combined Egyptian-Syrian attack across our borders caught us by surprise. After a few traumatic days when the thin red line of the boys of the regular army bore the brunt of the cruel battle and, often outnumbered ten to one, acted as a human shock absorber, the reserve army upon which Israel relies went into action, pushed back the Syrians, conquered new territories on the road to Damascus, crossed the Suez Canal, brought havoc to the soft underbelly of Egypt, and began heading westward toward the center of Egypt. The Egyptian Third Army, which had crossed the Suez Canal in the first days of the war, was encircled by the Israeli army and threatened with destruction. At this point the war was brought to an end by the combined pressure of the United States and the Soviet Union upon the combatants.

From a purely military point of view, the Yom Kippur War was our finest victory. Everything worked against us at the beginning: the element of total surprise, errors in logistics, command confusion. But the turnabout was swift and decisive. This war showed that Israel can—admittedly at a terrible cost—stand against many Arab armies and fight simultaneously on more than one front. It also showed how dependent Israel is for its weapons on the United States.

Israel will not and cannot forget what the United States did to help her in October 1973. Her very existence was saved. At the same time, Israel preserved the interests of the Western democracies in this area of the world.

We are still in the aftermath of the Yom Kippur War. Israelis call it an earthquake and are still feeling the aftereffects of its shock waves—politically, socially, economically, psychologically. They are asking one another, "Why did it happen? Could we have avoided it? Who is responsible? Where are we heading?" The government has lost much of its former prestige. In the December 1973 election it was significantly weakened by a sizable protest vote.

Israel today finds herself in a very fluid situation. On the one hand, her people very much want peace and are prepared to pay a heavy price for it; on the other hand, people are more suspicious than ever before of the Arabs and their "final" goals. But Israelis are not caught up in a "Masada complex"; rather, their mood can be best characterized as a "Samson complex." Israelis are saying to themselves, "If a war of this kind comes upon us again and we fall, then let all the others fall with us."

More than ever before, Israelis are searching now for new ideas, new faces, new leaders, new dreams.

We are at a crucial crossroads in our national life. Our current mood can bring to the foreground extreme elements from the Right and Left, most probably from the Right, and new charismatic warrior leaders. It can also bring a new renaissance to Israel. If we let honest, open criticism prune the dead limbs from the tree of Israel's social democracy, a new and healthy growth may spring from our trunk and we will come closer to the vision of the Land of the Hart.

*   *   *

To the Arabs the Yom Kippur War is known as the War of Ramadan. The political and psychological deadlock they had been caught in for decades was broken by this war. They regained their honor and pride. They began to use their oil as a latter-day Islamic scourge of Allah against the industrial world. It remains to be seen if they will use their increased wealth and regained prestige for the true improvement of the lives of their people or if their use of the weapon of oil will turn them into increasingly despised international blackmailers.

Are the Arabs now wise enough to come to terms with Israel? Will they agree to our existence in their midst? Will they compromise with us? There are contradictory signs. Sadat is talking differently from Nasser. But we have yet to see whether he will match his talk with deeds. There may be some second thoughts among the Palestinian Arab armed organizations. On the other hand, there are terrible omens of new fanaticism and extremism in the Arab world.

The Arab-Israel conflict has now gotten out of hand and has become global in nature. In 1973 it almost triggered a third world war. The United States, with the tacit agreement of the Soviet Union, is exerting, through the great skill of Dr. Kissinger, all the pressure it can to bring the two sides to negotiations and gradual arrangements leading slowly to peace.

Cruel reality and the great powers have brought the Arab and Israeli warhorses to the trough of peace. Will they drink from its waters?

2

THE ARABS AND "FALASTIN"

COMMON ORIGINS

The purpose of this book is to offer an assessment of our national situation and designate objectives for the future. In this task we shall be guided by the past and the present. So far we have discussed the struggle over this land from a Jewish point of view. But before setting ourselves goals for the future, perhaps we should first try to achieve a better understanding of the other side, its motives, and its attitudes in this struggle.

The legend of the common origins of the sons of Abraham— Isaac, forefather of the Jews, and Ishmael, forefather of the Arabs—undoubtedly contains a grain of truth. The environment, the landscape, the climate, the desert, and the living, breathing land, the tribal way of life, and the dress of the very early Arabs and Jews were similar, although not identical. Assyrian reliefs and Egyptian hieroglyphics depicting warriors, captives, bearers of tribute, and merchants, both Arab and Israelite, show a strong resemblance, both to each other and to their present-day descendants.

The original Arab tribes wandered through the desert in the two millennia B.C.E. They made their grand entrance on the world stage in the seventh century, and left their mark on hundreds of millions of people. The life of Muhammad, creator of the Koran, and the birth of Islam in the bosom of the Arab tribes and its emergence as a worldwide religion, borne by Arab warriors and believers to the four corners of the civilized world, are among the most remarkable phenomena in human history and a source of pride to Arabs to this very day.

The belief in one God—which gave the Jews the strength to exist in the Land of Israel and the Diaspora—also gave Muhammad and his believers the strength to come out of the desert and subdue peoples and nations. This unique history—small nomadic tribes possessed of burning religious ardor, disseminating that new faith throughout the ancient world, and founding a worldwide empire—this history remains indelibly stamped upon the Arab character even today.

Unlike other great conquerors in history—the Vandals, the Huns, the Mongols—the Arabs did not merely destroy; within a very short time they founded a glorious civilization of their own in which they blended the cultures of the conquered lands. This fact, no less than their actual victories in the name of their faith, imbued Arab hearts with a sense of pride in their past, a feeling of greatness and grandeur in time of war as well as peace, with a burning faith at once all-embracing and tolerant, with a sense of their being the descendants of the standard-bearers of Muhammad and also the bearers and disseminators of civilization. To this very day they are proud of having been the conquerors of ancient lands which were the cradle of world civilization, of having built splendid cities, of their rich, lilting, and poetic tongue and their enchanting and picturesque script. They are proud of their heroes, caliphs, kings, scholars, philosophers, writers, and poets, of their unique architecture, of the manner in which they cultivated the humanities and natural sciences, all at a time when medieval darkness had descended upon Europe. The Arabs have just cause to be proud of their rich past and their centuries-old role as bearers of progress in the world.

The original Arab tribes, who inhabited the Arabian Peninsula, succeeded in bequeathing their faith and culture to the world in two stages. At first they influenced those populations in the lands from the Maghreb to Iraq who are known today as the Arab peoples. They taught them their language and their faith. Then Islam spread and conquered tens of millions of people among non-Arab folk groups, who also adopted Islam as a religion and a way of life: Turks, Persians, Tatars, Uzbeks, Kazakhs, Baluchis, and others. Islam continued to spread over parts of Asia—to China, Bengal, Malaya, Indonesia. Its influence reached as far as the Philippines and the islands of the Pacific Ocean, to the African continent south of the Equator as far as Tanzania, and westward to Senegal and Nigeria. Today the number of adherents of the Islamic faith is estimated at hundreds of millions—also a source of pride to the Arabs.

Another pinnacle in Arab history was reached in the Middle Ages when Muslim warriors conquered the Iberian Peninsula and founded an Arab dynasty. In Spain they gave expression to their military and cultural superiority over the Christians; there they founded a form of government that was perhaps the most advanced of its day, and certainly far in advance of that of the Europeans. Under Muslim influence a golden age of art, literature, poetry, and science flowered in Spain.

After a few centuries Arab rule, which was beginning to disintegrate as a result of internal schisms and wars, was attacked by the Turkish peoples—Seljuks, Mamelukes, and, later, the Ottomans—who erupted from central Asia and saw in the Arabs and their lands a target for conquest. They overran and subjugated most of the Arab kingdoms. In Spain the Arabs were defeated and expelled by the European Christians. Before long they fell under the yoke of the Christians in other parts of the Arab world as well.

About five hundred years ago the proud Arabs had virtually ceased to exist as independent peoples and states. During the centuries that have since elapsed, the European Christian world has been swept by a succession of mighty social, cultural, scientific, and technological revolutions. New worlds opened up: the Americas were discovered, the globe was circumnavigated, and new horizons glimmered in all human and scientific spheres of activity. Then came the era of the industrial revolution and the modern period.

Throughout those centuries of change the Arabs and their creative powers were pent up within the great Turkish Empire which, having enjoyed its own golden age, also sank into degeneracy. Young, power-hungry European empires proceeded to tear it limb from limb. And thus, at the dawn of modern nationalism the Arab world lay sunk in a profound torpor, imprisoned within the Turkish Empire and the Muslim religion, which over the centuries had become increasingly conservative and narrow in its views.

The Arabs clung to their shining past more and more, while cultivating an attitude of acquiescence and fatalism toward the present. Only in the middle and late nineteenth century did young educated Arabs begin to bestir themselves and open their eyes to the world around them. New ideas, languages, and customs began to penetrate the Turkish Empire and the Arab world. Napoleon's invasion of Egypt, the Europeans who began to pour into the Middle East, and the opening of the Suez Canal all had a powerfully stimulating effect.

THE ARAB NATIONALIST MOVEMENT

At the end of the nineteenth and the beginning of the twentieth centuries, young Arab intellectuals began thinking and dreaming of a new age for the Arab peoples: an age of independence in which they would rid themselves of the yoke of the Turkish and European powers and create an Arab state or states which would restore to the Arabs their lost greatness and glory. Nineteenth-century Egypt was the first proof that there could arise an independent or semi-independent modern Arab state.

In Beirut, Damascus, and Baghdad too the Arab nationalist
movement began to develop and attempted to blend modern
European nationalist ideas with the Islamic faith and Arab consciousness.

As the Turkish Empire continued to crumble, Arab governors
began to shake off its yoke and rebel. The Wahabis on the
Arabian Peninsula rebelled and created an Arab state based on
a return to Arabism and an unadulterated desert Islam. The
thinkers of the new Arab nationalist movement understood that
upon their shoulders devolved the task of dislodging the foreign
yoke and at the same time bridging the centuries in order to
catch up and compete with the modern world around them.
They did not want to found a Levantine state, but aspired to a
unique social and political entity which would borrow from the
Europeans only what was good and useful, while preserving the
original ancient Islamic and Arabic foundation in all its majesty.

These dreams, like many dreams, were at first very obscure.
Some of the leaders of the Arab nationalist movement nursed
all-encompassing visions of a single, gigantic, united Arab state,
reaching across all the lands inhabited by Arabs, from Casa-
blanca to Basra. Others dreamed more modestly of a series of
independent Arab states, which in one way or another would
be linked together.

The pioneers of the Arab nationalist movement walked a
very thorny path indeed. Having themselves undergone a mental metamorphosis, they now had to sow the seed of modern
Arab nationalist consciousness among a population of which the
great majority were not sufficiently advanced to receive it. The
vast, thinly populated expanses, the opposition and persecution
of the Turks, and later the obstruction of both the British and
the French all hindered their progress. The Arab nationalist
movement, moreover, like any semiunderground movement of
fighters and ideologists, had its full share of quarrels, disputes,
and splits.

Most of the movement's founders at the beginning of the

twentieth century regarded the Turks as the prime enemy. When World War I broke out, they naturally pinned their faith on the British and French, in the hope that they would annihilate the Turkish Empire and enable the Arabs to build their independence on its ruins. Some of them actively helped the British in their war against the Turks, in the hope that with victory they would be granted greater rights and that the promises of political independence that had been made to them would be kept.

The end of World War I and the dissolution of the Turkish Empire brought the Arabs a galling disappointment. The victorious European empires—the British and the French—were by no means prepared to share the fruits of their victory with anyone else. What they wanted was to divide the defeated Turkish Empire among themselves and found their own colonies or protectorates in the Middle East.

The Arabs thus found, to their stupefaction, that although they had obtained release from the yoke of one suzerainty, they were now saddled with the weight of others. Morocco, Algeria, and Tunisia remained under French rule. The Italians were becoming predominant in Libya. The British continued to hold sway in Egypt and Sudan, as well as Palestine and Transjordan. Syria and Lebanon were under French rule, and Iraq was under the British. The changes that were to come about could be discerned even then. Whereas in the past most Arab countries had been subjected to the backward and disintegrating rule of the Turks, they were now subordinated to a modern European administration which would obviously also bring with it all the achievements of modernization. One side effect of this would be to impart renewed dynamism to the Arab nationalist movement, which would then demand liberation and independence. Thus, during the years between the end of World War I and the end of World War II, the Arabs, under British and French tutelage, achieved a tremendous forward leap into the twentieth century.

What also became apparent during that period, although indications of it had appeared even before World War I, was that the Arab countries possessed the greatest and richest oil deposits in the world. With the discovery and development of those oil fields, the importance of the Middle East was magnified tenfold.

The British and French did much to discover and develop these natural resources—primarily, of course, for the sake of profit. They also left a deep imprint on the educational, cultural, and services systems, as well as on other walks of life in the countries they ruled. Moreover, being from democratic countries and the cradle of modern nationalism, the British and French could not withstand the tidal wave of Arab nationalism. Many of them understood and sensed that the day would come when they would have to hand over their estates and colonies in the Arab countries to their Arab owners.

Following World War II the British and French Empires came to an end. Within a single generation, all eighteen Arab countries, stretching from the Atlantic Ocean in the west to the Persian Gulf in the east, achieved political independence. The Arab dream, so it appeared, had come to pass.

The total area of these Arab states is greater than that of the United States of America. Their natural resources are vast and plentiful. Their water sources are among the richest in the world. Their population, which numbers about a hundred million inhabitants, is sparse in comparison to the expanse of their territories except in Egypt. The Arabs gained their independence through frequently bitter, bloody strife, and on the face of it they could be proud of having realized their great national longings within two or three generations.

But there is another side to the coin. By the last quarter of the twentieth century the Arabs have only just arrived at the starting line of the modern, highly developed world; they are still not a part of it. Moreover, most of them are filled with deep frustration, and their society and states are being ceaselessly buffeted by severe crises.

This situation is the result of many factors, some of them

universal and others specific to the Arab world. Most Arab countries, like other developing states, are in the transitory stage from a technologically backward society to a modern and industrialized one; from a society subordinated to the colonial yoke to a nation-state. Other large parts of the human race are in a similar situation: the Latin American states, black Africa, the Indian subcontinent, and Southeast Asia. In one way or another all are undergoing the trauma of growth and adaptation to the late twentieth century. Their sociopolitical regimes are for the most part extremely shaky, and they are having scant success in raising up, on the ruins of the colonialist order, more stable regimes, either in the multiparty democratic style of Western Europe or in the Communist style of the Soviet Union or China. In most of them sole power is in the hands of the army, which installs and unseats governments, and when tired of civilian rule will (sometimes under an ideological guise and sometimes under no guise at all) put the country under rule of an officers' junta.

Another common denominator among the whole crisis-ridden Third World is a result of its artificial division into individual states. Dozens of new independent states were founded within strange, oddly shaped borders, following the generations-old arbitrary colonial divisions. In many cases these borders have no geographic, ethnographic, or demographic justification, and they cut right through tribes and folk groups. The result has been the creation of a multitude of Brobdingnagian and Lilliputian states. Many of these independent states still lack the unifying elements which would transform their tribes and folk groups into one people, whose loyalty to the new state would be greater than its loyalty to family, ethnic affiliation, or tribe.

Another characteristic of these states is the poverty and backwardness of vast segments of their population. Even countries rich in raw materials do not escape this poverty. In many of these lands the poverty exists alongside the dazzling wealth of small ruling groups. Where there is poverty, poverty-within-wealth, the atmosphere will be highly explosive, and ripe for social revolution.

Many of the new states, moreover, find themselves caught up in interbloc and interpower tugs-of-war, and ground between the millstones of strategic, ideological, and economic struggles for power positions, bases, and influence. Most of them adopt a bargaining stance with the superpowers, the Soviet Union and the United States: Who will pay a higher price? Who will offer a larger tip? Who will bribe them more generously?

There are additional factors which serve to exacerbate the situation of the Arabs and aggravate their frustration. The Arabs are going through a national identity crisis. Are they the sons of a single great nation, or of eighteen different peoples, each having its own state but united by a common language, religion, and origin? If they are the sons of a single nation, how and when will they unite into one state, and which of the existing states will be the leader in this all-embracing union? This crisis of Pan-Arabism, as opposed to particularism and the emergence of separate states, has plagued the Arab nationalist movement from its beginnings.

In reality, there exist separate countries, each of which is in search of its national identity, and all of which are prepared to fight one another over their separate identities and borders. At the same time, the dream of one vast nation continues to pursue the Arabs. Hence the dichotomy and confusion.

Another factor that aggravates the crisis in the Arab world is its geographic and geopolitical situation: more than any other group of states in the Third World, the Arab states are in a particularly sensitive position vis-à-vis the two-power or three-power struggle. The Arab states straddle some of the most important land, air, sea, and communications junctions in the world. Whoever possesses, influences, or rules them holds the keys to the African continent, the Persian Gulf, the Indian Ocean, the Mediterranean basin, eastern Asia, and southern

Europe. Moreover, the Arab countries are also sitting on the largest, most vital, and, even in today's energy crisis, the cheapest source of energy in the world. Middle Eastern oil today turns the wheels of West European and Japanese industry and technology.

It is true that within a generation or two this situation will be changed beyond all recognition by this very technology. Not only will great new oil fields be found in other parts of the world, but oil itself will come to occupy a less crucial status in world energy reserves. It is highly probable that by the use of revolutionary technology, coal will be reinstated to its former eminence, and there is no doubt that in spite of initial difficulties, atomic energy will come into ever-greater use as a source of power. Furthermore, it may be assumed that in the twenty-first century new sources of energy will be brought into play. But today oil remains the world's main source of energy. Small wonder that the importance of the Arab Middle East looms so large for the great powers and that their vested interests there appear to them to be so vital.

The Arab world's oil supply often impels the Arab states, especially the oil-producing states, toward egoistic separatism and renders them a prey to overt and covert threats from foreign powers and states. Thus they become pawns, quite unable to develop an identity, culture, or form of government integral to their own way of life; or they use oil as blackmail for political ends.

The form of government in the Arab states is also a cause of constant crisis. The modern Arab nationalist movement was mainly republican in character and aims. Yet at the time the Arab world began to be granted independence it was under the rule of kings, emirs, and princes, many of whom were artificially grafted (sometimes with the help of foreign powers) upon the Arab states. It is thus hardly surprising that the republicans, or military personnel advocating "republican freedom," rose against many of these rulers and deposed, killed, or exiled them. In most of the Arab states they founded either republics or else "peoples' republics" headed by acting or former army officers, who became presidents. Only in a minority of cases did the royal thrones remain unshaken. This crisis is still at its height. The revolutionary and often violent change from royalist to pseudorepublican rule will undoubtedly be visited upon other Arab states too.

One special factor working to aggravate the crisis in the Arab world stems from the Arabs' great pride in their past. Many Arabs are quite well aware of the fact that pride in the past, which can be a source of national identification, must be complemented by a worthy present. If they are to take pride in their present too, they must lay the foundations of a modern economy and society: a more even distribution of the national product, provision for education and public services to all citizens of the state, housing, urbanization, and particularly modern industrialization. None of these things are achieved in a year; all are a matter for generations. They require not only long periods of quiet and peace, but also great devotion and great humility on the part of those responsible. This kind of work offers no glamour, no glitter; it requires neither verbal sparring nor saber-rattling. But without them the Arabs will have nothing to show for their pride.

THE ARABS AND THEIR ATTITUDE TO THE JEWS

Another unique element in the crisis in the Arab world is the Arab-Israeli struggle. It is true that the existence of Israel and the Arabs' wars upon her are only one of a whole complex of causes. Although there is no truth to the Arabs' claim that Israel's existence is the only factor in the crisis they are undergoing, and that with Israel's liquidation the crisis will vanish, still there is no doubt that the existence of Israel greatly affects everything that occurs in the Arab world. To determine just how significant an influence it is, we should first examine briefly past relations between Arabs and Jews.

The love-hate relationship of Jews and Arabs can be traced

back to the feelings between Isaac and Ishmael at the dawn of
history. This relationship haunts Muhammad and finds expression in the Koran. On the one hand, there is admiration for the
Book of Books, for the common early ancestors, for the prophets
of Israel and the Jews' great spiritual assets. On the other hand,
there is great outrage at the fact that Muhammad's Jewish con-
temporaries did not become his believers, as well as at the
arrogance of the Jewish tribes of the Arabian Peninsula, their
wars against Muhammad, and their refusal to regard him as a
true prophet. This dichotomous attitude of great respect for the
people of the Book in the past and contempt for it in the present
has, over the centuries, become a distinguishing feature of
Arab-Jewish relations.

In the path of their conquests, the Arabs found many Jewish communities in all Middle Eastern countries—in Yemen,
Babylon, Persia, Syria, Falastin (as they called the Land of Israel), Egypt, Libya, the Maghreb, and Spain. They never developed among themselves the classic-Christian attitude of anti-
Semitism toward the Jews, either in theory or in practice.
Indeed, how could they when they themselves were the most
Semitic of Semites? The Islamic religion and the Arabs did
regard the Jews as heretics, but never as idol worshipers whom
they were forcibly trying to enfold beneath the wings of Islam.

Nor indeed were Jews seen as dangerous heretics like the
Christians, with whom Muslims felt they had to go to war over
the basic tenets of faith, as well as over territories and population. Against the weak, scattered Jews there was simply no need
to wage a jihad (holy war); they did not constitute a palpable
threat and challenge to Islam. Unlike the Christians, who developed a theory that the humbled Jews were a living "testimony"
to the truth of Christianity, and bore the mark of Cain as having
slain the son of God, the Arab Islamic believers developed no
all-embracing anti-Jewish theory; neither did they make the
Jews living in their midst scapegoats for their own failings.

Moreover, because of their special culture, language, customs, and appearance, the Jews who lived among Christians constituted a foreign body, a strange minority that was an easy target for hatred, whereas the Jewish minorities who lived among the Arabs were immeasurably closer to the local populace in appearance, dress, language, and customs. They "belonged" to the environment, the climate, and the landscape. The Jews who lived among the Arabs were indeed a minority, frequently deprived of rights; and there were also periods of anti-Jewish outbursts. But there were long periods in which the Jews found a common language with the Arabs and reached a plateau of social, economic, and cultural collaboration with them. A period of this kind occurred in the days of the geonim in Arab Babylon; another such period is known as the Jewish golden age in Arab-Muslim Spain.

It should not be forgotten that while Jews were being ground beneath the wheels of the Catholic Inquisition in Europe, they enjoyed almost uninterrupted cultural and community life in the Arab Muslim world. Some of the greatest Jewish religious teachers and philosophers, such as Saadia Gaon and the Rambam, and such great Jewish poets as Yehuda Halevi, Shlomo Ibn Gabirol, and Shalom Shabazi, lived and worked within the Arab Muslim world. Moreover, in their heyday the Arabs allowed the Jews to take part in administration, sciences, medicine, international commerce, discoveries, shipping, and finance—in all of which they rose to greatness. When the Jews fled before the Christian sword in Spain and Portugal, many of them found refuge in the Muslim Ottoman Empire and among the Arab people.

In view of the bloody dispute between Jews and Arabs today, it is very easy to forget all this. But without making an idyll of the Arabs' treatment of the Jews over the course of history, for the sake of the truth and for the sake of the future it must be stated that Arab treatment of the Jews was immeasurably better and more tolerant than that accorded the Jews by the Christian world.

There is a cruel irony in the fate of the relations between the two peoples: in the mid- and late nineteenth century the Arabs began to rouse themselves out of their abject state and emerge from their internal exile. They began to grasp at modern nationalism as a means of extricating themselves from subjugation. At the very same period, the hunted, oppressed Jews, scattered all over the world, also grasped at modern nationalism and made it an instrument for the realization of their dream of returning to their ancient land.

Until the end of the nineteenth century both movements were still in their infancy. Their respective objectives were still dimly perceived, and the relations between them were not yet clear. The Zionists had not yet hammered out a doctrine regarding the Arabs in general and the Arabs of this country in particular. And they certainly had not reckoned with the potential force of the Arab nationalist movement in the Middle East. Neither did the Arab nationalist movement, in the beginning, perceive the "Zionist danger." The initial rural Jewish colonization, about one hundred years ago, was something the leaders of the Arab nationalist movement could ignore, for one would have had to possess a fertile imagination indeed to have seen in the first dozen Jewish settlements a dynamic nationalist movement. The Arabs may well have assumed that within a great Arab state there would also be room for a small Jewish minority, similar to the other national and religious minorities that were part of the Middle East.

It was the founding by Herzl of the World Zionist movement, the creation of effective instruments for the purchase of lands, and Herzl's own definition of the final objective of Zionism—the founding of a Jewish state in the Land of Israel—that triggered a danger signal among the leaders of the Arab nationalist movement.

By the eve of World War I, the Arab nationalists began voicing their clear opposition to Zionism. The Balfour Declaration, which constituted the first recognition of Zionism by a world power, appeared to the Arab nationalist movement as a heinous act of betrayal. The disappointed Arabs produced a lengthy series of documents in support of their claim that the British had explicitly promised the Arabs that Palestine would be theirs.

The Arabs have neither forgiven nor forgotten what they regarded as a gross breach of promise on the part of the British. All British efforts during their rule in Palestine and the Middle East to win Arab hearts were fruitless. To this day the Arabs remember November 2, 1917, the date of the Balfour Declaration, as a black day for their nationalist movement.

After the fall of the Ottoman Empire the Arab nationalist movement was in for some more hard blows. It felt itself defrauded not only by the British, who ruled Palestine, but also by the French, who governed the cradle of the Arab nationalist movement: Syria and Lebanon. The fact that the British had installed an Arab king in Iraq and granted it limited independence; that from the original mandate entrusted them by the League of Nations, which included Palestine on both sides of the Jordan, they had themselves stripped off the whole of the East Bank and had there crowned an Arab emir, thereby restricting the applicability of the Balfour Declaration to western Palestine only—all this brought the Arabs no comfort.

During the 1920s the Arabs—both Palestinians and members of the Arab nationalist movements in the neighboring Arab countries—watched the Jews slowly advancing step by step toward the realization of their objectives. The anti-Jewish riots of 1920 and 1921, including the events of Tel Hai, may be regarded as the beginning of an armed and violent struggle on the part of the Arab nationalists (with the help of robbers and murderers) whose aim was to root out the Zionists and their settlements.

The acquisition of land by the Jews, although conducted legally and with due process, seemed to the Arabs to be a danger of the first order. They began fighting and boycotting the Arab land-sellers. They also looked with growing dread upon the steadily mounting wave of Jewish immigration to the Land of Israel. They did not try to understand Zionism, nor would they pay any heed at all to its doctrine that the Land of Israel had room for two peoples and two national liberation movements. All talk of this appeared to them so much humbug, mere casuistry and misrepresentation.

The Arabs were also dumbfounded by the kind of Jews who were coming to Palestine, by their ways, their customs, and their ideas. Their struggle to create "Jewish labor," to renew the Hebrew language, to set up tools for the state-in-the-making, including armed underground organizations—all this was conclusive evidence to the Arabs that the evil was upon them and that they were dealing with a foreign body forcibly implanting itself within the tissue of the Arab peoples.

The 1929 riots were another outburst of anger, violence, and murder against the Jews. This time the action was far more meticulously planned by the Arab nationalists, headed by the grand mufti of Jerusalem, Haj Amin Al-Husseini.

During the period between the 1929 riots and those of 1936, Arab nationalist resistance to the Zionist movement grew and took shape. The Supreme Arab Committee of the Arabs of Palestine mobilized money and support for their cause from the Arab and Islamic countries. The call to a jihad against the Zionists began reverberating throughout the Arab world. It was brought to the notice of the Arabs that the Jews were already tearing pieces out of their lands. The Muslims were panicked by the information that the Jews wanted to overrun their holy places, and especially the Holy City—El Quds (Jerusalem).

The continued settlement, the success of Jewish agriculture, and the waves of immigration during the 1930s again proved to the Arabs that they had to fight for their land (and Falastin—in its entirety—was considered by them as their land).

In retrospect, the 1936–39 riots can be regarded as a massive Arab effort and a national struggle against both the Jews and the

British administration. For three years the Arabs fought with all the weapons they could lay their hands on: general strikes, boycotts, guerrilla warfare, and terrorization. The Arab combatants were now immeasurably better equipped and armed than they had been in the 1920s. (These "gangs" or guerrillas are regarded by the Arabs as the forerunners of the fedayeen and the Fatah, just as the night squads of Wingate and the field units of the Hagana are seen by us as the ancestors of the Palmach, the Jewish Brigade, and the Israeli army.)

When those three years of rebellion were over, the Arabs clearly understood that without the participation of the independent Arab states and their armies, and without harnessing all the resources of the Arab world to the struggle over this land, they stood no chance against the well-entrenched and -organized Jews. The various proposals for partition were rejected out of hand by all the Arabs. The leaders of the Arab countries were by now deeply immersed in the struggle, and the British recognized them as a party to it. The Arabs justified their obstinately negative stand toward any attempt to partition the country on the grounds that they had opposed the whole Zionist cause from the outset. They did not recognize any Jewish rights over this land.

Following this logic, they would not even recognize the Jews as a party to the dispute. Moreover, they did not recognize Zionism as a national movement or the Jews as a people. Jewish immigration and settlement were seen by them as an international conspiracy against the Arab nationalist liberation movement. The English, the French, the Americans, and sometimes even the Soviets, the Arabs alleged, were using the Jews merely as "messenger boys" and pawns in their nefarious designs against the Arabs.

With the approach of World War II at least some of the Arabs and their leaders must have clearly realized that they were dealing with a small but courageous and desperate national movement. The great majority of them, however, still regarded the Zionist enterprise in the Land of Israel as something loathsome, something built upon stealth, cunning, and falsehood, a movement propped up by the bayonets of the British. They were confident that, given the chance, the regular Arab armies would easily deal a mortal blow to the Zionists and throw them into the sea.

In the period preceding World War II, the Arabs discovered that unyielding political pressure combined with military threats brought results. The White Paper of 1939 was the product of these pressures. It did not entirely satisfy the Arab leaders; but the fact that the British had at one stroke blighted those precious seedlings of the Zionist enterprise—immigration and settlement—proved to the Arabs the efficacy of their tactics. They felt that their Zionist enemy had been hard hit. Knowing how sorely the British would be in need of domestic peace in the Middle East as World War II approached, the Arabs understood that they would soon be in an even more favorable bargaining position than before.

When the war began to move toward the Middle Eastern arena, most of the Arabs remained on the fence, while the extreme nationalists among them actively aided the Germans and the Italians.

There can be no doubt that many Arabs hoped for the defeat of the Allies, who, they felt, had brought them nothing but trouble, colonialist rule, and, worst of all, the plague of Zionism. Well aware of the German attitude toward the Jews, they even hoped that when Hitler's armies occupied the country, the Nazis would exterminate the Jews of Palestine, thereby once and for all extracting the Zionist thorn from their side. The Arabs gazed with equanimity, and some indeed with frankly malicious pleasure, upon the atrocities that the Nazis were perpetrating upon the Jews of Europe.

The postwar struggle between the Jews and the British was seen by the Arabs as a further sapping of Jewish strength. They felt that it would leave the Jews even weaker and more exposed on the approaching great day when the British would get out of Palestine. Then strong regular Arab armies would enter the country, clear it out once and for all, and restore Palestine in its entirety to its Arab owners.

THE CRUSADER THEORY

The crusader theory is based on a highly simplified comparison of the Zionist movement and the State of Israel with the Crusades and the Christian kingdom of Jerusalem. To the Arabs, the scenario is a captivating one, especially as it plays itself out to a happy end—the overthrow of the crusaders. The Arabs developed this theory many years ago, almost when the struggle was first engaged, and they clung all the more tenaciously to it after their military defeats.

This is how the Arabs view the crusader scenario. The Christians wanted to conquer the Holy Land, lay waste its Muslim holy places, and drive out its Arab inhabitants. They mobilized warriors and capital from the whole of Christendom. They took advantage of the weakness of the Arab world in the eleventh and twelfth centuries. The crusaders enjoyed an initial advantage in modern arms and equipment. They took the Arabs by surprise, attacking from the north and from the sea, and they entrenched themselves along the coast. They fought and defeated the Arabs, and they conquered Jerusalem and desecrated the holy places of Islam. They humiliated and oppressed the Arabs; they founded the crusader kingdom of Jerusalem. They fortified the country, intending to hold it forever. They expanded to the north, east, and south, reaching east Jordan, occupied parts of Syria and Lebanon, and conquered the outlet to the Gulf of Aqaba and the Red Sea. From there they wanted to extend themselves southward across the sea; so they built up strategic outposts along the approaches to Egypt on the Sea of Bardawil in north Sinai. The crusaders were the lackeys of the imperialist powers—Genoa, Venice, and others—who were seeking strongholds, markets, and natural resources in the East. The great Christian world did its utmost to help them, and sent them a constant stream of money, arms, and volunteers.

The Arabs made a number of attempts to beat them off and liberate their land from the crusader yoke, but were defeated. About two hundred years passed. The crusaders weakened, began quarreling among themselves: this sect with that, one order with another. The Arabs did all the hard labor, while the crusaders grew soft. They never adapted to the climate and landscape because they were never an integral part of the land. They remained a foreign transplant in the country's soil.

From among the Arabs sprang a great leader and general: Saladin (Salah-al-Din). He welded the Arabs into a single fighting people. He studied the crusaders' weaknesses and developed new methods of combat. He learned from his predecessors' mistakes. He summoned up the courage to begin hitting hard at the crusaders. In the decisive battle at Karnei-Hittin, near Tiberias, he smashed their cumbersome armies and put an end to the crusader episode, thus delivering the country from their yoke.

What could be simpler than to view the Zionist scenario through the same prism: the Zionists wanted to conquer the Holy Land, lay waste its Muslim holy places, and drive out its Arab inhabitants. They mobilized warriors and capital from Europe and from the whole of Jewry. They took advantage of the weakness of the Arab world in the nineteenth and twentieth centuries. The Zionists enjoyed an initial advantage in modern arms and equipment. They took the Arabs by surprise, attacking from the west and from the sea, and they entrenched themselves along the coast. They fought and defeated the Arabs, and they conquered Jerusalem and desecrated the holy places of Islam. They humiliated and oppressed the Arabs; they founded the Zionist State of Israel. They fortified the country, intending to hold it forever. They expanded to the north, east, and south, reaching east Jordan, occupied parts of Syria and Lebanon, and conquered the outlet to the Gulf of Aqaba and the Red Sea. They occupied the whole of the Sinai Peninsula, reached the Suez Canal, and began threatening the heart of Egypt. They were the lackeys of the imperialist powers—Great Britain and later the United States—who were seeking strongholds, markets, and natural resources in the Middle East. The wealthy Jewish world did its utmost to help them, and sent them a constant stream of money, arms, and volunteers. The Arabs made a number of attempts to beat them off and liberate the country from their yoke, but were defeated.

Here the Arabs spin out their analogy to its happy end.

Years will pass, and the Zionists will sink into degeneracy. They will quarrel among themselves: this party with that, one bloc with another. The Arabs living among them will be doing all the hard labor. The Jews will grow soft. They will not adapt to the climate and the landscape, because they were never an integral part of the land. They were and will always remain a foreign transplant in the country's soil.

And then comes the longed-for denouement: from among the Arabs will spring a great leader and general; he will weld the Arabs into a single fighting people. He will study the Zionists' weaknesses and their vulnerable points. He will develop new methods of combat. He will learn from his predecessors' mistakes. He will summon up the courage to begin hitting hard at the Jews. In a decisive battle he will smash their armies and put an end to the Zionist episode, thus delivering the country from their yoke.

The crusader theory provides the Arabs with a psychological shelter in their flight from the hard and painful reality of the past, the present, and indeed the immediate future. For if salvation is to come in a distant future, what does it matter what happens today, tomorrow, and within the next year or two? The day will come, so the upholders of this theory believe and persuade themselves, when history will repeat itself. A new Saladin will be born and will bring redemption in the form of the annihilation of the Jewish state.

The crusader theory certainly meets the needs of present-day

Arab attitudes. It is difficult to argue rationally with the Arabs over this theory, because the theory itself derives from irrational feelings. But whatever the difficulty, an attempt at such an argument should not be evaded. Perhaps we should start by repeating the old adage that if there is one thing to be learned from history, it is that history does not repeat itself. Human history is so diversified, so arbitrary, its every event is governed by causes and circumstances that are so varied (Cleopatra's nose, Napoleon's bellyache, the hemophilia of the Russian heir apparent, and so on) that to believe that in the year 2100 there will occur a succession of events identical to ones that took place in the year 1100 is to believe in witchcraft and miracles.

It should also be repeated, although this is a truism which for the most part has not yet penetrated Arab consciousness, that the comparison between the Jews returning to their ancient homeland from east and west, from north and south, and the Christian knights of medieval feudal Europe is a highly superficial one, and attests to an utter misunderstanding of the motives of the return to Zion.

According to the crusader theory, the Arabs claim that after the Arab victory over the Jews, the Jews will return to their countries of origin. But with World War II and the holocaust behind them, it is clear that the Jews now have nowhere to return to. Europe is for them a graveyard. And the Arab countries of the Middle East as well as the Communist countries of Eastern Europe persecute, jail, and expel them from their midst.

The Jews of Israel, those who immigrated there as well as those who were born there (and the distinction the Arabs try to draw between the two is absurd) will fight for their state; they will live here and they will die here. The Arabs should begin to come to terms with this reality after a hundred years of strife with the Jews.

The parallel they draw between the religious campaigns of the crusaders and the struggle of two modern nationalist move-

ments is also totally unfounded. But even were all the components of the crusader and the Zionist scenarios similar or identical, which they are not, there is still one component that is so
different that it alone renders the analogy untenable. I refer to
the component of time.

Had the State of Israel been founded a hundred years ago and
had the Arabs sought to destroy it by force of arms, even at that
time any comparison between twelfth-century weapons and
those of the nineteenth century would have been absurd. But
the absurdity becomes total if we compare the weapons and
means of combat used by Saladin and Richard Coeur de Lion
with those of the end of the twentieth century.

In place of the kind of arms that determined the outcome of
the battle of Karnei-Hittin there will be laser-guided missiles or
even more unconventional weapons. The "decisive battle" in
the classic sense is a meaningless notion today. Should the
Arabs, with the help of a technological power or powers, ever
succeed in bringing Israel to the brink of annihilation, they will
themselves be annihilated: of this whole region and its inhabitants there will remain not a trace, not a surviving remnant,
neither Jews nor Arabs, neither conquerors nor conquered. All
that will remain will be dust and total destruction. There will
be no victory parades, either in Damascus or Cairo, because
after a modern Karnei-Hittin there will be no Damascus or
Cairo.

Is this what the Arabs are dreaming of? Do they understand
that they have lost out in the technological race toward decision
by force? Any Goliath plotting to destroy the David state must
now reckon with the ultramodern slingshots that David will
possess in the future, as well as the fact that if attacked he will
use them with murderous intent. Even if the motives of the
Zionist enterprise and the Jews' desire to live in peace and
compromise with the Arab world continue to be completely
misunderstood, it would be well for the leaders of the Arab
countries to grasp fully the import of technological deterrence.

The Jewish-Arab dispute maddens the Arabs, plunging them into deep frustration, imbuing them with virulent anti-Jewish feelings, and kindling in their hearts a burning hatred toward Israel. This new Arab "anti-Semitism," which finds expression in thousands of pamphlets and books, in tens of thousands of press articles and *Stürmer*-style cartoons, in radio and television broadcasts, is coming to bear an ever-closer resemblance to the Christian European style of anti-Semitism during the blackest days of Jewish history in Spain, Germany, and Russia. This anti-Jewish feeling proves that when priests so desire, even the Koran, like Christian dogma, can be made to provide material for ardent anti-Jewish propaganda. By giving imaginary descriptions of Jews and Judaism, it provides the darkest passions with an outlet and permits the murder of Jews to be an auto-da-fé—an act of faith.

The Arabs, who as yet have had no experience of murderous European-style anti-Semitism, should realize that the poison they are spreading has a boomerang effect. It poisons their own body first. Anyone who cultivates such fierce hatred, such uncompromising intolerance, who educates his children with such deep enmity to the Jews, cannot at the same time cultivate sentiments of tolerance, love, mutual compromise, and respect within his own society.

History furnishes many examples to show that the murderous sword of anti-Semitism brandished aloft by other peoples inflicted injury upon themselves. Are not the Arabs in dire need of every ounce of creative rather than destructive energy; should they not grasp eagerly at any cohesive rather than disintegrative force?

The human and social challenges facing tens of millions of Arabs are tremendous: to adjust to the late twentieth century; to raise standards of living; to deal with problems of housing, education, health, scientific development; to exploit natural resources for the common good; to develop agriculture and industry; to enhance the prestige of Arab civilization. None of these goals will be achieved by the destruction of the State of Israel. By channeling their economic and physical resources toward hatred of the Jews and Israel, the Arabs merely deplete their own energies without gaining even so much as a sense of relief, since Israel has not the slightest intention of offering itself up as a sacrifice on the altar of Arab hatred or of being butchered by the sword of Muhammad's heirs.

The Arab states attained independence only about a generation ago. Each one of them is still searching for its unique national identity. It will probably be a very long time before a stable supranational Arab framework comes into existence. But economic and international circumstances dictate to the Arab countries, as to other parts of the world, the creation of regional frameworks. Hence the Arab attempts to found various federations and confederations, in which each member state retains its independence and sovereignty. If and when the Arabs outgrow the crusader theory regarding Israel and reconcile themselves to its existence, then there will be room in the Middle Eastern supranational structure for Israel too, and Israel will bring to bear on such a body the full benefits of its vitality and talent.

3

FACE TO FACE WITH OUR NEIGHBORS: WE, THE PALES- TINIAN ARABS, AND JORDAN*

THE ROOTS OF THE CONFLICT

Our capacity as Jews and Israelis to affect world develop- ments is minute but significant. The Jews are scattered over most of the globe, and in many countries they carry more weight than their numbers would suggest. The Israelis are situ- ated in one of the most volatile areas in the world today. One move by Israel could trigger an explosion in our region which might set off a worldwide chain reaction. At the same time, it is within our power to try to neutralize the explosive material that has accumulated in our region and thereby remove one of the world's most menacing threats to peace.

It is difficult to disentangle the various threads of the Israeli- Arab conflict. Despite this difficulty, and despite the danger of oversimplifying the problem, we must treat each of the differ- ent elements of the problem separately for the sake of clear and thorough discussion. We must, therefore, deal separately with the possibilities that are open to Israel and with her objectives with respect to the Palestinian-Jordanians, the Egyptians, the Syrians, the Lebanese, and the other Arab peoples.

*   *   *

---

* This chapter was translated by Moshe Kohn.

The Palestinian aspect of the problem is the most delicate, the most tragic, and the gloomiest of all. It appears to be insoluble, but it also carries the greatest potential for peace.

There is no doubt that for the Arabs, for the nations of the world, and, finally, for many Jews the question of our relations with the Palestinian Arabs occupies first place in the broad question of our relations with the Arab world as a whole. Therein lies the key to the resolution of the struggle over this land.

The problem of the Palestinians—Do they exist at all? Who are they? What are they after? What is our attitude to them?— is so charged with emotional and political dynamite that it has virtually turned into an obsession, particularly since the Six-Day War. It is difficult—really, impossible—for us to be objective about this problem. For decades it has been linked to the question of our very existence here. It lives in our midst and follows us like a shadow. Anyone writing or talking about this problem without immediately trying to sweep it under the carpet— "There is no such problem"; "There are no Palestinians"; "It will all work out"—appears to some Jews as one possessed. But such an attitude can never by of any real help to us. The Palestinian Arabs live in our midst and within our borders. We are now responsible for the lives of more than one million of them. From their midst have come and continue to come our cruelest enemies. We are destined to go on living with them always. Even if in some miraculous way a temporary or permanent settlement is reached with the Arab states that are south, north, and east of us, the problem of the Palestinian Arabs will still not be solved. We will not achieve true peace, and the Jewish-Arab conflict will not come to an end, until a solution is found to this problem. It is wrong to brush it aside, for such a human and national tragedy must not be ignored. It would be better for us to face the problem head on; and—despite all the difficulties, the discomfort, and perhaps even the fear involved—we are duty bound to do so.

First, let us discuss the problem of names.

The extremist Palestinian Arab leaders have set the destruction of Israel as their goal. They lay claim to all of Palestine—that is, Mandatory (western) Palestine—and they contend that Israel is not a real state and that the Jews are not a real people. In their view, the Jews who live here—"the Zionist gangs" in their terminology—are no more than a rabble and have no rights whatever to this land. Since they have been repeating this argument for several decades, some of us try to answer them in kind, saying, "There are no Palestinian Arabs. Those who define themselves as Palestinian Arabs have no real rights to this country." And some of us refer to some of them as "gangs" or "rabble."

This approach is a grave error. For many generations Jews faced the identical problem and were often asked: By what right do you define yourselves as a people? You have no land of your own, no common language; you differ from one another in customs, complexion, dress; you are dispersed far and wide; you are refugees and wanderers—so how do you dare to request the right of self-determination?

We struggled for the right of self-determination of Jews, and succeeded. How can we deny this right to others then, to people who wish to see themselves as a nation? To be sure, this group —the Palestinian Arabs—wishes to destroy us. But this is irrelevant to the question of self-determination. If we do not recognize the enemy, or if we do not call him the name which he calls himself, will we thereby bolster the morale of those fighting him? Will the soldiers of the Israeli army engaged in a chase after armed Palestinian Arabs who have come to murder Jews fight better if they are told they are fighting "gangs"? When we were fighting the British, would our war have been any different if we had called the British "Bevin's gangsters"?

Some of us would like to solve the name problem by a semantic exercise in which we refer to the Palestinian Arabs by the neutral designation of "the Arabs of this country," while others use the formulation "the Arabs of the Land of Israel"—which is meaningless to the Arabs. We delude ourselves into thinking that we have thereby solved the basic problem.

WHO ARE PALESTINIAN ARABS AND WHAT IS THEIR UNIQUENESS?

We are strong and mature enough to call the baby by his right name. We must ask: Who are the Palestinian Arabs, how and from where did they come to this country, and what have they experienced in the past?

When the Zionist undertaking began a century ago, its pioneers found in this country a sparse Arab population of several hundred thousand people, most of them Muslim, a few of them Christian. This population had a history in this country that went back well before the Arab conquest. It is very likely that these Arabs were the descendants of ancient settlers: Jews, Samaritans, Idumeans, Nabateans, Greeks, Romans, Byzantines, and members of many other tribes and nations that lived in this country. The country was conquered by the Muslim Arabs who swept up out of the desert, and the overwhelming majority of its population accepted Islam.

The pure Arabs—the people of the Arabian Peninsula—assimilated over the generations into the indigenous population, and the two became one Arab amalgam. The same thing happened in many of the other countries conquered by the Arabs. In each country the Arab amalgam comprises different elements.

The grandeur and glory of the Arab empires did not bypass this country. Jerusalem became El Quds (The Holy), and the Mosque of Omar (Dome of the Rock) was built on the Temple Mount. Even though Jerusalem never became the capital of any of the great Arab dynasties, and notwithstanding the fact that this country was only a tiny province in the vast Arab world, the city was still a very special place to the Arabs. The Arabs preserved the sanctity of the land in their own way. Many Arab settlements reflect historical continuity and local traditions; many have biblical names.

More than thirteen hundred years have passed since the Arab conquest. The land and its Arab inhabitants passed from conqueror to conqueror: Seljuks, Mamelukes, Mongols, and Ottoman Turks. Each of these added something of their own to the Arab amalgam. It was this Arab population that the early Zionists found here.

A hundred years ago the indigenous Arab population of the country did not constitute a separate nation and had no separate political aspirations. Modern nationalism was barely beginning to make itself heard in the Arab world, and this little province was not too important to the nascent Arab nationalist movement. The Arabs of this country knew no allegiance—did not relate at all—to something called "Palestine"; their loyalty was to families, clans, tribes, to villages and towns.

The Arab national renaissance, which began about a century ago in Egypt, Lebanon, and Syria, reached this land only at the end of the nineteenth and the beginning of the twentieth centuries. (The Arab newspaper *Falastin* began to appear in Jerusalem in 1911.) From its beginnings the Zionist undertaking served as a spur to Arab nationalism. Zionism became an "enemy"—and there is no better catalyst for a national movement than a rival.

After World War I the Jewish nation renaissance movement faced a Palestinian Arab national movement. The latter was, to be sure, split by internal rivalries and contradictions, but it already had a clear objective: to rule the whole country, with or without the patronage of the British, and to turn it into a land named Falastin and eliminate the Zionist undertaking.

This Palestinian Arab movement was part of a greater Arab nationalist movement. In the 1920s this Palestinian Arab nationalist movement already had something that distinguished it. That something was us. So it may be said, paradoxically, that Zionism brought about the creation of the Palestinian Arab nationalist movement.

As the struggle over this land intensified, the distinctiveness of the Palestinian Arabs took on added significance. The "gangs" and the troubles of 1936–39, the general strikes, the formation of the Arab High Committee were unique to the Palestinian Arab national movement. Moreover, the human toll they took among us: their onslaughts on our settlements, our heavy counterblows against them, their blood that we shed, our constant contact with them, their day-to-day contact with Jews, their adoption of some of our life-styles and fighting methods— all this and numerous other major and minor factors made the Arabs of this country unique.

The Palestinian Arab national movement failed and was routed in 1948 because of its intransigence, its unwillingness to grant Zionism even an inch of ground under the common sun and in the common land. It was the Palestinian Arabs' own determination to "throw the Jews into the sea" that caused their debacle.

It behooves us—especially those of us who say that there is no such entity as Palestinian Arabs—to ask ourselves frankly: With whom were we living and against whom were we fighting in those decades before the establishment of the State of Israel? Wasn't it with Palestinian Arabs? Were we engaged in a life-and-death struggle with Egyptians? Syrians? Moroccans? Didn't the Arab High Committee belong to the Palestinian Arabs? Who were the members of the "gangs"? Wasn't it with Palestinian Arab leaders that the Zionist leaders sought with all their might to come to terms? Weren't the mufti's Husseinis—and the Nashashibis, the Dejanis, the Khaldis—all Palestinian Arab leaders?

When we agreed in 1947 to the partition of western Eretz Yisrael (Land of Israel) into two states, a Jewish state and an Arab state (as they were referred to in the United Nations partition decision), did we not imagine that when the Arab state obtained independence it would call itself Falastin? Weren't we prepared to live peacefully side by side with this Falastin? It is urgent that we debate this among ourselves. There is a certain lack of candor in the naiveté—especially since the Six-Day War —of people who ask: Who are the Palestinian Arabs? Where have they suddenly come from? When were they born? What are they doing here?

The Palestinian Arabs are our bitterest enemies—but we must call them by their right name.

The Palestinian Arab national movement did not accept the United Nations decision of 1947 and in 1948 rallied the entire Arab world to its side in a bid to destroy Israel. That effort failed. Instead of throwing us into the sea, hundreds of thousands of Palestinian Arabs became war refugees. Instead of their destroying hundreds of our villages, hundreds of their villages were destroyed. The State of Israel came into being—partly on the land of Palestinian Arabs who had just set out to destroy her. That was the price—and the Palestinian Arabs themselves know this well.

The Palestinian Arabs were hit so hard that they were unable to muster the strength to set up Arab Falastin in the parts of the country that remained in their hands. The Egyptians remained as conquerors in the Gaza Strip; the Jordanians—the people of the Hashemite kingdom—conquered and took control of the West Bank; a minority of Palestinian Arabs remained within the borders of the State of Israel.

After 1948 the distinctiveness of the Palestinian Arabs among the Arabs intensified: about half of them turned into refugees. The stamp of refugee leaves an ineradicable stigma on the individuals or groups who bear it. No one knows this better than the Jews.

The Palestinian Arabs have turned into the most tragic Arab national group in the Arab world. They were the biggest losers among all the Arab national groups: they were the only ones not to gain independence. Every other Arab group that crystallized into a national movement acquired a state. Moreover, no Arab state or nation besides the Palestinian Arabs has had to suffer the pain of refugeeism on such a scale.

The distinctiveness of the Palestinian Arabs is one of the reasons that the Arab states, the "sister" states—Egypt, Libya, Morocco, Algeria, Tunisia, Syria, Lebanon, Iraq, and others—have not really absorbed them.

There are many factors in the Arab states' leaving hundreds of thousands of refugees in such deplorable conditions in the camps. One of these factors is the refugees' own refusal to let themselves be absorbed by the Arab states, and their intense desire to return to their lands and homes. The Arab states wanted to turn the refugee camps on Israel's borders into a political, psychological, and military sword of Damocles over Israel's head. They did not wish to waste money and effort absorbing the refugees within their borders. They were quite cruel to them, leaving them to their fate as beggars living off the dole meted out by the United Nations Relief and Work Agency (UNRWA). Behind this attitude lie the Arab states' fears and suspicions of the Palestinian Arabs' distinctiveness. They had turned into wanderers and transients, and had acquired some of the characteristics of refugees: frustration, bitterness, suspiciousness. They carried with them a mood of intransigence and became the standard-bearers of extreme political radicalism. They were antiestablishment—any establishment, even that of their host country. Paradoxically, they acquired a similar image to that of the Jew as seen in the anti-Semitic stereotype: sowers of doubt, unstable, unreliable, security risks of whom one must beware.

This was true of all the Arab states save the kingdom of Jordan. Jordan could not help but "absorb" the Palestinian Arabs, who outnumbered the indigenous Jordanians. After the Hashemite kingdom occupied the West Bank in 1948 and annexed it in 1949, the Palestinians started to "annex" Jordan—demographically and socially. It may be said that if it had not been for the Six-Day War, the kingdom of Jordan would gradually have turned into the Palestinian Arab state on which the United Nations had decided in princple—and one occupying a much greater area than provided for in the United Nations decision (just as, following the 1948 war, Israel occupied a greater area than provided for in the UN partition plan).

In Jordan—unlike the situation in the Gaza Strip and the refugee camps of Syria and Lebanon—the Palestinian Arab refugees were integrated into the country's economy. Some of the camps took on a new character as refugees were moved into permanent dwellings. Many camps became city suburbs in every respect.

Palestinian Arabs—refugees and nonrefugees alike—began to occupy increasingly prominent places in Jordan's establishment. Some of them learned new professions and trades and made new lives for themselves in other parts of the Arab world, mainly in the oil principalities.

If all this had gone on for a generation or two longer Jordan would have turned into a Palestinian Arab state, and as she developed she would have attracted other Palestinian Arab refugees from the camps in the Gaza Strip, Syria, and Lebanon. It is also likely that—in evolutionary or revolutionary fashion— the Palestinian Arabs would have brought about a radical change in Jordan's governmental structure and would have turned her into a constitutional monarchy or even into a republic.

Before the Six-Day War about two-thirds of the Palestinian Arabs were concentrated in Jordan. Considering the importance and prestige of the cities that then constituted the Hashemite kingdom of Jordan, the holy places, the natural resources, and the development potential, that country could have served as a solution to the Palestinian Arab problem.

But this was not the desire of the leaders of the young Palestinian Arabs, of those who set up the Fatah and the other armed organizations. According to their "Falastin Covenant," they desired "return" and revenge. They wished to rally the Palestinian Arabs and the entire Arab world to a third, fourth, and fifth round against Israel. They wanted to destroy Israel and take her place.

After the Six-Day War the leaders of the Palestinian Arab armed organizations thought that their great hour had struck and that because more than a million of them were now living "inside" Israel they would turn her life into a hell and, by classical guerrilla warfare, bring her down. But their influence —as a result of their rout by the Israeli army and, after they turned on the Hashemite kingdom, by Hussein's Arab Legion —is now at a much lower point.

The Fatah and the other armed Palestinian Arab organizations at first gained considerable sympathy in the Arab world, which saw them for the moment as latter-day Saladins. They also gained sympathy in parts of the world at large, especially among Communists, New Leftists, and all varieties of guerrilla-sympathizers. In order to increase this sympathy, some of the Palestinian Arab leaders, under the leadership of the Fatah, sought to pose as "liberating revolutionaries" who desired, not to exterminate the Jews of Israel, but "only" to eliminate the State of Israel and set up in its stead a "democratic, secular, multinational Palestine whose Jewish inhabitants would dwell side by side with the Arabs." But in the end their desire for revenge and a war of extermination showed through this ideological mask.

Israel must under no circumstances underestimate the Palestinian Arab armed organizations. Despite the relative decline in which these movements now find themselves, it would be most dangerous to imagine that the terrorism and sabotage are over. To be sure, our assumption that the Palestinian Arab saboteurs would not constitute a serious military threat to Israel's existence has been borne out, but we must not for one moment forget how much blood we have shed in recent years.

We must also not deprecate these organizations with respect to their courage. It would be sheer stupidity for us to fail to see that they succeeded—temporarily at least—in raising the morale of the Arabs in general and of the Palestinian Arabs in particular, serving them as a symbol of heroism and self-sacrifice. Anyone who dismisses the thousands of armed Palestinian Arabs who have tried to kill us, by calling them "gangs" or "rabble" or "Arabooshes," is first and foremost doing a grave injustice to the soldiers of the Israeli army and the men of our security forces who have fought and are fighting them with skill and courage at the risk of their lives. This is a cruel war against cruel, embittered people who are certain that they are fighting for a cause, and who by no means lack courage and enterprise. To set out from bases outside Israel's borders, to infiltrate into Israel through a dense network of bunkers, fences, minefields, and electronic devices, and then to live in caves and wadis, hunted relentlessly by the Israeli army and our other security forces—all this requires no little courage. We ought to recognize this, and this recognition does not detract one whit from the credit due Israel's soldiers. On the contrary, it enhances it.

These armed Palestinian Arabs know that they are courting death, and that out of every ten setting out only one or two will return alive to their bases, while the rest will either be killed in battle or captured and sent to prison for long terms. Anyone who says that people going into battle under such circumstances are "yellow Arabooshes" or "rabble" doesn't know what he is talking about.

If I have stressed the activities of the Palestinian Arab extremist organizations, it is only because it is they who have given the Palestinian problem the character and dimension it has, turning it into a military and terror problem which we have reacted to mainly by the use of force, on the simple and self-evident principle of "When someone is coming at you to kill you, kill him first."

But let us not forget that these organizations and their attitude to us are only one part of the whole Palestinian problem and our attitude to it.

This brings us back to the matter of names. Are the Palestinian Arabs a nation? This is a question over which they themselves are divided. Some of them refer to themselves as the "Palestinian entity"—an unclear term whose coiners themselves have not adequately defined it. In the final analysis it is for the Palestinian Arabs to give themselves a name and define their essence. No one—neither the Jews nor anyone else—can deny them this right.

Actually they, or the past several decades of history, have already defined them as a distinctive people among the Arab peoples. If—and this is the growing tendency in the Arab world —the Moroccans are defined as the Moroccan nation, the Algerians as the Algerian nation, the Tunisians as the Tunisian nation, the Libyans as the Libyan nation, the Egyptians as the Egyptian nation, and so on for all the Arab peoples, then the Palestinian Arabs may certainly be defined as a nation, or as a nation-in-the-making. To be sure, the Palestinian Arabs do not as yet have a state in which they can express themselves as a nation, but who knows better than we Jews about the possibility of a "nation-on-the-way," nurturing dreams of a state of its own.

The Palestinian Arab nation has a history of its own, special memories of its own, wars, sacrifices, sufferings, and heroes of its own, poetic and literary expressions of its own. This nation also has a central continuous territory, including Jordan, occupied by a majority of its members. Numbering some 2.5 millions, this nation has a diaspora of its own. The Six-Day War intensified the Palestinian Arab identity—the consciousness of the shared disaster was heightened after this further debacle, in the wake of additional casualties and additional refugees.

NEW BORDERS—A NEW SITUATION

After the Six-Day War Israel found herself not only within new borders but also in a totally new situation with respect to the Palestinian Arabs. For more than six years now about a million of them have been under Israeli rule—some six hundred thousand of them on the West Bank and some four hundred thousand in the Gaza Strip. About one-third of the total are 1948 refugees, mostly in the Gaza Strip.

Israel has not yet given herself, the Arabs, or the world a clear statement of her position concerning these Palestinian Arabs. Israel has dealt with the Palestinian Arabs pragmatically. She set up military government in the administered areas. Through them she developed unconventional methods and operations. Local government offices in the towns and villages were activated. Educational, health, welfare, and other institutions were activated. Through her ministries Israel supplies services, guidance, and advice in all areas of life: agriculture, water, electricity, commerce and industry, public works, transport, mails, law, police, and so on.

Israel developed the system of open bridges across the Jordan, which makes possible business, transport and tourism, and the passage of relatives and students between the West Bank and the Hashemite kingdom of Jordan. All this developed at the height of the "war of attrition" and terrorist activity. And the bridges remained open all through the Yom Kippur War.

After the Six-Day War many tens of thousands of Palestinian Arab workers on the West Bank and in the Gaza Strip started crossing daily into Israel to work in construction, agriculture, industry, and services. In a certain respect it may be said that all of Israel is now serving almost all the Palestinian Arabs as a kind of huge school for high-grade vocational training—by guidance and training given in the administered areas, by jobs provided in new trades, or by the training and experience that make it possible for workers to improve their skills.

This policy has borne considerable fruit. The standard of living of the Palestinian Arabs on the West Bank and in the Gaza Strip has risen steadily. Compared to conditions under Jordanian and Egyptian rule, the administered areas are now quite prosperous. Daily life has become a more or less calm and tolerable routine; people no longer fear for their lives. It should come as no surprise that even among the Palestinian Arabs themselves there is a positive appreciation—sometimes concealed, sometimes open—of this policy. There is no doubt at all that laying the groundwork for a higher standard of living and providing vocational training are most important steps forward in the developing relations between Israel and the Palestinian Arabs.

But the Palestinian Arabs have not yet received any answers to the questions that they ask—and must inevitably ask—that are beyond bread and butter: What will their future be? What national options are open to them? What does Israel want from them? The reason that they have not yet received answers is that Israel has not yet given herself any clear-cut answers to these questions.

I have discussed the various opinions in Israel on the future of the administered areas. The views vary and debate rages, especially with regard to the territories of western Eretz Yisrael —the West Bank and the Gaza Strip—and the future of their one million Palestinian Arab inhabitants.

In dealing with this question from an Israeli standpoint, we touch an extremely sensitive spot. There is no question that in the Six-Day War, Israel conquered—some say liberated—the historical cradle of the Jewish people. In antiquity the Jews lived mainly in the mountains of Judea and Samaria—which today constitute the southern and northern parts of the West Bank. In Hebron, in Jerusalem, and in Shomron stood the palaces of the ancient Jewish kings; in Bethel, in Tekoa, in Anatot lived the great Jewish prophets; in these mountains and on these hills Jewish heroes fought—Joshua, Judah the Maccabee, Bar Kokhba.

And now these territories are ours! Who will ignore the feelings of the Jews upon reaching these precious areas after a bloody and valiantly fought war? It would seem that all that remains for us to do now is to settle these areas as quickly as possible, build Jewish villages and towns in them, annex them unequivocally to the sovereign State of Israel, make them a part of the body of Israel, and thus complete the historical act of restoring all of western Eretz Yisrael to the Jewish people. To those who think this way, the problem of the Palestinian Arabs living in these areas in such density is a problem, to be sure, but one that takes second place to the annexation and settlement of the areas.

Some among us seriously think that this problem will be solved more easily if we annex the administered areas. For then, they think, the Arabs living in them will know that they are destined to become a national minority in the State of Israel. The Arabs will then reconcile themselves to their fate, in due time acquire Israeli citizenship and full civil rights, and become fully integrated into Israel's economic and political life. And if they do not reconcile themselves? Well, say those wishing to annex areas of western Eretz Yisrael, they will have no alternative. And those who still do not reconcile themselves will eventually emigrate to Jordan or one of the other Arab states.

In the course of time, these people think, the administered areas will become depleted, especially of young people, who will settle in one or another of the Arab states, and the problem will be solved—with those of us alive today bequeathing a whole, historical Land of Israel to our children.

I do not doubt the sincerity of those who think this way. But now and then some of them sound a false note by pinning the label of heresy on those who think differently, on anyone who dares to suggest that we should return or relinquish the administered areas or some part of them to the Palestinian Arabs or the kingdom of Jordan. There is an extremist nationalist-religious school among us whose members have managed to find scriptural evidence attesting to the sanctity of every last inch of western Eretz Yisrael, and they have found rabbis to threaten the government and parliament of Israel with excommunication if they should ever dare even discuss the possibility of returning any of these areas.

Another sensitive aspect of the problem of the West Bank and the Gaza Strip has to do with security. For nineteen years we lived in a state with accidental, tortuous, and intolerable borders. Israel's backbone was extremely narrow, at some vital links no wider than about nine miles. Tel Aviv, the Dan region, and Haifa were all within range of the cannon of Jordan's Arab Legion. Jerusalem, Israel's capital, was divided, and the Knesset building could be reached by Arab snipers and machine gunners. The narrow corridor leading to the capital was, like the backbone of the coastal plain, vulnerable to attack. The Gaza Strip was pointed like a dagger at the Negev.

And now the Israeli army is encamped along the Jordan River. We hold the ridges of Judea and Samaria. Anyone wishing to invade us now must first come up the mountains which we control. We have sealed the invasion and infiltration routes. The border is now more natural and much shorter than it was before. We have pushed the threat far away from our capital and population centers. We are secure now. How—it is argued —can anyone think of withdrawing from these splendid strategic positions? If we withdraw we will again expose ourselves and our settlements to cannon and Katyushas. Our life will turn into a hell again, and sooner or later we will once again have to capture—and who knows at what price?—these vital strategic areas.

Did you ever, it is argued, see a nation that wishes to go on living return areas vital to its security and existence? Did any other nation anywhere ever relinquish excellent borders and return to an inferior and intolerable security situation? Didn't the big powers annex, and aren't they forcibly holding onto, strategic areas which they conquered in defensive wars? Didn't the Soviet Union annex—for security reasons—hundreds of thousands of square miles of territory inhabited by tens of millions of members of non-Russian nations and nationalities? Did she content herself with these annexations? Didn't she surround herself with a safety zone of states which she controls militarily and strategically? Didn't the Americans surround the United States with strategic bases—some of them nearby and some of them thousands of miles away? Isn't the history of mankind filled with struggles over vital territories?

Anyone who doesn't understand the magnitude of these emotions and arguments concerning western Eretz Yisrael cannot begin to understand present-day Israel. Anyone wishing to argue another point of view on the future of the administered areas must have the understanding and sensitivity to take these deeply rooted emotions into consideration.

And just as we must not go around pinning the label of heretic on those who reject the notion of "don't give up an inch," so must we avoid the indiscriminate pinning of the chauvinist or annexationist label on those who think that we should not give up any parts of western Eretz Yisrael. It will be a sad day when the debate is reduced to the mutual pinning of labels and hurling of epithets.

TWO NATIONS—TWO STATES

What Israel must do is declare her readiness in principle to return—"return," not "withdraw from"; there is a tremendous difference between these two terms—to the Palestinian Arabs most of the West Bank and a large part of the Gaza Strip, so that in these areas plus Jordan they may set up an independent and sovereign state of their own whose future form of government or name (Jordanian Palestine, Palestinian Jordan, or any other combination) will be up to them.

Anyone advocating this approach must answer some fundamental questions about history and security. He must also explain how such a position can be implemented.

The historical, undivided Land of Israel is the Land of the Twelve Tribes: the area, more or less, which the British acquired as a mandate from the League of Nations—in other words, western Eretz Yisrael (Mandatory Palestine) and the part of Palestine that is east of the Jordan River (Mandatory Transjordan). In this land—from the territory of the tribe of Dan on the Hermon slopes to the territory of the tribe of Simeon in the Negev; from the territories of Reuben, Gad, and Manasseh in Jordan to the territories of Zebulun, Asher, and

Judah in the Mediterranean littoral—our people was born and lived. The Jews have no historical-national rights to any other territory in the world, notwithstanding the fact that members of the Jewish nation are spread over nearly the entire globe and have given of their strength, talent, energy, and blood to the revival, establishment, and upbuilding of dozens of countries. But here, in these 20,000-odd square miles, we have full historical and national rights.

But this, too, must be said: to that very same number of square miles the Palestinian Arabs also have national-historical rights. Is there anyone who will deceive himself and say that these Arabs, natives of this plot of earth, are only "transients" here?

These "transients" have been living here for thirteen hundred years. Does it make any difference that they came here as conquerors? Didn't we, at the beginning of our history in this country, arrive here as conquerors? All of us contend, rightly, that it is not only our conquest that gave us our national-historical rights in this land, but also the remarkable national and religious culture that we built here; it is by virtue of both that conquest and culture that we lay historical claim to this land.

There are some among us who argue that the Arabs have not left any significant mark on this country. The Arabs even wrecked the country, they argue; the Arabs turned a blossoming land into a swamp and a wasteland, and therefore have no historical rights to it.

This is a half-truth, and thus worse than a lie. We must not deceive ourselves on this subject merely in order to assuage our conscience. It is true that Eretz Yisrael under Arab rule was not a center of the great Arab Empire; but this is a far cry from saying that the Arabs created nothing of cultural value here.

Aren't the tens of thousands of ancient graves scattered throughout the country proof enough that the Arabs had a life of their own and created a culture of their own here? And what of the dozens of Arab towns and hundreds of Arab villages—

some of which rose on the sites of ancient villages and towns, but some of which were built by the Arabs? The exquisite mosques on the Temple Mount in Jerusalem and the hundreds of other mosques—aren't they a great Arab creation? Didn't they build educational institutions here, palaces, baths, roads, bridges, and aqueducts? Didn't they leave a thousand and one other signs of their creativity here? Will someone say that this creativity was not great? Who are we to judge what is historically "great" or "minor"? Didn't the Greeks, the Romans, the Byzantines, and others scorn our national-religious-cultural creativity?

As to the desolation we found here when we started returning in the last century—is that entirely the fault of the Arabs of the land? Isn't the Bible full of stories about destruction in ancient times, when we were masters of the country? Wasn't it also destroyed by the Assyrians, Babylonians, Scythians, Romans, and others? Didn't we ourselves destroy our own land in wars between the tribes and kings? Do these terrible facts—which the Bible does not conceal from us—diminish our historical and national right to this country?

We ought to apply the same standard to the Arabs. To be sure, we found the country sparsely inhabited and quite wasted. But is that the exclusive fault of the local Arabs? Wasn't the land easy spoil for the armies of rival Arab dynasties passing through from the north or the south on their imperialistic campaigns? Wasn't the country laid waste again and again by rampaging Seljuk tribes, warring crusaders, Mamelukes, Mongols, the hosts of Tamerlane? Finally, weren't the Ottoman Turks, who ruled the country for four centuries, until 1918, one of the factors—perhaps the main factor—in the country's despoliation?

It is true that the local Arabs and the bedouins had a hand in all this, but by what right do we indict them for everything and tell them that therefore they have no rights whatever in this country? All that we are entitled to say without being hypocritical and self-righteous is this:

"Since, for historical reasons, we found here a century ago a half-ruined, sparsely populated land, and since this land—when we inhabited it two thousand years ago—had a population that reached five millions, and since we are now returning and wish to restore it to its former glory, there is room in this land for us and for you, for a state for us and a state for you."

This is both the minimum and the maximum that we are able to say. If on coming to Eretz Yisrael a century ago we had found a relatively modern and large population with a highly developed national consciousness, it is very doubtful whether we would have been able to launch the Zionist enterprise. This is another reason that we ought to deal humbly with the question of Palestinian Arab national-historical rights.

As a matter of fact, the attitude of the best of the Zionist leaders to the Arabs of the land was from the outset that of Abraham to Lot (Genesis 13:8–9): "Let there be no strife between you and me, between my herdsmen and yours, for we are kinsmen. Is not the whole land before you? Let us separate: if you go north, I will go south; and if you go south, I will go north."

In the 1930s our leaders said to the Arab leaders: "Let us divide up the land. In one part we will set up a Jewish state, and in the other part you will set up a Palestinian Arab state." But the Palestinian Arab leaders responded: "Never! The rights to this land are exclusively ours. We are its sole masters and there is not an inch for you—for you there is the sea to be thrown into."

On the eve of the 1948 war we again told the Arabs: "The United Nations has voted to partition the land. Let us divide it up accordingly and live in peace beside each other in our separate states." Again the Arabs responded with: "You have no rights whatever in this country, and—with the help of the Arab states—we're going to drive you into the sea."

After the establishment of the State of Israel we again said to the Arabs: "There was a war and there was killing. Now our state has come into being. Not in the way we wished—but it has come about the way it did. For eighty years you took a toll of casualties among us, and in 1948 you set out to annihilate us. You had no mercy on us. You went to war against the remnants of an exiled people, fugitives from war and holocaust who had only just set foot in this country. At the war's end you did not leave a single house in Israel that was not mourning some dead. We know that a heavy disaster has befallen you too, but now let us come to terms with each other. We will undertake to indemnify your refugees—we shall not permit them to return, for these refugees only just set out to push us into the sea. We will undertake to content ourselves with our present borders forever and never to seek to expand beyond them. These borders—the borders of the State of Israel—are not the borders of the undivided, historical Land of Israel. We know—and we will never forget—that we also have rights to other parts of the Land of the Twelve Tribes. We do not waive these rights, for we are not at liberty to do so. We will insist on the right to visit and pray at those of our historical sites that are in your control. But we will waive the implementation of these rights, if only you will make peace with us. We know that you, too, have rights in our part of Eretz Yisrael, but by the same token we ask you to waive the implementation of your rights."

This was Israel's position from 1948 to 1967. But the Arabs totally rejected it. Now it behooves us to return to its principles. We and the Palestinian Arabs will have no peace unless both sides waive the implementation of part of their respective national-historical rights in this country.

We must return to the principle—the truth—that we asserted up until the Six-Day War: there is room in the Land of the Twelve Tribes for the State of Israel and a Palestinian-Jordanian Arab state. In exchange for a full and permanent peace we will waive implementing part of our historical rights in this Arab state.

DECLARATION OF PRINCIPLES

Some ask what the point is to such a scholastic exercise in abstract principles concerning our and the Palestinian Arabs' national-historical rights in this country. Isn't it better to let sleeping dogs lie, they ask. Also, there is no one to talk to among the Palestinian Arabs. Those who might be ready to talk are afraid to do so, while those who do talk claim the entire land and are not ready to give up an inch. In that case, why should we expose ourselves? Why stir up internal debate and strife? As soon as we know that there is someone to talk to, let us talk. Meanwhile it is better to remain silent.

We would be committing a fatal error if we were to adopt this approach. For our own sake, for the sake of peace with the Arabs, we must speak up and declare in principle what it is we wish. For our entire undertaking here is based on principles—the deeds came afterward.

It is precisely we Jews who must begin discussing this subject in principle, because we, and not the Palestinian Arabs, are the victors; because we hold most of the good cards and not they; it is we, not they, who have the upper hand—and that is precisely why we can allow ourselves to rise to the occasion and discuss principles. And this continues to hold true even today after the Yom Kippur War.

To the standard argument that there is no one to talk to it can be said that this may be due precisely to the fact that we are not clearly stating any principles concerning the problem of the Palestinian Arabs and their and our national-historical rights, and are obscuring the subject of the future of the areas of western Eretz Yisrael. If we were to start discussing principles, first of all among ourselves, we might stir the Arabs into discussing them among themselves and then with us.

The Zionist movement was and is fundamentally an ideological movement. It is true that we often acted pragmatically. We did not merely adhere to abstract ideals and we did not wait for

the Messiah to come in order to actualize ours dreams; but our
entire undertaking was founded on principles. If a movement
of this sort does not lay down some guiding principles for itself,
it leaves itself open to suspicion. If, on the one hand, we do not
give any answers to questions of principle, and on the other
hand we continue—with crass pragmatism—to create reality in
western Eretz Yisrael by settlement, it is no wonder that we
arouse suspicion and that the Palestinian Arabs can also tell
themselves: "There's no one to talk to."

The pragmatists who argue that we should not get involved
in principles and ideology, and say, "Let things take their natural course," find themselves slipping into the following thought
pattern: "What does everybody want of us? The Palestinian
Arabs in the administered areas never had it so good. Everybody's happy. They're making money, they're all eating well.
Every morning they leave their areas and go happily off to work
in our fields and factories and on our construction sites, and
every evening they return happily to their homes in the administered areas. Their standard of living is rising. What's wrong?"
Here and there one also hears the argument, "Actually, the
Palestinian Arabs are better off than the Arabs of the other Arab
countries. See how the others quarrel with each other, make
war against each other, kill each other, fail to develop their
countries. While 'our' Arabs are living in peace and having the
time of their life."

This kind of talk has a terrible ring to it and calls to mind
echoes from our own exilic past—"Those Jews have it good."
This is the kind of talk one hears in countries where we would
not wish to live for a single moment. What is more, this kind of
talk does not enhance the prestige of the excellent work we
have done in the administered territories; on the contrary, it
diminishes it. If we are proud of what Israel has done in the
territories, this pride can have only one justification: that whatever we are doing there is being done on the premise of open

options in the future for the inhabitants of the areas: readiness by us to make concessions and compromises, and recognition in principle by us of the national-historical rights of the inhabitants of the areas. Only this premise can fully justify what we are doing and will yet do in the areas. Otherwise, all the bounty we are lavishing on the inhabitants of the areas will turn into a cause for the suspicion that what we are really doing is building deluxe reservations for unwanted nationals.

On the other hand, if we leave the Palestinian Arabs open national options, and if we speak of the principles of two nations and two states, then our positive activity in the areas has better prospects for the future. The work of laborers from the administered areas then assumes the aspect of vocational training for the future, when similar industries will be set up in their state. All our guidance in modern methods of agriculture, health, and education becomes training in the eventual use of these methods in their own sovereign state. Every new road, every new link-up to the electricity grid, every new waterworks signifies modernization for the future sovereign Palestinian-Jordanian Arab state.

If we do not discuss principles, then no act of ours in the territories can be understood; or, what is worse, every act is interpreted as part of a Jewish plan for "creeping annexation" by creating reality—and every road is a created reality, every electrical link-up is a created reality. Without principles and an offer of hope for the future, we cannot come with these created realities to the Palestinian Arabs or the world and say: "Look at the marvelous things we have done." For there is nothing new in all this; the world has already seen—and not been surprised by—development projects of administrators in the areas they occupied. Without principles, the work of Arabs from the areas in Israel is nothing more than the exploitation of cheap labor of one ethnic group by another—with all the frightening implications that attend so ugly an enterprise.

SECURITY AND DEMOGRAPHY

No less complex than the moral problem with which I opened, and whose consideration must precede everything else, are the problems of security in the territories of western Eretz Yisrael and the demography of that area. The latter, on the face of it, is not a security problem; but it has security as well as economic and social implications, for both us and the Palestinian Arabs.

There are those among us who are ready for concessions and for the repartition of western Eretz Yisrael only because they fear the demographic problem; the moral problem they take to be so much abstract talk. But I maintain that even if there were no demographic ghost stalking us we would still have to take a stand on principles.

The demographic problem exists whether we like it or not; it is reflected in a simple statistic: anyone who wants Israel to annex the one million Arabs of the West Bank and the Gaza Strip—without relying on those Arabs to "flee" or "wither away"—must realize that only an ongoing immigration of many tens of thousands of Jews each year will guarantee a Jewish majority in "undivided Eretz Yisrael" in the next generation. Without such a large-scale immigration, annexation will lead to a situation where, as a result of their birthrate, the Arabs will constitute about half the population of the State of Israel within two or three decades.

I believe in large-scale immigration and in the concentration of a majority of the Jewish people in Israel. But in order to absorb additional millions of Jews we must first create for ourselves and for them a state that is unmistakably Jewish and that has a distinctiveness all its own.

There are others among us who wish to annex the populations of the West Bank and the Gaza Strip without granting them full civil rights. Here lurks a great danger for us. We will not be able to bear such an act morally and psychologically; it will distort our soul beyond recognition.

The demographic problem, then, only strengthens the basic position that in this land there ought to be set up two states for two nations.

The security problem is a vexing one. Even if today we were to find an Arab partner who agreed in principle to the repartitioning of the country on the basis of mutual waiver of the implementation of historical rights; and even if this partner were ready to discuss the future borders of the two states with us, to sign a peace treaty with us and see this as the end of the bloody conflict between us and the Palestinian Arabs—the security problem would still remain. The establishment of a Palestinian-Jordanian Arab state occupying the territories of existing Jordan, most of the West Bank, and parts of the Gaza Strip would require not only the waiver of the implementation of our historical rights and the return of territories, but also guarantees of our security after the return of these territories. In exchange for peace with the Palestinian Arabs we will be prepared to pay a heavier price than has ever been demanded in the settlement of conflicts. But even those who are ready to pay this price will not agree to the return of territories without the assurance that those territories will never again be turned into bases for the renewal of war against us. Not even a binding contractual agreement will eradicate the fear of a "next round" from our hearts. Our fear is that such a peace treaty with the Palestinian Arabs will not even be worth the paper it is written on, and that it will merely be a camouflage for their desire to try again to destroy us. We are afraid that the Palestinian-Jordanian Arab who will sign that peace treaty with us and wholeheartedly make that great reconciliation will himself fall victim to extremist nationalists, who will declare that the treaty is null and void and that this new Palestinian-Jordanian Arab state has one major goal: to destroy the State of Israel.

And then where will we be? Instead of peace, economic cooperation, and an Israeli–Palestinian-Jordanian common market, we are likely to find ourselves facing the armies of that Palestinian-Jordanian Arab state and—even worse—armies of other

Arab countries as well. These armies will encamp in the Palestinian-Jordanian Arab state and once again threaten the State of Israel with destruction. Then our major cities and settlements will again be within range of cannon, Katyushas, and sniper fire located in that state whose establishment is, in principle, a necessary and just act.

We must, then, try to find a solution to this problem, which, even if it is immediately unacceptable to the Palestinian-Jordanian Arabs coming to negotiate a peace treaty and the establishment of their state with us, will at least be acceptable to us and give us maximal assurance that in our desire to do historical justice to our neighbors, we are not laying the groundwork for our own destruction.

Such a solution must be unconventional and flexible. It will depend on when the negotiations with the Palestinian-Jordanian Arabs take place and who represents them—monarchists or republicans; it will depend on whether the settlement with those Palestinian-Jordanian Arabs takes place before, during, or after a settlement has been reached with any or several of the other Arab states. It will also depend on the general situation in our region and on the relations between the superpowers.

Here it must be stressed that partition as a possible solution of the problem of Israel and the Palestinian Arabs does not mean dividing Eretz Yisrael into more than two states. In other words, I do not have in mind a Palestinian state in the administered areas separate from the state of Jordan; I am speaking of one Arab state which will contain the majority of the Palestinians. We should not sign a peace treaty with the kingdom of Jordan unless that country represents and offers a solution to the Palestinian Arab problem. But the system of government in the new Palestinian-Jordanian Arab state—monarchical, republican, federative, or some combination of these—will be for the Arabs themselves to decide.

In the short run, the establishment of a little Palestinian Arab state on the West Bank, perhaps together with parts of the Gaza Strip, might appear easier, more promising, and perhaps safer for Israel. But such a state will not solve the Palestinian Arab problem, because about half of the Palestinian Arabs will be outside it, mainly in Jordan, and this nation—split in two—will not consider this a solution to its problems. Such a state will be more an enclave than a real state, and will have no possibilities of development and rehabilitating refugees. On the other hand, a Palestinian-Jordanian Arab state comprising Jordan as well as most of the West Bank and parts of the Gaza Strip will, like Israel, have access to two seas: the Red Sea and the Mediterranean—Gaza being this state's Mediterranean port, with Israel permitting the transfer of goods and free passage through her territory.

This state will be larger than Israel in territory. The two will be very similar with respect to natural resources, water sources, arable land, areas for urban and industrial development, and so on. Precisely because this state will constitute a solution to the Palestinian Arab problem and because only in it will the Palestinian Arabs be able to express their national identity and turn their state into a progressive Middle Eastern Arab state with a technological potential—precisely for this reason must it be laid down at the outset that this state, to be set up with our consent, will have certain temporary restrictions pertaining to Israel's security. One of these restrictions will be that Arab military forces will not cross the Jordan River; further, the Gaza Strip will be separated from Egypt and no military presence will be permitted in it.

This categorical demilitarization of the West Bank and the Gaza Strip will be guaranteed not only by written agreements, but—with all due respect to written agreements—also by concrete guarantees. The most concrete guarantee possible is Israeli supervision or joint supervision by the two states. This can be done from joint bases or by joint patrols along lines to be drawn on the West Bank and in the Gaza Strip.

In order not to compromise the sovereignty of the Palestinian-Jordanian Arab state while according Israel maximum security, it will be possible to limit the operation of these joint bases or patrols to a decade or two, in the hope that relations between Israel and this state will become normalized and that at the end of the stated period the matter of bases and patrols will be open again for negotiation—until the day that both sides consider such matters superfluous.

Here it is worthwhile discussing the new Israeli rural and urban outposts and settlements that were established after the Six-Day War on the West Bank and in the Gaza Strip. There are those of us who would like to see these outposts and settlements used as a means of establishing irrevocable facts. Their thinking is that every spot on which a Jew sets foot will remain forever Jewish, and that since the areas containing Jewish outposts and settlements will sooner or later be annexed to the State of Israel, no options remain for the Palestinian Arabs in these areas. To those who see Jewish settlement in the administered areas as a continuation of Zionist policy in the decades before the state, the matter seems simple indeed. We will set up Jewish settlements in the areas, we will create facts, the facts will speak for themselves—and when the time comes to discuss the West Bank and the Gaza Strip there will be nothing or very little to discuss.

This line is based on a method that was valid when we were a "state-in-the-making"; but it is not seemly for a state already in existence. This method establishes political reality through settlement and leaves no door open. It affirms the feeling of the Palestinian Arabs that, slowly but surely, we are closing all options for reunification of the West Bank with Jordan, and that all our declarations about open political options are just talk while in fact we are effecting creeping annexation of all the territories of the West Bank and the Gaza Strip. This method does not deceive a single one of us or the Palestinian Arabs, the other Arab nations, or the rest of the world. It would be better if we said openly that we reserve the right to settle anywhere in the entire Land of Israel, anywhere in the Land of the Twelve Tribes, and that we now need security outposts—but that the future of all the Jewish urban and rural settlements established beyond the pre-Six-Day War borders is open to negotiation, and this settlement does not constitute de facto annexation.

Jewish settlement on the West Bank and in the Gaza Strip is open to several possibilities in the future: some settlements will be officially and finally annexed to Israel at the conclusion of negotiations between Israel and the Palestinian-Jordanian Arab state (the Etzion region, for example); some may be turned into temporary bases for military forces and patrols, under the security arrangements agreed upon by the two states; and some will remain within the borders of the new Arab state.

Generally speaking, it ought to be taken for granted that in the Palestinian-Jordanian Arab state—both on the West Bank, the East bank, and in the Gaza Strip—there will be Jewish settlement. It is unthinkable that of all the countries in the world, only our next-door neighbor, our "sister state," should be *Judenrein*. Reality will not tolerate this. The close ties—economic, business, and other—which will inevitably exist between the two states when peace comes will lead to a situation where, with the consent of the Arab state, Jews will in the course of time settle in the cities of the West Bank, the Gaza Strip, and Jordan. They will be Israeli citizens whose business requires them to live in the Arab state. Some may choose to settle there permanently; they will become citizens of the Arab state, with all the duties and privileges that will entail. Just as today in Israel there are several hundred thousand Arabs who have accepted Israeli citizenship, so should it be possible that under conditions of peace thousands or tens of thousands of Jews could live in the neighboring Arab state.

We must speak candidly to our Jewish settlers in these settlements and tell them, now, that when peace comes they may have to make new decisions regarding where and how they are to live. They have a right to know the truth. It may also be assumed that most of them will be prepared to see their efforts today as a bridge to peace, and will accept the idea that the piece of land which they prepared and to which they gave some of their best years is to serve as a security patrol base or as a training and experimental farm—even if, when peace comes, that land will be in sovereign Arab territory.

The possibility of a Palestinian-Jordanian Arab state alongside Israel may also alleviate the psychological problem of the Israeli Arabs. At present they face a terrible dilemma with respect to their identity: on the one hand, they belong ethnically to the Palestinian Arab nation and have no desire to assimilate with us (and we do not intend to assimilate them); on the other hand, they are citizens of Israel.

Only if a neighboring Palestinian Arab state living in peace with us comes into being will the Israeli Arabs be able to feel themselves both citizens of Israel and an extension of the Palestinian Arab nation with an identity of their own. Some of them might choose to move, temporarily or permanently, to the Palestinian-Jordanian Arab state, and that will be their privilege. It may be assumed that most of them will remain with us. They will constitute a bridge between the two states; and Jews and Jewish settlements in the Arab state will also constitute such a bridge.

All this seems rather utopian right now. But history is full of examples of neighboring nations living side by side in peace, with each having a minority of its members living in the other state.

It is too soon to discuss the future governmental systems of the two states. It is to be hoped that Israel will continue to be a multiparty democratic republic. It is impossible to prophesy now about the form of government the new Palestinian Jordanian Arab state will adopt.

AN ISRAELI DECLARATION

We have a tremendous task in the shaping of this future. Even though it appears that at this moment "there is no one to talk to," we must declare our truth: that we do not need the majority of the territories of the West Bank and the Gaza Strip for purposes of dense settlement, for it is not there that we will settle the millions of Jews whom we intend to bring to Israel; and that we are ready to accept the idea of a sovereign, independent Palestinian-Jordanian Arab state next door.

There is need for such a clear and public declaration—for ourselves, for the Arabs, and for the world at large. Such a declaration in the name of the Israeli government will itself serve as an impetus toward changing the situation in our region. I believe that such a declaration by Israel will find support among some Palestinian Arabs living in the West Bank and the Gaza Strip; and maybe in time even among those in Israeli prisons (it would not be the first time in history that leaders emerged from among men in prisons); among leaders in Jordan; and among some young Arabs studying in the universities of the Middle East, Europe, and other parts of the world.

It should be borne in mind that the process will be a very slow one, and that it will take time before they really believe and trust us and seize on our declared readiness to muster the courage to speak up.

To be sure, such an Israeli declaration today would be like a speech delivered from a lighted stage to a silent audience sitting in the dark. But there are signs that in that dark stillness some courageous Palestinian Arabs will stand up and proclaim, "We are ready to talk to you and make peace with you."

I believe that such a declaration by us will have a tremendous impact not only among the Palestinian Arabs but also in the Arab states. The Arabs will, in the course of time, become aware that the Jews are ready to give the Palestinian Arabs their due. They will also realize that the establishment of a Palestinian-

Jordanian Arab state alongside Israel is the maximum that Israel can concede, and that demands for any further concessions—such as the relinquishment of territory inside the 1948–67 borders or the return of Arab refugees to Israel—will be seen by Israel as part of an effort to destroy her.

It may be that at first this declaration will meet with no response, and that the Arabs—the Palestinians and the others (as well as the powers that advise them)—will say to us, "First return the areas, and then we'll see." We will simply not agree to this. We must declare again and again our readiness for the establishment of a Palestinian-Jordanian Arab state and continue being patient until we find true partners among the Palestinian Arabs. We must not allow lack of a response or a hostile response to cause us to despair. Again and again we must explain our aspirations and our objectives to the Palestinian Arabs, the Arab states, and the world at large. We must show ourselves and them how and where we plan to absorb additional millions of Jewish immigrants without expanding into territories populated by Arabs, without harming them in any way, and without expelling them. And we must do all this before a peace treaty is signed. We must also calculate for ourselves and prove to others how we will live as neighbors with a Palestinian-Jordanian Arab state in a manner that will solve our national and demographic problems and, above all, the problem of the Arab refugees. Such proof is possible if we use imagination, sociological data, and modern techniques.

First of all, it should be remembered that the Palestinian Arabs are among the most advanced of Arab populations. It is a fact that this population, half of whom are refugees, has one of the highest educational levels of all the Arab nations. There is comparatively little illiteracy among these Palestinian Arabs, and they have a relatively high number of university graduates and professionals. They are a relatively mobile and achievement-oriented people who adapt quickly to modern technological methods. They are in the main an urban population, with the potential for producing innovative leaders who will understand one day that their fate is in their own hands, and that they can no longer depend on the nations of the world or the Arab states. They will come to realize that in the past they have taken a beating not only from us but also from the Arab states. And they will realize that they must take their fate into their own hands and link it to our fate for life and peace.

If this nation-in-the-making is given a state, it is capable of turning it in a short time into a decent home for all the refugees and into perhaps the first Arab country to enter the modern era. The Palestinian Arabs are capable of developing a modern agricultural nation that will export most of its produce to Europe and Arab lands; they are capable of building new cities and expanding those that now exist on both sides of the Jordan River and in the Gaza Strip. With international assistance they are capable of setting up modern industries, building new seaports and airports, developing tourism, establishing research and scientific institutions, raising the level of culture and art in their land, and serving as a model Arab state. Moreover, in cooperation with us, this independent nation will be able to undertake vast projects which will benefit both its people and ours.

Israel and her Palestinian-Jordanian Arab neighbor, sitting beside the same two seas, will in time be able to establish a common market which will eventually attract other Arab countries—and non-Arab countries as well. Together they can develop their lands into sites for tourists which can be among the most beautiful in the world; they can integrate their shipping enterprises, their transport and air services, and provide services, technical know-how, and capital to the entire region—and perhaps to lands beyond.

Even today there are scientists and technologists with imagination who possess extraordinary plans for turning the treasures of the Dead Sea—which Jordan and Israel share—into a base for a chemical industry of world dimensions. What is more, there are plans to turn the geological depression of the Jordan Valley at the approach to the Gulf of Eilat and Aqaba into a new sea channel; to discover new major sources for the creation of cheap energy; and to explore various possibilities for the establishment of giant industrial and service enterprises.

In viewing the Land of the Twelve Tribes as the land of the Jewish state *and* the Arab state one should not be frightened by the problem of the million-odd Arab refugees. It may even be that in the long run this refugee population will prove a blessing for the developing Palestinian-Jordanian Arab state by serving it as a reservoir of highly skilled labor.

Even in the future Palestinian-Jordanian Arab state, the only possible solution for these refugees, most of whom are young and modern, is settlement in new towns or modernized existing towns, and employment in advanced industries and services. Any "pastoral" solution that involves creating additional peasants and farmers must inevitably lower the standard of living of this new state. One of the major problems of this future Arab state will be, not how to settle the Arab refugees on the land, but how to remove from the land tens of thousands of peasants now living in it on the West Bank and in the Gaza Strip in a density that prevents the efficient working of the soil, and to settle those peasants in towns and employ them in urban trades. The solution of the refugee problem can only come from such an urbanization program backed by the anticipated economic, industrial, and technological development.

Obviously, these solutions will require tremendous sums of money. We will provide some of the money—in the form of individual or collective compensation to the Palestinian Arab refugees, as well as the financing of integrated enterprises of the two states and technological know-how and guidance. The Arab states—mainly the enormously wealthy oil-producing states—will be asked to give their share. (Israel will in the future conduct a separate accounting with the other Arab countries. This will concern the vast property that was confiscated by them from the hundreds of thousands of Jews who left those countries.) In addition to the sums which we and the Arab countries will allocate for the solution of the refugee problem in the Palestinian-Jordanian Arab state, international fiscal institutions will be asked to give this undertaking very large grants and loans. There is no doubt that the bigger the plans, the greater will be the readiness of the international institutions to help implement them.

This way to peace with the Palestinian Arabs is difficult and tortuous. It may well be that along the way there will still be wars in store for us. The Arabs generally, and the Palestinian Arabs in particular, have not yet given up hope of defeating us in battle. The conflict between the Jews and the Palestinian Arabs does not exist in a vacuum; it is inextricably bound up with the struggle between us and all the Arab nations and with the interests of the great powers. Let us have no illusions that declarations alone will solve such a complex problem. But we must take the first step now, even if our path proves to be strewn with obstacles and disappointments.

We took the first steps in the right direction shortly after the Six-Day War: the opening of the bridges on the Jordan River; the provision of vocational training and guidance in various fields; the activation of the services in the West Bank and the Gaza Strip—those were all correct steps. But if they are not accompanied by a declaration concerning our future objectives, they will become nothing more than pragmatic acts unguided by principles regarding long-range goals.

ACTING ON OURSELVES

Simultaneous with the issuing of a declaration concerning our effort to solve the problem we must take certain other important steps in connection with our attitude toward the Palestinian Arabs.

The first step is to educate ourselves to the possibility of peace with the Arabs. There is no denying the difficulties involved in teaching our youth to regard the enemy—an extremely cruel, intransigent enemy—as a prospective peaceful and equal neighbor. Happily, we have so far avoided implanting in our youth deep hatred of our Arab neighbors. Hatred of the Arabs is as yet marginal among us. With proper education it is possible to prevent it from growing and perhaps even eradicate what little does exist.

What is worse is the contempt some of us have for the Arabs. This has taken on frightening dimensions. The Arabs, who used to scorn the Jews, have become our enemy; now they no longer scorn us. We, on the other hand, have begun to scorn them. We must fight this ugly phenomenon with all the educational means at our disposal. We have enough reason to be proud of ourselves without having to support this pride with scorn for our enemy. The scorn which many of us feel toward the Arabs is apt to twist our minds and souls. The weapon of scorn can boomerang, as any history book will show us: the Mamelukes who sneered at Napoleon's Frenchmen, saying they would "trample them under the hooves of our horses"; the Russians who sneered at the Japanese, whom they were going to "cover . . . with our caps"; the Germans who sneered at the "inferior Slavic Russians"; and others. How can Jews, who were objects of scorn everywhere all through history, now look with scorn at another nation? This lesson was bitterly brought home to us in the Yom Kippur War.

I do not mean to say that we should adopt a false love of the Arabs. There is a great deal of insincerity in the overly righteous Christian idea of "Love thine enemy." This is especially true when we consider that the conflict between us and the Arabs is by no means over. What we must do is educate our younger generation to understand the Arabs in general and the Palestinian Arabs in particular. Anyone who understands and objectively studies his neighbors—their past, their language, their culture—probably will not regard them with contempt—which generally stems from lack of understanding and ignorance.

The very fact that there are as yet very few schools in Israel in which Arabic is taught as a required language alongside English attests to a very serious gap in the way we are educating our children—not to mention the fact that our failure to teach our children spoken Arabic has caused a depletion in the significant reservoir of Arabic knowledge which our Jewish immigrants from the Arab lands brought with them. Arabic was the mother tongue for about half a million immigrants—a language rich in written and spoken rhetoric, in poetry and song. Taken together they had a mastery of the many dialects of Arabic: Iraqi, Syrian, Egyptian, Libyan, Moroccan, Yemeni, and others.

What did we do with this great treasure? As a result of our unjustified, destructive "Europistic" contempt, we squandered it. Instead of encouraging Jewish parents from the Arab lands to transmit their knowledge of Arabic to their children and grandchildren in a natural way, we impressed it upon them that Arabic was not an important language. In that way hundreds of thousands of children of parents who came here from Arab lands forgot what Arabic they knew, or were never taught it by their parents to begin with. The parents, seeing that our schools did not teach Arabic—a subject in which their children could have excelled—and that Arabic had no "value" in our society, stopped transmitting it to their children.

It is too late to undo this, but we still can—and must—introduce Arabic as a required course in our school curriculum. We must train cadres of Arabic teachers, both Jews and Arabs. We must also introduce the study of Arab history, religion, tradition, poetry, prose. To this day we are still teaching considerable European history and very little of the rich history of the region in which we are living.

It may be said that the history of the Arabs is a "poor" one. But who will dare to say that the history, poetry, and prose of the centuries of Arab grandeur are poorer than, say, that of medieval England? Do the terms "poverty" and "richness" apply at all to such categories?

It is a fact that, except for a small number of youth majoring in oriental studies in our schools and an even smaller number in our universities, the overwhelming majority of our young people, destined to serve in the Israeli army and then to be the backbone of our society, have no notion of the Arabic language, of Arab history, literature, religion, tradition, custom. They are, therefore, totally in the dark as to Arab longings, aspirations, hopes, moods. This is a gap that we must repair even while we are engaged in our struggle with the Arabs; it is one of the steps toward peaceful existence with them.

No less important from an educational standpoint—and I am now speaking not of the youth alone but of the entire nation—is the task of the country's political and social leadership to alert the nation to the possibility, and even the need, of eventually handing back to the Arabs areas on the western side of the Jordan River where they might establish their state. In the years since the Six-Day War some of us have been infected with tendencies that are alien to Zionism, with "blood and soil" concepts. I have no complaint against those who state clearly their contention that we ought not to give up an inch. I am opposed to this position, but its proponents are fully entitled to propagate it in a lawful and parliamentary manner. My complaint is against my own party, the Labor party. The confusion in the minds of the public and of our youth regarding Israel's position toward the Arabs is the outcome of the muddled manner in which my own party has been dealing with the matter.

The nation does not know what it is we wish of the Arabs. Are parts of the West Bank and the Gaza Strip open to the possibility of one day becoming an Arab state, or are they destined to be annexed by us—de facto at first, and then de jure? The present generation of our youth is highly critical and wants to hear the truth, no matter how bitter it may be. An unequivocal declaration concerning our intentions toward the Palestinian Arabs may lead to polarization in Israel. But it will bring some order into our thinking and will enable discussion to replace our present confusion and the notion that we ought to leave matters to the government because it knows best.

The Zionist-socialist Labor movement must discuss this matter thoroughly and come up with clear-cut decisions. This movement cannot continue to avoid this fundamental issue. Significant elements in the Labor movement, mainly its youth, believe that socialist Zionism must compromise with the Palestinian Arabs and grant them the right of self-determination and the possibility of setting up their own independent state. The very soul of the Labor movement is at stake here, for it is simply inconceivable that socialist Zionism can accept the idea of a state containing reservationlike enclaves inhabited by one-third to one-half of the members of another nation seeking self-determination. In my opinion, this is inconsistent with socialist Zionism. Some members of the Labor movement think otherwise—therefore, the great debate of principles which has now begun must continue.

The religious Zionist movement, too, must come to a decision on this issue. With regard to the administered territories, many religious Zionists are drifting in a direction that is alien to Judaism—toward the sanctification of trees and rocks against which the prophets inveighed. And there is a certain inner contradiction here: if the territories of the West Bank—Judea and Samaria—or the Gaza Strip are holy, then the mountains of Gilead and Bashan in eastern Jordan are holy, too. In this fashion the religious Zionist movement is apt to arrive at extremist, uncompromising, dogmatic positions from which it will then not be able to budge.

The religious movement therefore must decide if its task is to teach Jewish love and love of Eretz Yisrael, or if it is going to drift into a position entirely inconsistent with Judaism and give unreserved, indiscriminate support to the sanctification of any and every military conquest that is forced upon us. It must ask itself whether the essence of the Bible is expressed in the territorial promises that God made to Abraham in their covenant (Genesis 15) or whether its cardinal tenets are not rather the Ten Commandments. Is the essence of the Bible certain sections of the Book of Joshua—for example: "And all the spoil of

these cities, and the cattle, the children of Israel took for a prey
unto themselves; but every man they smote with the edge of
the sword, until they had destroyed them, neither left they any
that breathed" (Joshua 11:14)—or is it rather in the words of
Isaiah (2:4): "And they shall beat their swords into plowshares,
and their spears into pruning-hooks; nation shall not lift up
sword against nation, neither shall they learn war any more,"
and of the other great prophets with their messages of ethics
and peace?

The Jewish religion has many extremely important tasks to
perform in the Jewish state. Total sanctification of the administered territories is not one of them.

Liberal Zionism also has to consider the matter of the territories, of readiness to make concessions, and the Palestinian Arab
problem. The principle of "not an inch" is no more consistent
with liberal Zionism than it is with socialist Zionism. What kind
of liberalism is it that would commit an Arab population to
permanent second-class citizenship, annex this population to
the State of Israel against its will, and deprive a national-ethnic
group of its right to self-determination?

So it would seem that the three main Zionist trends—the
socialist, the religious, and the liberal—must have the courage
to ponder this matter deeply, discuss it, and decide. If moderation prevails—and loyalty to the original ethical ideas of Judaism, socialism, and liberalism will cause it to prevail—the leaders of these movements will come to realize that there is a need
to educate the nation toward moderation and readiness for
compromise.

ACTION ON THE REFUGEES

Besides issuing a declaration and educating the public to
moderation, there are a few other steps that Israel must take in
order to advance peace. The most important of these is to begin
to tackle in a serious way the Palestinian Arab refugees under
Israeli rule in the Gaza Strip and on the West Bank.

After the Six-Day War some four hundred thousand Arab refugees—who constitute a major part of the total number of Palestinian Arab refugees—came under Israeli control. About two-thirds of them live in crowded, miserable camps in the Gaza Strip; the remainder live on the West Bank. I have already spoken of how the Arab leaders made political, psychological, and military capital of the million Palestinian Arab refugees, and how they let them rot in the camps.

In June 1967 nearly half of them came under our jurisdiction. Here I must point to a strange, inexplicable failure on Israel's part in connection with the refugees. To be sure, the refugees have also benefited from the general rise in the standard of living and the provision of work for the populace on the West Bank and in the Gaza Strip. But Israel has never given considered, methodical, long-range thought to the question of what to do with the camps and how to deal with the problem in a significant way. After the Six-Day War the Israeli leadership was well aware that the refugee camps, particularly in the Gaza Strip, were a sore spot and a kind of ghetto-within-a-ghetto. The Jews, who very recently had themselves sat in German, Russian, British, and other camps, should have been the first to realize the urgency of dealing with these camps, the humanitarian challenge they posed to us, and the political and security problems inherent in this situation. Instead, mental paralysis and even indifference prevailed in Israel on this issue. There were some who spoke up, but they went unheard. Our insensitivity on this matter remains incomprehensible.

Of course, it is possible to justify Israel's leaders on the grounds that they were totally preoccupied with other matters: the struggle for survival, the war of attrition, strengthening the army, immigration and absorption, economic development, and so on. But there was no shortage of people in Israel who were willing to assume the burden of planning solutions to the Arab refugee problem. But the government showed itself unwilling to take on the challenge.

It may be that some cabinet ministers were intoxicated by our victory in the Six-Day War and believed that matters would straighten themselves out somehow: the refugees would "disappear"; they would cross over into Jordan or go elsewhere, and the problem would solve itself. Perhaps they imagined that if Israel assumed the burden of thinking, planning, and initial implementation in this matter, it would imply that Israel was admitting to having created the problem or was undertaking sole responsibility for solving it.

In fact, Israel left the camps and the conduct of day-to-day affairs in them to UNRWA. This agency, set up after the Arab-Israel War of 1948, turned into a bureaucracy employing thousands of Palestinian Arabs whose main concern was to preserve the camps as they were—"till the 'return,' and the liberation of Palestine." Many of these UNRWA officials were hostile to any new initiatives in the matter of the refugees. They flourished by virtue of the preservation of the status quo. Even the attempts of some of the non-Arab UNRWA heads to do something unconventional ran up against this conservatism and vested interest.

In 1967 Israel did not take constructive advantage of the unique situation in which the Palestinian Arab populace in general and the refugees in particular found themselves after the Six-Day War. They were then in a state of psychological shock, like people after a severe earthquake or flood. Anyone who has dealt with people who have survived a disaster knows that they are likely to accept unconventional treatment that is aimed at bringing about a drastic change for the better in their situation. From my own experience in the Qazvin earthquake zone in Iran a decade ago I know that extremely conservative, tradition-bound Iranian farmers, who had for years persistently refused to learn modern agricultural and irrigation methods, suddenly became excellent pupils after the earthquake and were very receptive to the technological innovations that were offered to them. The Jewish refugees who came to Israel en masse after 1948—a typical crisis-population—were also very receptive to modern methods in matters pertaining to vocation, housing, nutrition, and the like.

If Israel had set about dealing with the Arab refugee question with some fresh, vigorous thought and implementation after the Six-Day War, we would now be at the beginning of the road toward a solution to this problem. After some quick surveying and planning, most of the camps could have been broken up and, as an interim step toward the solution of the problem, the refugees could have been settled in an orderly fashion on the outskirts of the West Bank and in Gaza Strip towns. There is no doubt that if the government had set up a crack team of planners and implementers, a team that had the power to deal with the problem in practical terms on a full-time basis, within a year or two it could have drawn up a whole variety of plans for solutions in the areas of housing, social and psychological treatment, education, health, and employment. There is no doubt that if we had submitted such plans to international agencies, the financing would have been found.

Instead, ad hoc teams were set up consisting of people for whom this was only a part-time task. From time to time they came up with better or worse proposals, all of which had one thing in common: they were pigeonholed.

And so it happened that Israel—which with complete justification prides herself on the way she settled her own refugees in towns and villages, on her agriculture and industry, on the planning and execution of rural and urban settlement undertakings, carried out on a large scale under her supervision, in Asia, Africa, and Latin America; which has delivered relief and aid to stricken populations throughout the world—Israel stood there empty-handed and tongue-tied when it came to dealing with the Palestinian Arab refugees within her borders and under her jurisdiction.

To be sure, there have been some stirrings lately; there has even been some small-scale sporadic action on the refugees. The fact remains that we still cannot explain our inaction to ourselves or to the outside world.

It may well be that the failure to act stems from our general inability to think clearly regarding the administered territories and the Palestinian Arabs. This makes it all the more urgent for Israel to come up with a declaration of intent.

We must begin to deal with the refugee problem in an open and unconventional manner. Clearly, the difficulties now are much greater than they were before. The refugees are no longer in shock, the patterns of life under our rule have become deeply rooted, and the terrorist activities in the Gaza Strip have taken their toll. But it is not too late. We ought to set up a central authority that will consist of outstanding experts who will draw upon the latest knowledge and experience in the planning and execution of solutions to this problem. Significant budgets should be put at the disposal of this authority, which should be empowered to deal with the entire matter, including the complex problem of reparations to the refugees.

The issue has to be dealt with in an imaginative manner, in a daring manner. Experience shows that a program of this scope involves thousands of gray, petty details and components. Its execution is attended by disappointment and frustration at almost every step. So far we have made no attempt to walk this difficult path, but the time has come to make the effort. It is important for ourselves, as an indication of our approach to the entire Arab problem; and it is important also vis-à-vis the world at large. Above all it is important for the Arab refugees, those hundreds of thousands of men, women, and children who hate us and hate the world. Their minds are completely twisted; their pain will not be eased all at once; there is no miracle cure for their illness. But we are in a position to start applying first aid.

A personal note: Some may say that my stand on this matter is detached from everyday reality, so I state that after the Six-Day War I engaged in a months-long intensive effort to study the matter at first hand, through personal contact with the refugees. I visited all the refugee camps in the Gaza Strip and nearly all the camps on the West Bank. I tried to check my ideas against the experience I had acquired in working with stricken populations in Israel and abroad. Immediately after the Six-Day War I indicated to the prime minister that I was willing to head a team that would study the problem of the refugees and come up with a plan for their rehabilitation. I am still prepared to put my experience to the test.

JERUSALEM OF THE JEWS

Another major issue which has Arab, Muslim, and worldwide implications is Jerusalem. This is, both for us and for the Arabs, perhaps the most delicate problem in the entire complex of problems.

The Jewish people carried Eretz Yisrael in its mind and heart through the two thousand years of its exile. All of Judaism has been a "Zionism-on-the-way," with Zion—that is, Jerusalem— at its center. If Eretz Yisrael as a whole—the Land of the Twelve Tribes—was an extremely unclear geographic concept, Zion—Jerusalem—was, for the Jews, a supremely clear, brilliant, radiant concept, so radiant that in our literature and world literature it has turned into a synonym for something unique, mystical, almost metaphysical—a focus of longing. The Jews invested most of their longings, desires, prayers, hopes, dreams, and legends in Jerusalem. Jerusalem lit up the darkness of their lives in exile with the precious light of messianic hope. In the gloomy caverns of the ghettos Jerusalem was a beacon to the Jews. Their finest poetry in Hebrew and in the hundred and one other languages they spoke was dedicated to Jerusalem. It was on Jerusalem that they always had their hearts set; it was to Jerusalem that they always tried to return—to mourn her destruction, to die within her, and to be buried opposite her walls on the Mount of Olives. The final redemption was to come from Jerusalem; the Messiah was to appear in Jerusalem at the End of Days and make her again "fair in situation, the joy of the whole earth . . . the city of the great King" (Psalms 48:3). From "Zion shall go forth the law, and the word of the Lord from

Jerusalem" (Isaiah 2:3). There is no parallel in history to this identity between a country and a city, a religion and a city, a nation and a city as that between Eretz Yisrael and Jerusalem, Judaism and Jerusalem, the Jewish people and Zion. Zion came before Zionism. The Zionist hymn—the Israeli national anthem —is a hymn to Jerusalem: "The eye looks to Jerusalem—to be a free people in Zion's land, Jerusalem."

I was an emissary to the remote Jewish communities in the Caucasian mountains, in the Uzbekistan steppes, on the Kurdistan peaks, on the Atlas slopes, and I know what Jerusalem is to the Jews, all the Jews.

When we Israelis would come to the synagogues of the Jews of Tbilisi or Kutaisi, Sochumi or Batumi, Derbent or Baku, Tashkent or Samarkand—Jewish communities which had never seen an Israeli—we knew that it was not important that we were Israelis, and we would say that we were from Jerusalem. "From Jerusalem?" the murmur would flash through the entire congregation. "From Jerusalem!"—and the men in the congregation would wave their prayer shawls at us the way the prayer shawl is waved at the Torah scroll when it is removed from the holy ark. They would kiss the palms of our hands—hands that had touched the stones of the Western Wall—and if we had allowed them they would have kissed the soles of our feet that had trodden the city's pavements. This Jerusalem, this earthly Jerusalem, Jerusalem between the walls, Jerusalem of the Western Wall, was almost never without a Jewish community, however poor and wretched its members might be. It lacked Jews only in those few short periods when its conquerors forbade Jews to live in it.

No wonder, then, that when Zionism became briskly active a century ago, the construction of the New Jerusalem was the cornerstone of the whole undertaking. The Jews emerged from amid the walls of the Old City of Jerusalem and started ringing it with Jewish neighborhoods. On its surrounding valleys and hills were built Jewish agricultural settlements. In the city itself

there arose the cultural, religious, and governmental institutions of the Zionist state-in-the-making: the Hebrew University,
the Chief Rabbinate, the Va'ad Le'umi (National Committee),
the Jewish Agency. We already knew then that Jerusalem was
unlike any other city and had a unique destiny, for she would
always also be the focus of the ardent desires and aspirations
of the Arab and Muslim and Christian worlds. We knew from
the outset that if we wished Jerusalem to be the crowning glory
of our undertaking, we might have to forgo exclusive rule of the
city, because others also loved her and were devoted to her.

We dreamed that Jerusalem would be ours and would be a
city of peace for the land and its peoples and for the entire
world. At the same time, in all our political plans we took into
consideration unconventional solutions, including the setting
aside of certain extraterritorial sites for other religions and in
order to satisfy the national aspirations of the Arabs.

But this matter, like all of our bloodstained history in this
land, was decided by the sword in 1948. All the high-sounding
talk of the international community concerning the internationalization of Jerusalem and the need to safeguard her against
the ravages of war proved to be worth nothing.

The Palestinian Arabs, followed by the Jordanian Arab Legion and the Egyptian army, laid siege to Jewish Jerusalem and
tried—almost successfully—to put her to death by famine,
thirst, and cannon. They subdued Jerusalem's defenders in the
Old City's Jewish quarter and led them away into captivity—
slaying many of them. By an extraordinary effort and at a high
price in blood, we held on to new Jewish Jerusalem and linked
her with a narrow corridor to the body of the State of Israel,
while the Hashemite kingdom of Jordan kept the Old City and
East Jerusalem. The city was sundered in two. On her ancient
walls the Jordanians placed machine guns and mortars. For
nineteen years Jewish Jerusalem, the capital of Israel, was fair
game for snipers and machine gunners. From time to time
civilians in Jerusalem streets and homes were fired upon and hit

by some Arab gunman who—the Jordanian authorities would
always announce—had had a fit of nerves. The Knesset building, the prime minister's office, the home of the president, and
the Supreme Court building were all in the sights of Arab Legion gunners.

We resigned ourselves to this frightful situation, but we never
reconciled ourselves to the vandalism of the Arab Legion and
the Hashemite kingdom, and to the destruction they wrought
in the Old City's Jewish quarter. They razed nearly all of the
quarter's old synagogues; again and again they desecrated the
Jews' holiest burial ground, the Mount of Olives Cemetery. In
violation of the Jordan-Israel armistice agreement and of all
standards of decency, for nineteen years the Jordanians pe-
remptorily rejected all our requests that we be allowed, under
the supervision and protection of the Arab Legion, to pray at
the Western Wall without in any way affecting or challenging
their sovereignty, without requesting any kind of permanent
corridor to it, without asking to be permitted to fly the Israeli
flag there. All we asked in those nineteen years was to be permitted to come to the Western Wall, and even that was denied
us. We would do well to remember this when discussing the
future of Jerusalem.

We gritted our teeth and lived with this painful reality, because we did not wish any more bloodshed. And the following
should also be remembered: on the morning of June 5, 1967,
Israeli Prime Minister Levi Eshkol sent a message to Hussein,
the Hashemite king, advising him that if he did not open hostilities in Jerusalem and on the West Bank, nothing would happen
to him. In other words, Israel would not launch a war to liberate
the Old City of Jerusalem. The reply of the Jordanian king came
in the form of machine-gun bursts and mortar shells. Only then
did our soldiers enter the Old City.

Shortly afterward, Israel, by an act of the Knesset, annexed
all of the Old City and East Jerusalem. This was Israel's only

territorial annexation. It was a very small piece of territory, to be sure; the Old City is less than one square mile in size. But three world religions and hundreds of millions of people regard that tiny piece of territory as sacred.

JERUSALEM AND THE CHRISTIANS

Jerusalem is sacred to the Christians. Yeshu—Jesus the Nazarene—was born in Bethlehem near Jerusalem. He lived and was active in Nazareth and the Galilee, but his life had its culmination in Jerusalem: in the hills facing the Temple Mount he was revealed to his disciples; there he ate his Last Supper; there he was judged and sentenced; there—in the Via Dolorosa—he carried the cross on his back; there—at Golgotha—he was crucified and buried. In the Old City of Jerusalem the first Jewish-Christian community arose, and from there the apostles set out to propagate Christianity in the pagan Greco-Roman world.

It is no wonder, then, that in the centuries up to the Muslim conquest, the Christians, whose faith had become a world religion, built in Jerusalem some of their holiest and most beautiful churches, and Jerusalem became a lodestone for myriads of Christian priests, monks, believers, and pilgrims.

Following the conquest of Jerusalem by the Muslim Arabs, most of the Christian holy places were destroyed. The Christian world never forgave the Muslims and tried again and again to regain the Terra Sancta. The Crusades were the culmination of this effort. Jerusalem and the Holy Sepulchre returned to Christian hands for a few generations. But when the Muslims recaptured the city they once again destroyed many of the holy places of the Christians and barred the city to them. Before long Christians of numerous denominations and schisms began to return to Jerusalem. Under Muslim rule, they built new institutions and succeeded in enlarging and expanding them in the centuries that followed.

The rights of the Christians in Jerusalem was a serious problem during most of the period of Muslim rule. Toward the end of Turkish rule, about a hundred years ago, this problem became one of the causes of the Crimean War.

After the British conquest, the significance of Jerusalem as a center of Christian activity and pilgrimage was heightened. In the Arab-Jewish wars both sides were careful to avoid damage to the Christian holy places. After 1948 both Israel and Jordan opened their gates to Christian pilgrims and tourists.

After 1948 the Christian world looked coldly upon the fact that the Holy Land and its Christian shrines were in territories that were ruled either by Jews or by Muslims. But the various churches reconciled themselves to the status quo. In fact if not in principle, and for lack of any alternative, they have also reconciled themselves to Jewish rule of united Jerusalem since the Six-Day War. After centuries of Christian religious wars, Christian bellicosity in the Western world was replaced by nationalistic bellicosity. We do not see on the horizon any latter-day crusaders ready to invade us in an attempt to recapture the Christian holy places. They are open to all; in fact they are controlled by various churches, which often engage in rivalry with each other—sometimes to the point of physical violence—over their respective rights in the different holy places.

It appears that many Christian groups feel that they owe the Jewish people a debt—not because the founder of Christianity and his disciples were Jews, but because they know full well that Nazism sprouted in Christian civilization.

The churches also feel—or should feel—a sense of guilt over having been found wanting with respect to what happened in the Old City of Jerusalem and the Jewish holy places there between 1948 and 1967. Where was the Christian world when the Arabs destroyed the Rabbi Yehuda haHassid Hurva Synagogue, the Ramban (Nahmanides) Synagogue, the Rabbi Yohanan ben Zakkai Synagogue, and dozens of other synagogues in

the Old City? How many Christians protested? How many
Christians demanded that the Jordanians desist from their vandalism? How many Christians protested against the ban on Jews
going to the Western Wall? How many protested against—how
many cared at all about—the destruction of centuries-old
graves on the Mount of Olives and the use of gravestones to
pave Jordanian army camps and latrines? Where were the
popes, bishops, patriarchs, priests, and monks during those
nineteen years? This guilt feeling is perhaps the cause of the
relatively tolerant attitude of the Vatican and the other
churches toward the fact that the Christian holy places in the
Holy Land are now under Jewish protection.

There is also a feeling—mainly among the Protestants, but
also among many Catholics—that the establishment of the State
of Israel was an act of historical justice to the Jews, and that the
Jews should now be allowed to live in peace in their land.
Another element in the attitude of the churches is the fact that
under Jewish rule the Christians are enjoying in the Holy Land
and in Jerusalem a degree of freedom of worship which they
had not enjoyed there for a long time.

Nevertheless, there is no doubt that there are Christian interests working for the internationalization of Jerusalem, or at least
for special arrangements regarding their holy places. The influence of the churches should not be underestimated. Any settlement of the Jerusalem problem will have to take into account
the feelings that the world's Christians have about this city.

But this problem may be easier to resolve to everyone's satisfaction than the problem of the Muslim holy places in Jerusalem
and the relationship of the Arabs to the city.

JERUSALEM AND THE ARABS

Jerusalem—El Quds, the Sacred—is, after Mecca and Medina,
the third holiest city in Islam. To be sure, Muhammad never
lived in Jerusalem, and Jerusalem was never an object of Mus-

lim pilgrimage on the grand scale of the *haj* to Mecca. But in their traditions and legends the Muslims linked Jerusalem and the Temple Mount to Muhammad's life, and this was sufficient to make the city holy to them. On the Temple Mount the Arabs built the magnificent Dome of the Rock (Mosque of Omar). Nearby stands the Al-Aqsa Mosque, one of the most sacred edifices in Islam. Thus for more than thirteen centuries Jerusalem has been sacred to many millions of Muslims. Again and again the Muslim Arabs fought fiercely to capture the city from the Christian infidels. Like the Christians, they built in Jerusalem, in addition to the two great mosques, beautiful religious and cultural edifices, sanctified the city's palaces, invested its antiquities and graves (including Jewish graves) with holiness, rebuilt its walls, sang liturgical songs to it, recounted its glories, and—like the Jews and Christians—integrated it into their "End of Days" visions. They, too, doubtless are pained that their holy places are now ruled by "aliens" and "infidels"—the Jews.

In any peace settlement we will have to grant the Muslim holy places in Jerusalem, especially the mosques on the Temple Mount, special status—that is, grant the Muslim religious bodies complete freedom to administer them without any interference by the State of Israel. We will have to consent to this special status despite the fact that on this holiest of Jewish sites, where the holy of holies of the Temple stood, another religion has erected shrines of its own. We shall never do what others have done to us and our shrines; we shall not behave as members of the great religions have behaved toward religious shrines they have conquered, the way the Muslims behaved when they destroyed Christian churches or turned them into mosques (Al-Aqsa in Jerusalem, Hagia Sophia in Istanbul, and countless others) or the way the Christians behaved against the Muslims. We shall in no way alter what is holy to others. We shall not wreak vengeance upon the Muslim sanctuaries for what the Arabs did to us and our synagogues in Jerusalem in 1948. We will uncover and reconstruct the glories of Jewish Jerusalem in the Old City, but we shall not dare to lay a finger on the holy places of others. Happily, there is no debate in our midst on this issue: the Jewish religion views the reconstruction of the Temple as an act to be performed by God in His own good time.

But the complex, unique problem of sacred Jerusalem does not end with the question of the Muslim holy places. We must understand that even secular Jerusalem is more than merely another city to the Palestinian Arabs. It is true that Jerusalem was never an important secular city in the Arab Empire. Damascus and Baghdad, Cairo and Granada, Fez and Marrakech have been inestimably more important than Jerusalem. It is true that under the Abbasids and Ummayads, the Fatimids and Ayyubids, the Mamelukes and Ottomans, Jerusalem was just another small provincial city. It was not a governmental or administrative or military center; it was not the site of any of the great schools in which the Arabs take such pride. But it should be remembered that for about a century now Jerusalem has been important to the Arabs not only because of its holy places but also as a center of the Palestinian Arab national movement. The more the Jews enhanced the significance of Jerusalem by the various endeavors of the Zionist undertaking, the more the Arabs stressed its importance to them. When we started building modern neighborhoods outside the walls of the Old City, the Arabs did the same. When we established in Jerusalem the institutions of the state-in-the-making—the Va'ad Le'umi, the Jewish Agency, the Hebrew University—the Palestinian Arabs set up the Arab High Committee in Jerusalem, and their leaders began to be active in the city.

After the 1948 war and the division of Jerusalem, a substantive change occurred in the political significance of Arab Jerusalem. The kingdom of Jordan spared no effort to expand, develop, and elevate its capital, Amman, and in effect turned it into the capital of both Jordan and the West Bank. Arab Jerusalem had no special administrative status in the Hashemite kingdom; it was just another city.

The Jordanian defeat in Jerusalem in the Six-Day War and

Israel's conquest and annexation of all of Arab Jerusalem kindled in Arab hearts a flame that was fed by two sources: the terrible feeling of degradation over the fact that their shrines had fallen into the hands of infidels, and the sense of loss of a city that had acquired national-secular significance of the first order.

To the heads of the Palestinian terrorists the goal is clear: erase Israel from the political map and establish an Arab Palestine in its place. Once this is achieved, Jerusalem will ipso facto cease to be the capital of the Jewish State of Israel and become the capital of Falastin. One may assume that more moderate Palestinian Arabs—and, of course, the leaders of the Hashemite kingdom of Jordan—would like to see the return of the pre-Six-Day War situation, with Jerusalem divided again between them and Israel.

The Arabs—all of them, not just the Palestinians—feel very strongly about Jerusalem. In talking to them and listening to their emotional response about "our Jerusalem," one can sense a drift toward irrationality. In view of our own highly charged feelings toward Jerusalem for thousands of years, we ought to make an effort to understand the Arab attitude toward this city. We should not mock them when they speak of the city with such longing.

THE FUTURE OF JERUSALEM

In this complex issue of Jerusalem, so charged with irrational emotions, we must make a few things clear: united Jerusalem is the capital of the State of Israel and so she shall remain. For nineteen years Jerusalem was divided into two cities. We will never again accept such a situation. We will never allow this city to be split in two. We will not allow it to be restored to Arab rule, nor will we again expose its streets and buildings, its inhabitants and institutions, to snipers and machine gunners. This price—and it is a heavy one—the Arabs will have to pay for peace with us.

This might seem to settle the matter; after all, the Muslims can pray in their mosques in Jerusalem, and the Arab nations have fifteen magnificent capitals.

But fate has decreed that Jerusalem is not only the city of David and Solomon, Isaiah and Jeremiah, the Hasmoneans, Herod and the Zealots, Bar Kokhba, the men of the Jerusalem Talmud, Nahmanides, Rabbi Yehuda haHassid, and one of my ancestors—Rabbi Mordechai Ettinger, a Lubavitcher Hassid who came to Jerusalem five generations ago and was buried on the Mount of Olives (his grave was desecrated by the Arabs and restored by my family)—and of tens of thousands of pious Jews like him: the city of the Yellins, the Eliashars, the Salomons, the Rivlins, and the Navons, of the city's Zionist builders and defenders who have fought for her and died for her these hundred years, of the entire Jewish people. Fate has decreed that Jerusalem is also the city of Jesus and Peter, of the thousands of Christians who built their churches within her, beautified her, and made her name sacred. Jerusalem is also the city of the Arabs who fought under Khalid ibn al-Walid and Osama ibn Zeid, of Abdel Malek who built the Dome of the Rock, of the sultans of the Ummayad dynasty who built the palaces, of Saladin and his warriors, of the men of Suleiman the Magnificent who built the city walls that stand today, of the Husseinis, the Nashashibis, Khaldis, and Nuseibehs—the city of tens of thousands of Arab inhabitants, Muslims and Christians, who lived within her, worked within her, and fought and died for her.

This is Jerusalem. There is no other city like her, in antiquity or today; no other city has her glorious and tragic history; no other city has her problems; no other city will have the difficulties that any solution to her problems is likely to generate. But we have no choice. We must find unconventional solutions to Jerusalem's problems; we must offer a modicum of satisfaction for the religious sensibilities of the Christians and Muslims and the national sensibilities of the Arabs.

The solution of the religious questions lies in some sort of Vaticanization—the establishment of a clearly defined holy area within the secular city. This area should receive all municipal services from the city but should enjoy a symbolic sovereignty and its affairs should be conducted independently by clergymen. Of course, this kind of solution may have many variations. The difficulty with the Christian holy places is that there does not exist a Christian world body to whose administration they could be assigned, and there is no way of knowing whether or not such a body will ever be formed.

The Muslim-Arab question, comprising at once religious and national aspects, and therefore being all the more delicate and complex, might be solved by the creation of a territorial corridor from the Palestinian-Jordanian Arab state to be established when peace comes; the borders of this state would be very close to Jerusalem. This corridor would lead to the area of the great mosques, over which the Arab state would have sovereign control. Their buildings would fly Arab flags, and Muslims and Arabs would be able to feel at home there.

At the same time, we must make it clear to the Muslims and Arabs, as well as to the whole world, that we will be ready to deal with the Jerusalem issue only at the end of the process of reconciliation and peace, not at the beginning. Any proposed solution before the end of this process will fail. Only after we have found a partner for true peace on the principle of two states for two nations, only after we have discussed total disarmament of the West Bank and have reached agreement on the guarantees of disarmament—only then will we be able to discuss special solutions for the Jerusalem problem. Nevertheless, it is urgent that we now make clear to the Muslims and Arabs our general intentions and our readiness to talk with them even on the issue of Jerusalem—an issue which is so important to us, to them, and to the whole world.

THE "GREAT *SULHA*"

What could be easier than to say about a defeated and divided nation—half of which consists of refugees either under our occupation or hounded by the Arab states; whose leaders are at odds with each other, whose terrorists are insane; many of whose people are steeped in daydreams about Israel's destruction and serve as pawns in the rivalries between Arab countries and foreign powers—considering all this, what could be easier than to say that an Israeli declaration supporting self-determination for this nation and accepting the establishment of such a nation as an independent, sovereign state is premature and unrealistic? What could be easier to dismiss as "castles in the air" than a vision of two countries, both relatively small in territory but great in human resources, living side by side with each other in peace and capable, by the end of the century, of supporting millions of inhabitants, like Holland and Belgium, and cooperating in development, economics, trade, culture, and science, and together serving as a bridge to a much greater regional league of states bordering on similar regional leagues in Europe, Asia, and Africa? Apparently it is the easiest thing in the world to say, as many of us do, that there will never be peace between us and the Arabs, and that what we have to do is go on strengthening ourselves, consolidating our position in the field, and gaining time.

But this is an utterly sterile, pessimistic approach. In the past there have been bitter conflicts between nations in the course of which much more blood was shed than in our conflict with the Arabs and lasted longer than the conflict in our region. The English and French kept invading and killing each other for hundreds of years before finally making peace. The Germans and French fought each other bitterly for many generations, until they wearied of the slaughter and made peace. The Americans and the Japanese made peace after Pearl Harbor and Hiroshima. What is more, we Jews have come to terms with (not forgiven; only come to terms with) the Germans—the sons and brothers of the murderers of our people.

In Arabic culture, a blood feud is terminated by a *sulha,* a grand reconciliation; this custom predates Muhammad. Why should we not believe that the time will one day come for the "great *sulha*" and an end of the internecine struggle between us and the Arabs?

Even if we cannot bring about peace immediately, we must try to bring it nearer and advance ourselves toward it. We must begin by adopting a new way of using words. We must try to talk to anyone claiming to represent the Palestinian Arabs. We must address our words to Arabs under our jurisdiction on the West Bank and in the Gaza Strip, to Arabs of the kingdom of Jordan, even to saboteurs and terrorists being held in our prisons. We must not stop trying. At first the seeds we sow will fall on rock. For every ten wells we drill for peace, nine will prove dry. The path of dialogue is strewn with disappointments. But there is no other way.

If we speak, the chances are that someday we will find partners for dialogue. We must foster such dialogue among the Palestinian Arabs of the administered territories and grant them the rights of free assembly and free debate with us, however bitter-tasting such a debate may prove to be. When this struggle is over we do not wish to have as neighbors humiliated, obedient, cowering Palestinian Arabs, but a proud people. Helping them attain this pride does not mean that we should relax our vigil against those among them who bear arms against us; it means that we should sponsor their elementary right to national self-determination and to an independent, sovereign state of their own.

4

ISRAEL AND EGYPT

THE MOST DANGEROUS PROBLEM

The Palestinian Arab issue is the most difficult and tragic aspect of the conflict between us and the Arabs, and the one whose resolution may require the longest time. However, the conflict between us and Egypt is the most volatile of all with respect to the magnitude of the forces involved; it is fraught with immediate danger, both for our region and for the world.

Before the Yom Kippur War, the components of the Israel-Egypt problem were the Israeli army sitting on the Suez Canal; Egypt, the largest and most powerful Arab country, facing Israel with a huge army equipped with the latest and best Russian armaments; the Sinai Peninsula, serving Israel as a modern military base; and the Soviet presence in Egypt. The situation was clearly potentially volcanic. Hence all the world's sensitivity concerning this arena of conflict; hence the concentration of international effort to dampen this powderkeg.

In antiquity we had very close ties with Egypt. It was to Egypt that our shepherd ancestors went to obtain provisions when Canaan was stricken by famine. In the land of the Nile, the land of a rich and remarkable civilization, Joseph was viceroy to one of the pharaohs. There the children of Israel lived for many generations, and tasted slavery and tyranny for the first time. There, under Egyptian oppression, the ancient Hebrews first created their tribal confederation. And the father of Jewish prophets—Moses—was born in Egypt, was raised in her palaces, began his career in her cities, roamed her wildernesses, and was influenced by her great culture.

In Egypt one of the most memorable events in our history occurred—the Exodus. This event echoed through the centuries and became integral to the religions and literatures of the Western world. The Exodus from Egypt became a universal symbol of human liberation, of the eternal striving for freedom.

After establishing their state in the Land of Israel, the Hebrews developed an attitude to their great southern neighbor which was sometimes realistic, sometimes irrational. Relations between Egypt and little Israel were always complicated by the fact that Israel sat on the main road up along which the pharaohs went to fight for Egypt and down which the great northern kings and emperors came to attack and conquer Egypt.

The Land of Israel, situated as it was on that crossroads of the ancient East, would seek alliances now with Egypt, now with Egypt's enemies. There were frequent differences between the advocates of *Realpolitik* and the prophets as to whether to form an alliance with Egypt or to fight her; whether to join an alliance with her or against her (although many a time it was the prophets who proved to be the *Realpolitik*ians). Solomon married the daughter of one of the pharaohs and signed a treaty with him. King Zedekiah rejected the prophet Jeremiah's advice not to rely on Egypt in his struggle with Babylonia and brought about the destruction of the First Temple.

Generations passed. Egypt and Israel both came under the yoke of conquerors from the West—the Greeks and the Romans. By the time of the First Temple there was already a Jewish Diaspora in Egypt, which included colonies of Jewish soldiers garrisoning border posts in the service of Egyptian kings. There were Jewish communities in Egypt under the

Greek Ptolemaic kings and under the Roman and Byzantine emperors. After Egypt was conquered by the Arabs some thirteen centuries ago, and most of its inhabitants were converted to Islam, the Jews remained in the country. Under the great Arab dynasties Jews were prominent in medicine, science, administration, philosophy, and research. As a non-Muslim urban minority, the Jews of Egypt suffered in different periods at the hands of Arab, Mameluke, and Ottoman rulers, but many of them found a safe haven in the country.

From the time of Mehemet Ali, the founder of modern Egypt, early in the nineteenth century, Jews started coming to Egypt in large numbers and establishing large, important communities, mainly in Cairo and Alexandria.

The modern Egyptian nationalist movement, one of the first in the Arab world, came into being in the middle of the nineteenth century. Its leaders had a tremendous task: liberation from the yoke of Turkish and British imperialism, and independence for their country. From the outset the Egyptian national movement contained opposing tendencies. To this day there are differences of opinion between those seeking the Arabization of Egypt and Egyptian hegemony in the Arab world, and those preferring to preserve the country's unique Egyptian nature. The leaders of the movement grappled with the problem of bridging the gap between Islam and modern nationalism. They knew that Egypt's central problem was an internal, specific one: modernization of this unique country, 90 percent of whose populace live in frightful density on the two banks of the Nile and at the mercy of that river's waters.

To be sure, the modern Egyptians had expansionist ambitions, mainly in order to protect the country's flanks. This was true during the reigns of Mehemet Ali and his son Ibrahim, who conquered Palestine and Syria on Egypt's northern flank. Their successors sought conquests in Sudan on her southern flank, but modern Egypt's leaders devoted most of their energy to throwing off the yoke of alien rulers.

At first the leaders of the Egyptian nationalist movement and the Egyptian masses were much more indifferent to the Zionist enterprise in Eretz Yisrael than were the leaders of the Arab nationalist movement in Syria. Even after the Balfour Declaration and the disturbances of 1929 and 1936, when the Arab nationalist movements and the Arab countries became increasingly involved in the Jewish-Arab conflict, Egypt remained aloof. But eventually she was thrust into the conflict by Arab centripetal force. As the largest Arab state, Egypt—willingly or unwillingly, knowingly or unknowingly—assumed the role of leader of the all-Arab struggle against the Zionist enterprise.

Although Egypt was the leader of the Arab League, her leaders were not as rabid in their hostility to Zionism as were the Palestinian Arabs, Syrians, and Iraqis. This was not due to any love of the Jews and Zionism—although Egypt *was* quite tolerant toward the Zionist activity of Egyptian Jews—but to her preoccupation with her own struggle for national liberation.

Owing to shortsightedness, their failure to understand the motives of the Jews, and their underestimation of Jewish strength, the Egyptians joined the war against Israel in 1948.

The Palestinian Arabs—and all the other Arab states as well —gazed with hope at the columns of Egyptian armor and artillery crossing the Suez Canal eastward and setting out northward on a military campaign—the first independent Egyptian military campaign since the campaigns of Mehemet Ali and Ibrahim Pasha.

The Jews, who at the beginning of their undertaking in Eretz Yisrael did not dream that they would one day be engaged in a life-and-death struggle with Egypt, now realized that the major military threat to their existence came from this big modern army, and concentrated most of their strength against it. When the Royal Egyptian army was routed at the southern approaches of Tel Aviv and Jerusalem and driven into Sinai, Egypt suffered an infinitely heavier blow than any other Arab country. The debacle and the ensuing shock roused hatred and the desire for revenge against the Jews, who had touched the pride of the great Egyptian nation to the quick. The frustration and shame that followed set off—or at least speeded—the officers' revolt of 1952, the ouster of the king, the proclamation of the Egyptian republic, and the rise of Nasser.

GAMAL ABDEL NASSER

The 1948 war led to serious involvement by Egypt in the Israel-Arab conflict. The new rulers found a scapegoat for the defeat of the Egyptian army: King Farouk and the ministers of his rotten regime, who, it was said, had failed to prepare the army for war, fostered corruption, and pocketed the money that had been allocated for the purchase of arms.

In 1948 the Egyptians discovered that they were confronting a small but modern Israel that had the capability of striking at the heart of Egypt. The Israeli army thrust into Sinai toward El Arish and, but for the intervention of the British and the Americans, could have taken the entire Sinai Peninsula. This convinced the Egyptians not only that they were not going to destroy Israel, but also that Israel was capable of invading their country along the classic route of the country's historical invaders.

Another element in Egypt's growing involvement in the conflict was the fact that the Egyptians found themselves ruling the Gaza Strip and being responsible for several hundred thousand Palestinian Arabs, most of them refugees—something they certainly had not bargained for when they had set out to "help their brothers." As a result, the Egyptians remained inside the borders of what had been Mandatory (western) Palestine.

Upon assuming power, Nasser promptly embarked upon what he thought to be Egypt's destiny. If he had set civilian goals for Egypt and concentrated on achieving them, in all likelihood Egypt's situation after his death would not have been as bad as it was. In any case, at the outset Nasser understood—

and he said as much in his speeches and writings—that the real threat to Egypt was not defeat by Israel. He knew full well that the real problems were the backwardness, poverty, population density, poor health, and illiteracy of the Egyptian masses, and that first and foremost the Egyptian nation's backbone had to be healed—namely, the peasantry, who have always constituted the overwhelming majority of the Egyptian nation.

This great task of righting a five-millennia-old wrong that had made the overwhelming majority of Egyptians into serfs, with the Nile as their only source of livelihood, ruled by despots and for long periods by foreign conquerors, required a massive concentration of effort by the group of revolutionary officers that had seized power. This was the first time in centuries that the reins of government in Egypt were held not by a Mameluke, Albanian, Circassian, Turkish, or colonial European ruling clique, but by Egyptians born of Egyptians in Egypt.

But Nasser was in a hurry. He decided to deal radically at one and the same time with domestic matters—health, education, agriculture, agrarian reform, urbanization, industrialization, and so on—and with Egyptian imperialistic aims: building up a large modern army, wreaking vengeance on and destroying Israel, and turning Egypt into a center of influence of the first magnitude in the Arab, African, and Muslim worlds. This ambitious undertaking caused him to spread the few human and natural resources at the disposal of Egypt very thin. Like anyone who tries to grab too much, he ended up holding very little.

Instead of building up the pyramid of modern Egypt from a broad and solid base, Nasser rapidly built a pyramid whose base was sand; he used a very heterogeneous ideological cement to hold the sections of the pyramid together: part Egyptian, part pan-Arab, part African, part Islamic, part "socialist"—with the entire edifice groaning under the burden of an enormous military superstructure.

This is not to say that Nasser accomplished nothing for his people and the Arab world. On the contrary, he gave them, first of all, his glamorous and proud personality. For the first time since the distant days of the great caliphs, an Arab leader of world stature had arisen, had represented the Egyptian and the Arab cause to the world, and had sat as an equal with the leaders of nations. Utilizing a combination of boldness, shrewdness, and exploitation of international situations, he succeeded in freeing Egypt from the British yoke. For a long time he did very well in the "game of nations." He succeeded in turning military defeats, such as the 1956 war, into great psychological successes. In the time and with the strength that remained to him he even managed to carry out some developmental, educational, and health projects.

But the general balance sheet of his career is negative—above all because of the many goals he set himself without having priorities. The important roles he tried to play—great social reformer, pan-Arab leader, African leader, leader of the Third World, latter-day Saladin who would break the backs of the latter-day crusaders, the Zionists—were too much even for him.

Very quickly Nasser managed to get Egypt more involved in the anti-Israel struggle than she had ever been before. The greatness of the man, the fact that he had become the admired leader of tens of millions of Arabs outside Egypt, gave him enormous influence in everything he did pertaining to Israel. In choosing the path of revenge and war, he became Israel's prime enemy. He began to offer active, unequivocal support to the Gaza Strip fedayeen in their attacks on Israel. When he started equipping his army with the latest Soviet weapons and harassing us in the Straits of Tiran in the mid-1950s, we struck back at him in 1956 and conquered the Sinai Peninsula.

After May 15, 1967, when Nasser massed his great army against Israel, our withdrawal from the Gaza Strip and Sinai in 1957 came to be regarded as a reminder of our past errors. We had proved that we were not bent on expansion; we had returned territories—all the territories—that we had conquered, without any agreement whatever with Nasser—and see what happened! Did Nasser become more moderate? Was he ready to accept our existence?

Because of the great debacle of the English and the French, Nasser was able to turn his own debacle in Sinai into a "great Egyptian victory" and appear before the Arab world as someone capable, if given the opportunity, of defeating the Jews and destroying Israel. Didn't he continue to build up his army more vigorously than ever? Didn't he go about preparing Sinai as an assault base against Israel, laying more roads and building more airfields and army camps? Finally, didn't he send the United Nations packing from Sinai and the Gaza Strip, and in May 1967 concentrate about one hundred thousand armed troops and about a thousand tanks on the Israeli border? Didn't he close the Straits of Tiran once more? Didn't he galvanize Egypt and the entire Arab world for war against Israel? And the feeble promises of the Western powers, especially those of the United States, that the Straits of Tiran would remain open—what happened to those promises in May 1967?

THE GAZA STRIP AND THE SINAI PENINSULA

Anyone who does not understand the psychological shock we underwent in the second half of May and the beginning of June 1967 will never understand why, after the Six-Day War, Israel and her leaders reacted the way they did every time the question of another withdrawal from Sinai and the Gaza Strip came up, of even a token presence of the Egyptian army in Sinai, and of stationing a United Nations force between us and the Egyptians. The trauma of one hundred thousand Egyptian soldiers, a thousand tanks, and hundreds of war planes and guided missiles in Sinai is something we could not and did not wish to forget.

The matter of the Gaza Strip was also clear to us. Egypt's control of the Gaza Strip for nineteen years had been only a passing episode in the long conflict between us and the Palestinian Arabs. The Egyptians never had any rights in the Gaza Strip or Eretz Yisrael. Only we and the Palestinian Arabs have rights in the Gaza Strip. If evidence was needed that the Egyptians and the Palestinian Arabs are two separate nations, the years of Egyptian occupation of the Gaza Strip are conclusive proof. The Palestinian Arabs were never granted Egyptian citizenship. Egypt never wished to annex the Gaza Strip and its inhabitants. The Egyptian army and administration behaved like conquerors there. They did nothing to help the Palestinian Arab inhabitants in general or the refugees in particular. They held on to the Gaza Strip as a trump card and as a permanent military threat against Israel. The port of Gaza served as a source of revenue for senior officers, who became wealthy smuggling luxury items from the Gaza Strip into Egypt.

Any Egyptian demand, now or in the future, to return to the Gaza Strip is a challenge to the very existence of Israel. The fate of the Gaza Strip must be determined solely by us and the Palestinian Arabs. The question of whether or not the Gaza Strip—or any portion of it—will be part of a Palestinian-Jordanian Arab state is subject to negotiation between us and the future Palestinian-Jordanian leadership. The Gaza Strip must remain politically and geographically separated from Egypt.

The Sinai Peninsula is an altogether different situation. Concerning historical rights—it is difficult to say that Sinai ever "belonged" to any nation. On the one hand, most of it was a wilderness without water or arable land. On the other hand, it was crossed by highways vital to nations and states west, east, south, and north of it, and for thousands of years it served as an almost totally uninhabited thoroughfare. It became a springboard into Egypt on the south or into Eretz Yisrael and Syria on the north.

Since the dawn of history Sinai was a huge land bridge through which armies, caravans, traders, and pilgrims passed, and, in their wake, cultures and languages of great significance to human civilization.

There were always small settlements in Sinai, mainly along its coasts and in its oases. Across its expanses there always roamed nomadic tribes. For several thousand years Sinai has also had religious significance. It was the great, virtually impassable desert close to the cradle of human civilization in Egypt and Eretz Yisrael. Hermits, monks, God-seekers, mystics, and prophets sought inspiration and spirituality in its vast stretches of sand and awesome mountains.

Here Moses came. Here God revealed Himself to Moses in the bush that burned but was not consumed. In Sinai the Torah was given to the Jewish people.

But the Sinai Peninsula was not included in the Land of the Twelve Tribes, and thus does not come into the discussion of Jewish national-historical rights. The Jews in exile never longed or prayed for Sinai, and it was not included among the objectives of modern Zionism. If the Egyptians had not turned the Sinai Peninsula into a base for military attack on Israel, it would never have occurred to us to conquer it and incorporate it into our territory.

Since the establishment of the ancient Egyptian state, the Sinai Peninsula has served either as an Egyptian buffer zone and defensive base against invaders, or as a base for Egypt's northward offensives. The armies of the great pharaohs passed through Sinai on their way north. Hyksos cavalry and Assyrian, Babylonian, and Persian troops crossed from the north on their way to Egypt. The soldiers of Alexander the Great passed through Sinai in order to conquer Egypt. The Ptolemaic kings passed north to Eretz Yisrael and Syria. Roman legions, Byzantine hosts, Arab holy warriors, crusader knights, Mamelukes, Ottomans, Napoleon's armies, the battalions of Mehemet Ali and Ibrahim Pasha, General Allenby's expeditionary force, the armies of King Farouk in their campaign against Israel, the Israeli army under the command of Yigael Yadin and Yigal Allon in 1948 and under Moshe Dayan's command in 1956, Nasser's army in 1967 and the Israeli army under the command of Yitzhak Rabin and Yeshayahu Gavish in the Six-Day War,

Egypt's army under General Gamasi and Israel's army under General Elazar in the Yom Kippur War—all of these and more saw Sinai chiefly as a thoroughfare and base for their armies.

In antiquity it was not possible to maintain large permanent bases in the Sinai Peninsula. There was not enough water along its roads, and the towering mountains in the south formed an impassable barrier. In the nineteenth century, with the beginning of technological development and innovations in fighting methods and the transport of armies, Sinai began to serve as a permanent base and its strategic importance grew.

A tremendously potent factor in this change was the opening of the Suez Canal. The canal immediately became an international waterway of the first order and a focus of imperialist rivalries. Henceforth anyone holding the Sinai Peninsula became the defender of—or a menace to—the Suez Canal. This was perhaps the main reason that in 1906 the Egyptians and the British (the effective rulers of Egypt at the time) compelled—almost by force—the Sublime Porte in Istanbul to draw the international boundary between the Ottoman Empire and Egypt from Rafa to Taba, leaving the entire Sinai Peninsula in the control of Egypt (that is, the British Empire).

World War I proved to them how right they had been. They committed the serious error of not entrenching themselves in Sinai with a network of fortifications; thus, when the Turks invaded it under German direction, they came only one step short of victory. When General Allenby advanced toward Palestine in 1917, he did not repeat this mistake. This time the British troops were preceded by engineers and a quartermaster corps that firmly established their control along the routes of the advance; laid roads, water pipes, and railroad lines; set up provision and ordnance stores; and made certain that it would be possible to continue moving the army forward.

Between the two world wars, when the British did not yet foresee a new threat to Sinai and the canal, they did not do very much to entrench themselves in Sinai. But with the outbreak of World War II, when Egypt and the canal were threatened by the German-Italian forces who invaded Egypt from the west and there was a threat of a German flanking movement and conquest from the north, the British invested tremendous resources in laying new roads in Sinai, widening the existing ones, and building military installations, fuel stores, and new watering points.

By the time the Egyptian army took over Sinai from the British some years after the war, the peninsula had all the components of a modern military base: two good arterial roads—one from Kantara to El Arish, Rafa, and Gaza, and the second from Ismailia through Abu Ageila and Bir Asluj to Beersheba. It had a railroad from Port Taufiq at the southern end of the canal which linked up with the Cairo-Kantara-Lod international railway. It also had other east-west and north-south roads of varying classes, including the Et-Tur–Sharm el Sheik road. And there were military installations at the peninsula's major crossroads.

In 1948 the Egyptians used all this to transfer their armies northward with the aim of invading Israel, destroying the Zionist undertaking, and establishing themselves on its ruins. That year, and even more in 1956, we learned that the Sinai Peninsula was able to serve not only as a modern highroad for the invasion of our country but also as a permanent forward base for the Egyptian army.

In those same years the Israelis showed that the Kantara-Rafa road is also the Rafa-Kantara road; that an army can come on the Ismailia–Abu Ageila road from Abu Ageila to Beersheba, but also from Beersheba to Ismailia; and that good watering points can serve both an army going north and one going south. The Egyptians suddenly realized that the Sinai Peninsula is a two-way threat: a threat to Egypt's heart as well as to the heart of Israel.

Israel's withdrawal from Sinai in 1957 was accompanied by the demolition of roads, rail lines, and army camps by the Israelis, who went back to their country with the clear intention of having Sinai remain militarily neutral. Israel did not wish a large Egyptian army to appear suddenly on her borders again.

The destruction of the military installations and roads proved to be only temporary. In the ten years between 1957 and 1967 Nasser rebuilt not only his army, but also the roads and camps in Sinai.

In 1967 we underwent for a third time the trauma of a threat of annihilation by Egypt. In a matter of days Nasser moved a large, modern army to ready-made camps and bases close to the Israeli border. In a matter of hours his jet fighters and bombers were parked in the airfields of Bir Gafgafa, El Arish, and other places, and were being tended and fueled by waiting crews. Nasser ordered the United Nations forces out of Sharm el Sheik and Ras Nasrani and once again sent cannon and warships to block the Straits of Tiran.

In a matter of four days in 1967 the Sinai Peninsula was turned into a vast graveyard for the Egyptian army, its vehicles, armor, aircraft, ships, and thousands of soldiers.

For more than six years the Israeli army sat on the canal and in the entire peninsula, converting it into a base for the defense of Israel and an offensive base against Egypt in case war broke out again. The Israeli Bar-Lev Line of fortifications along the Suez Canal represented only a tiny fraction of Israel's investment in the military infrastructure of the Sinai Peninsula. After Israel's capture of Sinai many miles of roads were put down and new traffic arteries were opened. Existing take-off strips were enlarged and new airfields built. Many additional water lines were laid, new sea bases built, existing military camps enlarged and new ones built, and many fuel, provision, and ordnance reserves stored up. A modern communications network was set up, and modern infantry, armor, artillery, and missile bases established. The Sinai Peninsula became a military base equipped with the best, most sophisticated, and most variegated fighting systems available, and—at an investment of billions and all the engineering, scientific, and operational know-how and enterprise at Israel's disposal—was turned into a gigantic military base of international dimensions.

There was no doubt (and this is not just a subjective, emotional judgment) that the Egyptians felt that the Israeli army constituted a very real threat to all of Egypt. A modern army sitting on the east bank of the Suez Canal and throughout the Sinai Peninsula, drawing its strength from a solid and broad base in its rear, relying on a modern supply network, sustained by a highly technological state and society, was like a sword of Damocles hanging over the head of Egypt, the largest of the Arab countries.

Then came the Yom Kippur War and the subsequent cease-fire and separation of forces in the Sinai Peninsula. Now Egypt once again sits astride the Suez Canal, with the Israeli army pulled back to a line a few score miles east of the canal.

THE FUTURE OF SINAI

Concerning the Sinai Peninsula we must tell ourselves and the Egyptians a few elementary things.

Zionism never claimed any historical or national rights in Sinai, and we do not claim any today. Egypt does have national-historical rights in Sinai which we do not have. Sinai was defined as sovereign Egyptian territory more than sixty-five years ago, and nobody has since challenged this. We were prepared to consider this international boundary as the permanent border between us and Egypt and to sign a full and genuine peace treaty with Egypt on the basis of this boundary in 1948 and all the nineteen years of Israel's existence up to 1967.

We must declare that this is still our position in principle. At issue between us and Egypt, then, is not the question of national-historical rights or of recognition in principle of Egyptian sovereignty, but a security problem of vital importance to our existence.

If, in some way that today even after the start of the Geneva talks seems unlikely, an entirely new situation were to come about in which Egypt not only sat down at the negotiating table and signed a full and genuine peace treaty with us but also exchanged ambassadors with us; if our ships passed through the Suez Canal, our merchants sat in Cairo, and Egyptian merchants sat in Jerusalem; if our tourists climbed the pyramids and their tourists strolled in Tel Aviv's Dizengoff Circle; if we played soccer and basketball against each other; if their scholars taught in our universities and ours sat in their scientific institutes—if all this came about and true peace existed between us and the Egyptians, then, except for an Israeli presence in the Straits of Tiran, we would return the Sinai Peninsula to Egypt in stages, after it had been totally demilitarized under mutual inspection and bilateral and international guarantees.

All this is still a long way off—in the realm of dreams and mirages in the arid, sterile desert of the relations between us and Egypt. Sadat's Egypt is still demanding that we withdraw completely from the Sinai Peninsula. In exchange for peace she is ready to declare—ambiguously, and with some added stipulations concerning "justice to the Palestinians"—that she will make peace with us. But she does not make clear just what kind of peace she has in mind.

In other words, what Egypt now desires is that, solely on the basis of her word, we should hand over to her the biggest, strongest, and most sophisticated military base that we have set up (on her soil, to be sure) for the purpose of safeguarding ourselves against the possible danger of annihilation by her.

Nevertheless we say to the Egyptians: We are still sitting in your territories—but we are ready to return them to you. The Suez Canal is now once again yours; we are prepared to declare in principle that the entire Sinai is Egyptian. At the same time we declare that the entire peninsula is vital to our security. We will seriously be able to consider returning Sinai only after a clear, categorical, unqualified declaration by you that you are

entering an era of true peace with us, and—even before that—
that you are ready to sit over maps and discuss with us when and
in what stages Sinai is to be returned to you in such a manner
that it will never again constitute the slightest military threat
to us. We have every right to be wary of anyone who refuses to
sit with us to discuss a peace treaty and the details concerning
the return of territories, and instead tells us to give everything
back. In fact, we would be fools not to suspect that such a stance
harbors the worst kind of intentions against us. Only through
face-to-face dialogue will we both be able to ascertain what we
need to know: what will happen in every square mile of the
Sinai Peninsula in the future; what will be the fate of every mile
of road; what will become of every army camp, every base;
what will happen to every airfield and watering point. If Israel
does not know all this in advance, if we are not certain about
every single detail of the treaty between us, and if we do not
have guarantees that these details will be implemented—how
can we be asked to return this base? Returning it in any other
fashion would mean nothing less than turning the spearhead
away from your heart to our own. No nation can be expected
to behave in so irrational a way.

It would be best to clear the entire Sinai Peninsula of your
soldiers and ours. How is this to be done? How is this to be
guaranteed? By words, or by third-party agreements? We have
had our fill of third parties: Turks, French, British, the United
Nations, Americans, Soviets. And do you really believe that we
are going to agree to a third-party guarantee of the demilitarization of this huge base?

Can't you see that the guarantees of demilitarization must be
mutual between us? We understand your desire to check our
borders, for we know that you will fear that we will again invade
the Sinai. By the same token, we will want to see to it that you
don't move your troops toward our border again.

It may be that negotiations between us will lead to a solution
involving two-way inspection, or joint inspection, or integrated

patrols throughout Sinai with or without U. N. elements, which, for a specified number of years at least, will oversee all the sensitive arteries in the peninsula. It may be that at the negotiating table your representatives and ours will come to the conclusion that total demilitarization requires—before we hand Sinai back to you—the destruction of all the army camps, airfields and bases, and even all the roads and bridges, every well and water pipeline. But it may also be that through negotiations the two sides will find another way: not to destroy what exists, but to turn the peninsula with all its installations and its immense infrastructure into a peninsula of peace. It may be that the experts of both sides will reconnect the road and rail networks and the bridges of Sinai, so that they will lead westward to Egypt and eastward to Israel, and merge the airfields into an Egyptian-Israeli civil aviation combine, so that the peninsula will become an immense crossroads of international tourism, with millions of tourists stopping off there on their way to Cairo and Luxor, Jerusalem and Tel Aviv.

All this may sound utopian, but it is no less unrealistic to think that one fine morning Israel will announce, "Please take back this base and everything it contains. We're counting on your generosity and fair play. We'll just go quietly home and see how everything turns out."

IS THERE A WAY OUT?

We say to the Egyptians: The mutual suspicion between us is so deep that we are not prepared to make such a grandiose gesture or anything like it. We live with the annihilation complex you have imposed on us, and you live with still sullied pride and your fear of Zionist expansionism.

Is there a way out?

You still declare even after the Yom Kippur War that you will go to war again and "return by force what was taken by force." But after the Yom Kippur war one may hope that Egyptians from all walks of life and all ranks of government and the military will realize the terrible implications of going again to a total war against Israel. Another showdown battle is likely to turn into a flaming vortex that will suck into itself our country, your country, and perhaps the whole world, as it nearly did in October 1973.

Egypt, with one of the densest populations in the world, with more than 90 percent of her population living in the long, narrow Nile Valley, a country whose survival depends almost entirely on one river and one dam, should not get caught up in a torrent of flowery talk about wars of annihilation and showdown battles—especially in our day and age, when total war and the weapons that go with it are on the threshold of Egypt, Israel, and our entire region.

We, too, should not engage in such frightful saber-rattling, for total war will not bring us anything except death and destruction. A battle that ends with Israel sitting on the ruins of Cairo will be worse than a Pyrrhic victory; it will mean for us the loss of our human, Jewish, Zionist, and Israeli countenance.

If Egypt and Israel wish to live, their leaders must restrain the weapons of their armies. At the same time, the two sides must find temporary solutions in the hope that dialogue will be created and mutual trust will grow. To achieve even partial and temporary solutions the two sides will have to resort to the good offices of others: the United States, the Soviet Union, the United Nations, European countries, countries of the Third World, or combinations of these—anything to prevent the lighting again of the fuse that is apt to blow up all of us. Mediation between us and the Egyptians has to be unconventional. It may be direct or indirect, open or secret. We, the Egyptians, and the mediators must propose a variety of compromise solutions and offers of mutual compromise.

If we say, for example, that a presence in the Straits of Tiran is vital for us, the Egyptians must realize that we are not talking about the same Sharm el Sheik that they left us, but a Sharm el

Sheik with the modern harbor and airfield that we built and the naval base that we established and which we must maintain not only against a possible Egyptian threat but also against threats from anyone, today or in the future, who may wish to throttle us in the Straits of Tiran or in the Red Sea approach at Bab el Mandeb. On the other hand, if the Egyptians say that Sharm el Sheik is part of Sinai and all Sinai is part of Egypt, a solution must be found that will satisfy both sides. Such a solution might involve our leasing Sharm el Sheik for a long period of time, or some such similar arrangement.

History is full of instances where nations ended quarrels between them by adopting unconventional solutions. In Sinai, it is better to have any interim "anomaly" that both sides will accept than a situation in which each side sticks to a policy of "not an inch"; such a policy will drag us all into the chasm. Such arrangements can be created throughout the entire Sinai, as stages toward peace, as girders in the edifice of peace. It may take many years to complete this edifice, but we are duty bound to start. True peace will come when the Sinai Peninsula has been turned into a two-way bridge between Israel and Egypt and never again serves as a jumping-off point for armored brigades and a base for lethal missiles.

Egypt is a great and proud country. Her history, both in antiquity and since Islam, is one of the most glorious in the world. The Egyptian nation has suffered much and undergone many conquests, but it knew how to absorb and assimilate all its conquerors. It is a unique nation, and although it sometimes goes into a fit of madness (and what nation is totally free of this? Certainly not the Europeans!), it is basically a gifted, congenial nation. It was perhaps the first to harness nature to its needs; it was one of the greatest of ancient civilizations; it not only built great pyramids but also created an entire culture—engineering, medicine, literature, poetry, agriculture, industry, astronomy, seafaring—which earned the admiration of Greeks and Romans; it was the first Middle Eastern nation to try to absorb, in its own way, Western European culture and amal-gamate it with Islamic culture. It has been fighting for its inde-pendence and freedom for some 150 years.

What I said about our relations with the relatively young Palestinian Arabs and their national aspirations and values ap-plies all the more to the Egyptians—not only to the descendants of the pyramid builders but also to the descendants of those who fought against Napoleon, who tried to cast off the Mameluke yoke, who fought against the Ottomans and the British, who built the Suez Canal; the founders of modern Alexandria and Cairo, Port Said, and Suez; the builders of great universities; the seekers of the way to modern nationalism; the pathfinders of modern educational, health, and social service systems. Let us not sneer at the Egyptians!

The Egyptians have serious problems, problems of national identity and pride, the problem of Islamic religion in a modern state. They have frightful problems of very rapid population growth: at the present rate Egypt will have a population of about eighty million by the end of the century. They have urgent and tremendous problems of urbanization and industri-alization, of further radical changes in village life and structure.

We must try to explain to the Egyptians that *we are not their problem,* that their dreams of our destruction are not going to solve a thing for them. We must explain that after a full peace treaty has been signed and the Sinai has been returned to them, the Sinai Peninsula is not where they are going to solve their demographic and social problems. We must also tell them in no uncertain terms that we have no expansionist aims in Sinai, and that we have no desire to hold on to it forever—since for us, too, the Sinai is not where we are going to solve the problems of our additional millions of immigrants. Let us demand of the Egyp-tians that they understand us, study our past, our destiny, our uniqueness, and our aims. Let them believe us when we say that we do not wish to expand at their expense, that the Palestinian Arab problem is more our problem than theirs, and that we will solve it in an unconventional manner when we have found partners among the Palestinian Arabs. We must hope that in the course of time, after the initial stages have passed and peace exists, the Egyptians will agree to establish ties with us that will bring a new flowering to the region in which we all live.

The conflict between us and Egypt is, for the time being—despite wars and much killing—essentially smaller and less bitter than the bloody conflicts between other nations in the past. Why, then, can we not envision together that within a generation or two we will be cooperating in science and education, seafaring and aviation, engineering and commerce; that we will send our students to engage in Islamic studies at El Azhar University and theirs will come to study science in the Weizmann Institute?

In all likelihood some people will say that such rosy dreams will weaken our resistance against Egypt. But the opposite is true. Our youth, our soldiers, will be stronger if they know that they face a large enemy but not an eternal enemy, and that they face soldiers who are as proud and patriotic as themselves. If our young people dream that one day they will go strolling in the shade of the pyramids and that they will in turn be host to young Egyptians in our towns and settlements, they will not turn soft as a result. Our youth will know that the battles over Sinai were for Israel, and that if Suez and Ismailia had not been destroyed, Ashkelon and Beersheba would have been destroyed. At the same time, they will look forward to the end of the killing and destruction and to returning home to Israel.

Our supreme victory will come when a grandfather with a battle scar acquired in the Sinai will hand his grandson a pair of train tickets, and say, "Go and spend your honeymoon at the Semiramis Hotel in Cairo."

5

THE SYRIANS FACING US

THE NERVE CENTER OF INCITEMENT

On the face of it, Syria ought to be one of the quietest Arab states. She is not overcrowded, she has ample land and water, and she could develop her natural resources without any special hardships. She should not have become involved in constant quarrels with her Arab neighbors on forms of government and could easily have devoted herself to economic and social development. But the fact is that in all the years of her independent existence, Syria has been a seething caldron of unrest.

The causes of this unrest are doubtless rooted in her history. Syria has experienced a constant procession of nations and conquerors moving across her soil and leaving behind their offspring and influences. She has been inhabited by many hate-driven tribes and nationalities competing with each other for hegemony; she has served as the cradle of the most extreme Arab nationalist movements and pan-Arab groups The gap between the great expectations of the founding fathers of the Arab nationalist movement in Syria ("Greater Syria," "the Fertile Crescent" with Syria at its center, Ba'athism) and the petty reality of ceaseless interpersonal, intertribal, and intercommunal rivalry is certainly one of the factors—perhaps the main factor—in Syria's national schizophrenia. Hence Syria needs an external enemy who will serve as scapegoat for her fury and frustration and help unify the disparate elements of her population.

It was the Syrian nationalists who, more than any other group, invested Zionism and Judaism with a demonic image. Palestinian Arabs, with all their hostility to us, came to know us as human beings through day-to-day contact; the Egyptians were at first relatively tolerant toward Judaism and Zionism; but the Syrians saw us as the archenemy of the pan-Arabism that they preached.

Another element in the raging attitude of the Syrians toward us is their view of the Zionist undertaking, the Balfour Declaration, and the Sykes-Picot Treaty as the factors which prevented them, after World War I, from realizing their grand dream of setting up a Greater Syrian state which was to include all of Palestine. The British Mandate in Palestine seemed to them an imperialist plot which indirectly led to Syria being "sold" to French colonial rule.

From the beginning of British rule in Palestine, the Syrians were among the main agitators for Arab armed resistance against both the Zionists and the British. In the 1920s, and especially in the 1930s, Syria served as a training ground and shelter for the Palestinian Arabs who fought us. In 1947, even before the establishment of Israel, the battalions of Fauzi el Kawukji and other Syrian fighters entered Palestine and seriously threatened our settlements in the Plain of Sharon, the Jezreel Valley, and the Galilee.

With the establishment of Israel, the Syrian army exploited its topographical advantage on the Golan Heights and began shelling the settlements of the Jordan Valley and Upper Galilee. After this softening-up by artillery, armored and infantry battalions moved down into the valley, intent on wiping out the settlements, slicing through the Jezreel Valley, conquering

Haifa, and linking up with the other Arab armies that had invaded the country from the east and the south.

The defeat of the Syrians in 1948 underscored a character trait that appeared again and again in the years that followed: the vast gap between Syrian talk about total war against Israel and their performance on the battlefield. The readiness of the Syrians to fight "to the last Palestinian" (or Egyptian or Jordanian), despite their topographical advantage over Israel, became a byword among the Arabs themselves. Even though in 1948 Israel's effort was concentrated against the Egyptians and the Jordanian Arab Legion, and even though Israel had only small forces with light weapons facing the Syrians, the latter were incapable of exploiting this advantage; as soon as they encountered stubborn Israeli resistance they turned and fled. Compared to the significant losses suffered by the Palestinian Arabs, the Egyptians, and the soldiers of the Arab Legion, the Syrians were not prepared to give very much; instead, they hurried back to their mountain fastnesses. Their fighting was in inverse proportion to their braggadocio. In the years since 1948 Syria has undergone a revolution and a counterrevolution about once a year, and has yet to achieve a stable government.

In the Sinai Campaign of 1956 this Syrian trait appeared again. For all their big talk, the Syrian army did nothing to help Nasser when Israel penetrated deep into Sinai and crushed the Egyptian forces. About two years after the war the United Arab Republic came into being—a short-lived, short-tempered Egyptian-Syrian political union which lasted until 1961. In this union Israel saw the creation of a north-south vise whose main purpose was to crush Israel by means of one great army under a single command. It turned out—as the Egyptians and the Syrians both learned very quickly—that this union was completely artificial, for the character, life-style, and aspirations of the Egyptian people are diametrically opposed to those of the Syrians. It wasn't long before the Syrians were accusing the Egyptians of tendencies to dominate all the governmental, economic, and military bodies of the United Arab Republic. And the Egyptians also discovered how annoying the Syrians can be.

After the union was dissolved and Syria regained total political independence in the early 1960s, her leaders began to direct all their energy and anger against Israel. More than any other Arab country, the Syrians permitted the Fatah and other Palestinian armed organizations to develop and operate. In Syria these organizations found a solid base for their operations. In 1965–67 the Syrians and the Fatah cooperated very closely in applying pressure along Israel's northern border. Much Israeli blood was shed there, especially in the Galilee.

Armed with modern Soviet weapons, the Syrians learned to exploit their great advantage—the mountains of Golan— against the Jewish settlements in the Hulah Valley. Every settlement—every kibbutz, moshav, and town—became an easy target for Syrian cannon, missiles, mortars, and machine guns.

Under cover of this shelling, Fatah terrorists, encouraged by the Syrian army, started making night raids on the Jewish settlements in the Hulah Valley and along the borders, planting mines, killing settlers, and returning to their safe haven in the Golan Heights. The initial successes of the Fatah in the two years immediately preceding the Six-Day War turned the heads of the Fatah leaders and led to the creation of other armed organizations. These were also helped by the Syrian army and even turned the Syrian army and its leadership (which was, in fact, also the country's political leadership) into the chief defender of the Palestinian cause. The Syrians became a major factor in the escalation of terrorist activities and the call for a third round against Israel.

It was not Hussein's Jordan or Nasser's Egypt which, in the two years before the Six-Day War, pushed for total military confrontation with Israel. It was the Syrians. The disaster which Egypt and Jordan suffered in the Six-Day War was brought on by the Syrian leadership of that period.

In the Six-Day War the Syrians repeated their customary

tactics. When the fighting broke out in Sinai and the West Bank, they made no serious attempt to relieve the pressure on the Egyptian and Jordanian armies. Their armored and infantry divisions did not move from the Golan mountains but contented themselves with intensified shelling of the Israeli settlements below, assuming that the Israelis, even after routing the other Arab armies, would not dare to attempt a penetration of the massive fortifications on the Golan Heights. But this time Israel decided to bring an end to the Syrian menace. The Israeli army conquered the Golan Heights and routed the Syrian army.

THE GOLAN HEIGHTS

The conquest of the Golan Heights brought about a totally different strategic situation between Syria and Israel. We now had a hold on the Golan Heights at the very same altitude as the Syrians and we canceled out—at least in part—the considerable topographical advantage which they had mercilessly exploited over the years. With the Israeli army now dug in on the Golan Heights, Syria faced a potential threat to her capital, Damascus, from Israeli armor brigades only some thirty miles away. For the first time in the history of Syria as an independent state, the Six-Day War turned thousands of Syrians into refugees, and they paid the full price of this short and cruel war.

As might have been expected, after the Six-Day War the Syrians again placed themselves at the head of the most intransigent extremists among the leaders of the Arab states. The Khartoum Doctrine of 1967—"No negotiations, no recognition, no peace with Israel"—was too soft for them. In the years after the war they again gave unlimited support to the Palestinian Arab armed movements, and did so in characteristic fashion. They were careful to prevent these organizations from setting up a government-within-a-government and an army-within-an-army in Syria, and made certain that the armed Palestinian Arabs knew just who ruled in Syria.

The Syrians, in typical fashion, did not join Egypt in the war of attrition of 1968–70, and were careful not to heat up their own cease-fire lines with Israel. In the Yom Kippur War they were severely mauled by the Israeli army's counteroffensive, and they agreed to a cease-fire soon after the Egyptians and Israelis stopped fighting.

Such behavior, which runs through all of Syrian policy and military reactions, shows the level of realism of the Syrian leadership. This realism for the time being dictates to the Syrians that they not become involved in armed conflict on their own with Israel; that they not permit the creation in Syria of armed enclaves of Palestinian Arabs, because they know that their country, consisting of many ethnic groups, nationalities, and tribes, already has enough seedbeds of rebellion, and there is no need to add to these the Palestinian Arabs; and that they not join any all-embracing unions with other Arab states in which there is a danger that their partners will swallow them up and turn them into junior partners (this does not apply to tenuous federations in which Syrian sovereignty and independence are not threatened).

Paradoxically, this Syrian realism shows that even though the Syrians display extreme hostility to Israel, they may be the greatest realists and the least "insane" when it comes to their own self-interest. This character trait may hold hopes for a future settlement even with Syria.

To be sure, it appears after the Yom Kippur War that Syria will be the last of the Arab states bordering on Israel to reconcile herself to Israel's existence. To all appearances, they will be the last to come to any kind of arrangement with Israel. Unlike the Egyptians, the Jordanians, and the others, Syrians seem at this moment unwilling to talk about meaningful peace under any terms. They stick to the old idea that there is no Israel; there are only Zionist gangs that have to be thrown into the sea.

One day there could yet be a turnabout. If one day Israel should arrive at some kind of real settlement with one of her neighbors, it is not impossible that Syria might decide to follow

204 / LAND OF THE HART

suit and enter into some similar arrangements—out of the realism I have referred to. In preparation for this day we must clearly formulate our position on the major—in fact the only—bone of contention between us and the Syrians: the Golan Heights.

Israel must retain military domination of this mountain range. Even those who think in terms of unconventional warfare in the decades ahead cannot ignore the "conventionality" of cannon aimed at our heads. The return of the Golan Heights would constitute a serious threat to the security of Israel.

At the same time, we ought to tell the Syrians that though the Golan does come within the Land of the Twelve Tribes, they and we both have historical rights in the Golan Heights. We were prepared to forgo the realization of these rights; in all the years up to the Six-Day War we never mentioned them. But now we must consider, in return for full peace, a partition which will guarantee us military control of the fortifications in part of the Golan Heights while at the same time allaying Syrian fears about our presence so close to Damascus. This solution must give us a stronghold on the Golan Heights, and at the same time allow the Syrians to bring back their refugees—or at least some of them. By using modern methods, there will be room to resettle them there.

As in the resolution of the conflicts with the Palestinian-Jordanian Arabs and the Egyptians, this solution will also require negotiations, signing of a peace treaty, and intermediate stages, including full demilitarization, mutual and international guarantees, and joint supervision.

The future of the Jewish settlements in the Golan will be the same as that of the Jewish settlements in Judea, Samaria, and the Gaza Strip: with the advent of peace, some of them will be included in the State of Israel, some will become army and patrol bases, and some—fantastic as this may sound today—will be part of a Syria that is living in peace with Israel.

Syria today is an extremely unstable country with a very loose political and social fabric. Because of this instability Syria is the country that is most vulnerable to Soviet or Chinese infiltration. But it is possible for a different Syria to come into being, one that will use her vast expanses in a modern fashion, harness the waters and power of the Euphrates to develop agriculture and industry, and begin to solve her population's economic problems. The time is sure to come when Syria will know how to exploit her special geographic location between the Mediterranean Sea and the Arabian Desert, join a regional seafaring, aviation, and trade network, develop tourism, and serve as a bridge between Turkey, Iraq, Iran, the lands of the Fertile Crescent, and Europe.

Such a Syria will have no cause to fear Israel, just as Israel will not fear her. With the passage of generations, the bunkers in the Golan Heights will turn into tourist sites and symbols of a dark and terrible past.

6

OUR RELATIONS WITH LEBANON

Lebanon is an example of the kind of relations that could have existed between Israel and her neighbors. I do not say this contemptuously, or on the assumption that Israel can get along only with small and weak Arab countries. For even little Lebanon, if she had so wished, could have invested all her resources, strength, and energy—and she has plenty of all of these, both absolutely and relative to the other Arab states—in building a large army, a powerful air force, and a modern navy. She could have devoted all her attention to the war against Israel. If she had so wished, Lebanon, with her long serpentine border adjoining Israel, could have caused Israel a great deal of trouble. That she did not do so is not because Lebanon is short on Arab patriotism. On the contrary, Lebanon has been the home of some of the most outstanding Arab ideologists and intellectuals. Lebanon's sense of dignity and self-worth is no smaller than that of any other Arab state.

Lebanon's attitude to Zionism and the State of Israel apparently stems from special circumstances: Lebanon's historical structure as an Arab state whose population is half Muslim Arab and half Christian Arab created a very delicate balance which has required the Lebanese, since the beginning of the country's independent existence, to devote all their spiritual energy and political wisdom to keep the system from collapsing. Ceaseless war against Israel, which would have brought destruction to villages and towns and paralysis to the economy, might have toppled the complex, delicate structure called Lebanon. The country's leaders sought to prevent this. They correctly saw what the ceaseless war against Israel was doing to the other Arab states, and determined—despite the continuous provocations of the Palestinian armed movements—not to be drawn into it.

Lebanon's economic structure is another factor in her position on Israel. It is a modern economy dependent on international and inter-Arab commerce and banking, as well as on a prosperous shipping industry and on international and Arab aviation. Summer and winter tourism from both the West and the East, entertainment and recreation industries, and some manufacturing and agriculture for export also play a part in her economy. The advancement of all these economic branches requires organic development and continuous calm.

Lebanon did pay lip service to the Arab cause against Israel. But she never showed any desire to be the "noble conqueror" of the western Galilee and Haifa or to be included in an all-Arab eastern or northern front against Israel.

The Lebanese—scions of Hiram and the Tyrians, descendants of Greek, Roman, and Byzantine seamen and merchants, heirs of Arab traders and sailors, spawn of Genoese and Venetian dealers, all of whom settled at one time or other along the country's beautiful coast—developed a sense of history which made them aware that the world is a big place, that the seas are an unlimited, unbounded source of livelihood, that great states and cultures have come into being not merely by virtue of the number of square miles they possess but also by virtue of the number of their ships, the extent of business aptitude and activity, and the openness to a free and steady flow of goods, money, culture, languages, and various other influences. This sense of history led them—or at least some of them—to the realization that in the eastern Mediterranean basin there is room for a flourishing Beirut and a prosperous Tel Aviv, and that there is no need to murder and destroy in order to live a good life.

Another factor in Lebanon's attitude to Israel has to do with the country's Christian Arabs. Although they are half of Lebanon's population, they constitute a tiny minority in the Muslim Arab world. To be sure, many of the Arab nationalist leaders in Lebanon and other Arab countries are Christians. Some of them try to surpass the Muslims in their extremism, but there is no doubt that most of the Christian leaders and common people are well aware that a wave of extreme Arab nationalism will generate a wave of Muslim extremism. They must know also that a holy war against the Zionist-Jewish "infidels" is apt, under certain circumstances, to turn itself against the Christian Arabs as well.

Be that as it may, the fact remains that the Lebanese army was hardly involved in the 1948 war. The Israeli army, in chasing irregulars who fled into Lebanon, entered the country and occupied thirty villages. But when the Israel-Lebanon armistice agreement was signed, the Israeli army withdrew to the international boundary. From then till the Six-Day War our border with Lebanon was quiet. Israeli plowers and Lebanese plowers would meet at the border markers. During the Six-Day War, too, the border was absolutely quiet: not a single shot was exchanged.

Following the Six-Day War, the Fatah and the other Palestinian Arab armed organizations started moving into Lebanon and making it a base for sabotage and terror activities. They did so for several reasons: first, because they could not tolerate the fact that there was an Arab state which had maintained a quiet border with Israel. Second, it was strategically better for them to scatter their bases in a large number of Arab countries and strike at Israel from all directions, so that Israel would be forced to spread her forces thin. Third, there is no doubt that the

Syrians were interested, for internal political reasons and because of their relations with Lebanon, in pushing the Fatah and the other terrorist organizations into Lebanon so that Lebanon rather than Syria would be an object of reprisal actions by the Israeli army. It should be added here that after the disastrous defeat suffered by the terrorists in Jordan in 1970, Lebanon became a convenient shelter for them both for their forays into Israel and as a base for their international acts of terror.

As terrorist activity from Lebanon mounted, the Israeli army took reprisal action. The Lebanese are now beginning to realize that playing host to Palestinian Arab terrorists in their country is apt to lead to an internal explosion, to the rise of a government-within-a-government, and finally also to the temporary occupation of their territories by the Israeli army and the loss of their independence.

If Israel signs permanent or provisional peace agreements with the Palestinian-Jordanian Arabs, the Egyptians, and perhaps also the Syrians, there will be no problem about arranging a peace between Lebanon and Israel. There are no questions about where the international border lies. All that we and the Lebanese will have to do is open this border (at Rosh Hanikra, Marj-Ayyun, and other points) to two-way traffic of people and goods.

The standard of living and the level of economic and political activity in Lebanon is already high and unique compared to the other Arab states. One may say that the Lebanese Republic is today the most open and relatively the most liberal in the Arab world. Her press is almost completely free. Her political system is a variegated, multiparty one. Elections take place virtually without interference, and civil rights are observed.

In the future constellation of states in the eastern Mediterranean and in the Fertile Crescent, Lebanon will occupy a special place—not only as a model of normal relations with Israel, but also as a possible example to other Arab states in other areas of life. Under peacetime conditions, we can order our relations with Lebanon on a basis that will be of supreme value to both nations. A considerable number of Lebanese Arabs know this. Here and there, beneath the torrent of anti-Israel talk and writing in Lebanon, there are also wellsprings of understanding, reconciliation, and a real desire to live in peace with Israel.

7

FACE TO FACE WITH THE ARAB WORLD

ISRAEL—A UNIFYING BOND?

So far I have discussed Israel's four enemy-neighbors—the four states or nations directly involved in the struggle with Israel. I have dealt with the borders we share with them, the administered areas, the bloody struggle between us, and our blood ties with each of them. I have also discussed the geography and the ancient and modern history we have in common with them, and the possibility of reaching peace agreements with them.

In addition to these four, there are about a dozen other Arab countries which contend that they are also at war with us, not because they have common borders with us but because they claim to be part of an undefined entity called the Arab world. They say that there is a war also between us and Mauritania, Morocco, Algeria, Tunisia, Libya, and Sudan in Africa, and with Saudi Arabia, Yemen, South Yemen, the Persian Gulf principalities, Iraq, and Kuwait. They warn us that in the struggle against us are aligned not only the fifty million Arabs whose countries border on ours, but also another fifty million Arabs in countries that are hundreds or thousands of miles away from us. It is said that our very existence serves as a unifying bond—perhaps the only one—for the entire Arab world, which sees us as the common enemy of them all.

On the surface, this appears to be true: the Arab League, embracing—however tenuously—all the Arab states, is preoccupied mainly with us. A variety of treaty organizations, leagues, and federations have been created by different Arab countries with the declared aim of helping the four "front-line countries" in their war against us. The Palestinian organizations get money and encouragement from and maintain bases in a number of Arab countries that are far from us. The oil-rich Arab countries are contributing hundreds of millions in currency to the war against us. The oil embargo after the Yom Kippur War was perhaps the climax of this united anti-Israel front.

This picture—if it is all true—seems terrifying. Over the years we have learned to live with this menace and to deal with it. Iraqi forces invaded Palestine in 1948. The Iraqis went to war against us again in 1967, landed their divisions in Jordan after the Six-Day War, and shelled our settlements from the Gilead Heights. The Saudis sent battalions against us in 1948. Volunteers from all the Arab countries serve in all the armed Palestinian units. Libyan rulers threaten to send soldiers and aircraft to fight us. In the Yom Kippur War, contingents, both token and real, from many Arab states fought on the Egyptian and Syrian fronts.

It is true that the Arab world is united against us. But this is only a half-truth.

From the beginning of their independent existence the Arab states have been a mass of divisions and segments. There is considerable internal friction and conflict of interest, stemming partly from bitter border disputes, partly from the tension between utterly different regimes: "progressive," quasi-"socialist" and pro-Soviet, "monarchic" and pro-Western, sheikdoms, and military junta regimes. Some of the differences stem from diametrically opposite mentalities.

It is impossible to unify all of these differences on the basis of just one negative bond: hatred of Israel and the desire to destroy her. This bond is too insubstantial to unify the Arab world. The Arabs themselves have seen this time and again. Hatred of Israel did not suffice to consolidate even the Palestinian Arabs into one bloc against us during the days of the mufti and his opponents. Today, in the period of Yasir Arafat and his rivals, the genuine hostility of the Palestinian Arabs to the Zionist undertaking is not enough to fuse the Palestinian Arabs into one camp. The aims and objectives of the Palestinian Arabs have always been negative: not to allow the Jews to enter the country; not to allow them to develop; not to sell them land; and, above all, not to let them live. These negative objectives turned out to be like shifting sand dunes. The Palestinian Arabs were never able to build any sort of foundation of ideological and practical unity on them.

Hatred of Israel did serve as a firm bond to consolidate Egypt and Syria in the Yom Kippur War. But it did not serve to keep the Egyptions from arranging their own cease-fire and disengagement with Israel. And hatred of Israel did not suffice to impel Lebanon to participate actively in the war against Israel.

If this hatred of us cannot unite the Arab nations along our borders, then it certainly cannot be expected to unite the other more distant Arab countries. Of course, nothing is simpler than to use hatred as incendiary material, spread it over popular consciousness, and ignite it with the flame of demagogy. This is what the leaders of a number of distant Arab states (principally Libya, Algeria, and Iraq) have done and are doing with considerable success. But it is a far cry from this to the readiness to fight and make sacrifices.

THE ARAB CALDRON

The Arab states not bordering on Israel developed, each in a way appropriate to it, their own version of the anti-Israel bond, and, of course, there has been transparent exploitation of the

Arab-Israel conflict for legitimate but fundamentally selfish objectives. This situation makes it possible for the big and medium-sized powers to do some stirring of their own in the Arab
caldron, and eases their infiltration into the area—under the
guise of pro-Arabism and anti-Israelism—for the purpose of
achieving aims which have nothing whatever to do with the
Israeli-Arab conflict.

The Soviet penetration is certainly a blatant example of this:
at the relatively cheap price of a little military and economic aid
(and I am not now referring to Egypt and Syria, which border
on Israel) and an abundance of anti-Israel talk and anti-Zionist
propaganda, the Soviets, in the role of "defenders of the Arab
cause," gained a great deal of goodwill and sympathy, and in the
course of time also bases and economic and political influence.

The Chinese are playing the same game with the Arab countries, gaining sympathy at an even lower price. The Yugoslavs,
too, as well as other East European states, are exploiting the
conflict in our region for purposes of their own. Even the
French have learned well that in exchange for anti-Israelism
one can gain markets, influence, oil concessions, and the like in
the Middle East. And after the Yom Kippur War other European and African countries followed suit.

It is difficult to make a precise projection for the future on the
basis of the past. However, the history of the wars between us
and the Arabs shows that in 1948, 1956, 1967, and 1973 the
Arab countries far from the theater of war were not prepared
to pull the chestnuts of Israel's neighbors out of the fire. These
countries were well aware that this was live fire, and that real
involvement and the dispatch of large national armies to the
theater of war was apt to bring them disaster on a par with, or
even greater than, that visited upon the four countries bordering on Israel.

The Algerians, who are justly proud of their liberation war,
know that if they are routed in the Sinai they will not only lose
their national pride but also endanger their country. The

Iraqis, too, know that if their army is crushed by an Israeli vise on the eastern or northern fronts, it will mean the collapse of their country's wobbly, strife-ridden, multitribal structure.

It ought to be remembered that at this stage in the development of the Arab countries, the army of each of them is not only the strongest instrument of rule (and in many of them the only one), but also their crowning glory. The heads of these armies are therefore very careful not to expose them to defeat in faraway places. One may assume that in the future, even more than in the past, thanks to the lesson of the wars between us and the Arabs, this realism will guide the rulers of the Arab countries that are far from Israel. If another war is forced upon us and we have to move our forces beyond any cease-fire line, we will not hesitate to do so. The same applies to the borders of any distant Arab countries that involve themselves directly in such a war.

It seems that here and there, especially among some of the Palestinian-Jordanian Arabs and Egyptians, the elementary truth is beginning to strike home that only those who over the years have fought or now are fighting Israel will make peace with her; that only those who have spilled Israeli blood and had their blood spilled by her—only they and she are capable of saying one day: Enough! With the Palestinian-Jordanian Arabs, with the Egyptians, with the Syrians, with the Lebanese—with these we will sit down at any time and any place to talk, openly or secretly, about peace. The moment the first sign of any real arrangement appears, with any one of these or all of them together, the all-Arab bond of anti-Israelism will disappear. Then the Arab nations and states will have to search carefully for a different unifying bond, one that will fuse them into some kind of regional league or federation.

This bond already exists potentially: common language, culture, religion, tradition, and history. There are common regional economic problems. In time the Arab countries will have to realize and accept the fact that when some kind of supranational regional structure comes into being, it will not be able to be exclusively Arab. Like other regional leagues, it too will be multinational and will have to include non-Arab countries like Iran, Turkey, Israel, and others. It is precisely this variegation that will give the Middle East the possibility and prospect of being all the more modern and possessed of many areas of contact—geographical, political and economic—with the rest of the world. All the world will be the better for such a revitalized Middle East. And Israel can serve as a major area of contact between the world and the Middle East—once peace comes to our troubled region.

8

THE UNITED STATES
OF AMERICA

FACE TO FACE WITH THE POWERS OF THE WORLD

We deeply and fervently desire to achieve peace with the Arabs, to be a part of the regional checkerboard, to make our special contribution to the Middle East, and to be a people like all other peoples. As part of the human race in its march toward the future, we wish to grapple with universal problems and also to contribute something of our own toward the solution of these problems. Whatever our hopes for a better life in the future, we now live in a threatening present which allows us not a single moment's respite.

Our region has always been both a meeting place and a hunting ground for the powers of the world. Through it pass international waterways, and it is the site of vast deposits of oil, that liquid so vital for the existence of all nations, great and small.

For purposes of discussion this topic must be reduced to its component parts. Each individual international factor and our mutual relations with it must be discussed separately, while bearing in mind that all are interwoven and ceaselessly changing.

We shall therefore scrutinize our relations with the United States, the Soviet Union, the countries of Europe, and the Third World.

"NEW JERUSALEM" AND "BLACK GOLD"

In a discussion of the complex of relations between the United States and ourselves, we should first note a phenomenon that we shall encounter, differently formulated, in our discussion of the Soviet Union and the countries of Europe. These relations are conducted on two planes that are sometimes convergent and sometimes divergent, each of which has a different derivation: first, the great-power–global level—the whole gamut of American interests in the Middle East and its attitude toward Israel within that context; and second, the American domestic plane—the attitude of the United States to the Jewish-Zionist cause, and the way she relates in practice to the Jewish-Zionist cause within the states.

Our relations toward the United States also follow this symmetry: in one sense we relate to a superpower having vested interests of its own in the region, and in another sense we are dealing with a state where six million Jews, constituting about one-half of the Jewish Diaspora, now live.

In the nineteenth century the United States was a mighty and burgeoning state, but still inward-directed, still busy building up the country and developing its resources and industry at a breathtaking pace. It was even then beginning to flex its military biceps, especially to protect its new half-continent from the designs of old imperialist Europe. American interest in the Middle East was marginal.

The Americans knew that in this area there was a deep and direct involvement of the great powers of the previous century —the Ottomans, British, French, Russians, and to a certain extent also the Germans and the Italians. They knew who owned and who controlled the area, and they did not try to stir this caldron, which was in any case very remote from them and their concerns.

The real beginnings of American interest and involvement in the region date from World War I. The United States joined in the war against the Germans and the Turks and appeared, under the leadership of President Woodrow Wilson, as a world power with a say in the world that was to arise after the Allied victory and in the division of the spoils of the Ottoman Empire. At that time the odor of Middle Eastern oil began to reach American nostrils, and American capital and know-how began penetrating the area to prospect for "black gold." American interest in the Arab countries became keener.

The United States of the nineteenth century, with its gates open wide to admit the persecuted of the whole world, and itself building a new and progressive society, acted like a powerful magnet, drawing millions of Jews from Europe. Even in their new land the longing for Zion remained with those Jews. At the end of the nineteenth century a Zionist movement began to come into being in the United States. Few American Jews immigrated to Israel, but the movement did begin remarkable work in the form of financial support, while at the same time providing the Zionist enterprise with political backing.

Some of the first to take Zionism to their hearts in the United States were the non-Jews (the Jews, strangely, gave them little encouragement at first, because Zionism, which preached the upbuilding of the ancient homeland, seemed to be at cross-purposes with the Jewish community's efforts to carve out a new life for itself in America). Christian Americans—second-, third-, and fourth-generation descendants of the pioneers who had fled from religious clashes in Europe, and had come to this new, unsown land wanting to found a "New Canaan" and a "New Jerusalem"—were receptive to the Zionist idea. The first American pioneers were deeply and strongly influenced by the Bible. The life and behavior patterns of many of them were founded on values drawn from the Bible.

Since the American pioneers were thoroughly conversant with the narratives of the Bible, it is not surprising that Zionism should have found a way to the hearts of many of these people.

They began to entertain a sense of fellowship with the new Jews that were building up the ancient land of the Bible. They evinced deeper and truer understanding for and sympathy with the Zionist cause than the Europeans had.

Between the two world wars American Jewish interest in the Zionist undertaking grew, while, at the same time, American economic penetration of the Arab world increased immensely. Oil companies were awarded concessions, invested fortunes, and developed in the Middle East some of the greatest oil fields in the world.

The Americans quickly learned that the oil deposits in the Arab countries were enormous and that the region would become increasingly important for the supply of energy to the industrialized states. At first they felt themselves to be the tenants of the British, who in most Arab countries were still the local suzerains. Gradually they too began creating a political presence based on their great vested interest in these countries. A certain contradiction had already begun to emerge between American support for the Zionist enterprise and a pro-Arab lobby, which argued that if the Jews wanted to return to their homeland, good luck to them, but as a world power, America should not damage its own interests in the region by offering them unqualified support.

Before World War II, United States Jewry had become the strongest and richest Jewish community in the world. It boasted thousands of large and small communities, synagogues, diverse public associations, a press and literature, and many Zionist organizations. The influence of Jewry upon American society was proportionate to its "presence" and numerical predominance in a few key areas of economic, political, social, and spiritual life.

The Zionist movement of America did its utmost to provide help, mainly in the form of money, for the Jews of Palestine in their struggle against the Arabs and British, who were disgruntled and indeed irate at Jewish and non-Jewish American intervention in the dispute between them and the Jews.

The European holocaust showed up the weakness of American Jewry. In the face of the holocaust this great sector of Jewry was confused and powerless. Tens of thousands of American Jewish soldiers fought Hitler and the Japanese, but when the full extent of the horror of Nazi atrocities became known, American Jewry knew in its heart that it had not tried hard enough, had not pitted every ounce of its strength, had not protested as vigorously as it might have while the slaughterer's knife was descending upon a third of the Jewish people. This nightmare—the sense of having done too little—to this very day pursues that generation of American Jewry that was active during World War II, and it hands its guilt feelings down to its sons.

These pangs of conscience were first indicated at the end of World War II, when American Jews began stepping up their assistance to the Yishuv in its struggle to bring the surviving remnants of European Jewry into Palestine. They donated generously to the financing of illegal immigration and arms procurement. Moreover, they began to take part personally in these activities: Jewish volunteers from the United States engaged in rescue work and arms procurement; some served on illegal immigrant ships. But American Jewry concentrated its efforts mainly on exerting pressure on the political establishment in their country—the White House, both houses of Congress, state governors, and mayors of the large cities. The Jews of the United States found a thousand and one ways to influence their government to help the Yishuv in its struggle for the founding of the State of Israel.

UPS AND DOWNS IN AMERICAN POLICY

In 1947 the United States was at the height of its power and influence in the world. The nations of Europe, including victorious Britain, were in ruins, nearly reduced to bankruptcy. The great and victorious Soviet Union was still bleeding profusely, and her economy was half destroyed. Occupied Japan had also been laid waste. China was in the throes of a civil war, and

Africa was still entirely under colonialist rule. The only power possessing nuclear weapons, a prospering economy, and a civil population that had suffered none of the ravages of war was the United States.

Even in this situation, when many people in authority were truly sympathetic to the Jewish struggle for political independence, American Jewry achieved only partial and limited assistance for the Zionist cause from the United States. Only the unique coincidence in 1947 of Soviet and American support for the founding of the State of Israel gave American Jewry room to maneuver. But even this coincidence did not lead the United States to give her full support to the founding of the state, to say nothing of rendering military assistance at a time when Israel was fighting for its very existence. In contrast to the sympathy we gained from part of the American public, mighty forces were even then working against us.

The cold war drew nearer. American leaders understood that they would have the Soviet Union to contend with in all parts of the world, including the Middle East. They clearly perceived that the British and French empires were crumbling, and that a political vacuum would be created, a vacuum that the two new superpowers—the United States and the Soviet Union—would struggle to fill.

American investments in the Middle East were constantly increasing at that time, especially in the oil-producing states, and the vector of powerful American interests in the Arab countries began working against the vector of support for Israel. One should not forget that American recognition of Israel came only at the last moment, and then only as a result of tremendous pressure exerted on the White House by U. S. Jewry, and perhaps out of awareness that the Soviet Union intended to recognize Israel too.

Moreover, both before and after recognizing Israel, the United States maintained the strictest embargo on the delivery of arms to this region—either to Israel or to the Arab states. It is true that American Jews did manage to purchase a small quantity of arms and supplies for Israel, but they did so in defiance of their government.

Whatever the debt of gratitude that Israel owes to the American administration of President Harry Truman, it should not be forgotten that in those fateful months of the spring and summer of 1948, when the Arab armies could, by all laws of military logic, have razed the entire Zionist enterprise, it was Soviet, not American, weaponry that stood us in good stead. The United States could have altered our almost desperate military situation without difficulty had it even slightly relaxed the embargo laws and sent Israel a small shipment of arms. A few dozen fighter aircraft, tanks, and guns would have sufficed to change our situation overnight. But she did not do so.

America was by no means "in our pockets" even then, and there was and is a limit to the pressure and influence American Jews can bring to bear on their government and to the sympathy of non-Jewish American public opinion toward our undertaking. Today too there are strong American interests working for what they (and not we or American Jewry) regard as good and useful for the United States. In 1948, when the Israeli forces pushed through the northern Sinai in hot pursuit of the Egyptians, it was the Americans, together with the British, who exerted heavy and perhaps decisive pressure on Ben-Gurion and his government not only to halt our advance, but to retreat to the international boundary.

During the first years after the establishment of the state, American Jewry continued to aid Israel. Its ties with Israel grew stronger and American Jews' pride in Israel increased. With loans and grants, the American government also helped Israel to put its young economy on a sound footing, to absorb Jewish immigrants, and to build up agriculture and industry. As to American government aid, we should remember that this large-scale assistance came at a time when America was handing out vast sums of money under the Marshall Plan, not only to individual states, but also to whole continents. The United States' economic contribution to Israel was thus proffered through an accepted post-World War II framework, and Israel was in very good company in receiving large-scale economic aid: Britain, France, Germany, Japan, and dozens of other countries. The Arab states also received loans and grants from the United States. Had they submitted concrete, broad plans for the solution of the Palestinian refugee problem, the United States would undoubtedly have footed the bill.

In 1956, when it came to another military confrontation between Israel and the Arab states (which on Israel's part was combined with an Anglo-French military operation), Israel once again ran afoul of American interests in the area—and this time far more seriously. During that period, the Eisenhower-Dulles era, the United States was already envisioning herself as an international policeman whose job it was to see to it that order was maintained everywhere. Since the Israelis, as well as the British and the French, had failed to consult it, the American government was in a blazing temper when the Sinai Campaign began, and in an ungovernable fury by the time the Anglo-French invasion of Port Said got under way.

The Sinai Campaign was unleashed with such swiftness and surprise that the United States was unable to prevent it. But it did act with all its massive strength to block the path of the British and the French, and was also responsible for braking the operation, thus causing its shameful failure. One can say, and this should be remembered for the future, that it was the United States and not the Soviet Union that saved Nasser's regime and enabled him to convert his military defeat into a psychological victory. The Soviet Union then threatened Israel and also Britain and France; but as she was involved in putting down the luckless uprising in Hungary, it is now apparent that her threats were quite idle. Had they not strangely and suddenly coincided with the American threats, they would not have been sufficient to defeat the Anglo-French operation.

What was then done by an American president—or more precisely by a resolute American secretary of state—in an effort to guard global and regional American interests is something we should commit to memory. It seemed to us at the time that the Americans had made a grave and fatal error. Now we feel that had they not intervened as they did, the face of the region and the world would be totally different today. But our opinion on the subject did not make the least impression. Even the attempts of American Jewry to alter the strategic decisions of their government proved futile, and we indirectly put American Jewry in the dangerous quandary of having to decide between the good of their homeland (as seen by the American government) and the good of Israel (as seen by the Israeli government).

After the Sinai Campaign, the American authorities stepped up their pressure on Israel to recall her troops from the Sinai Peninsula. In return for this withdrawal they offered Israel lukewarm verbal promises of support. In May 1967, when the time came to redeem those promises, they proved to be worth very little.

AMERICAN JEWRY AND THE SIX-DAY WAR

In the years between the Sinai Campaign and the Six-Day War, the bonds between Israel and American Jewry grew stronger and more extensive, as did the ties between Israel and the American government. During that period the Soviet Union forged ahead with her penetration of the Middle East, and the American government began to regard Israel as a bulwark against further Soviet penetration. But some of the American governing bodies began to develop an "Israel complex" which came to bear an ever-closer resemblance to the British government's "complex" regarding the Zionist enterprise. Through the prism of this complex, Israel and Israel alone is seen as the source of American troubles in the Middle East, including that of Soviet penetration. This view, which to us appears narrow and malevolent, is held even today by certain of the architects of American policy, whether wittingly or unwittingly, whether they express it openly or only think it.

Toward the end of that ten-year period the Americans began, albeit hesitatingly and slowly, to take into consideration Israel's arms balance, but only when they realized, after ceaseless affirmations on Israel's part, that the Soviets were penetrating Egypt, Syria, Iraq, and other Arab states with quantities and types of armaments that the Israelis could not procure elsewhere.

The second half of May and the beginning of June 1967 ("the waiting weeks") revolutionized the relationship of American Jewry toward Israel. There had previously been a strong emotional identification with the Zionist enterprise by large numbers of American Jews. During the first nineteen years of Israel's existence, up to 1967, they grew accustomed to the existence of "their" state: just like Americans of Irish, Italian, or Polish extraction, the American Jews now had an "old country" of their own. Israel became for them a fair and shining fact of life. They related to Israel as to a beloved sister, the remnant of a great family, raising children in the old ancestral home that she had undertaken to revive.

In 1956, during the Sinai Campaign, the Jews of the United States were proud of the Israeli victory (although undoubtedly somewhat embarrassed by the "collusion" between Israel and the Anglo-French "imperialists"), but they had no presentiment of danger to the existence of their sister Israel.

An entirely different reaction came from them in 1967. Suddenly, during three short weeks, they had to endure the shock of their lives. The mass media brought into the home of each of the six million Jews of America the horrific feeling that savage and crazed enemies were about to attack their sister, intending to rape and murder her. The sounds of alarm from Israel, and much more emphatically the exultant cries of revenge emanating from the Arab masses that appeared on television screens in Cairo, Damascus, Amman, and Baghdad, gave rise to the dread feeling that another holocaust was about to be visited upon Israel, the second holocaust in the life of the Jewish people within one generation. The wound of the European holocaust was reopened. American Jewry, all of American Jewry—Zionists and non-Zionists and anti-Zionists, simple folks, New York taxi drivers, Chicago butchers, and senators in Washington, scientists at Harvard and in Los Angeles, even Jews who had forgotten they were Jews, half-Jews, and quarter-Jews—American Jews suddenly discovered that Israel's struggle was a matter of life and death for themselves. They understood that their life would be no life, or would be completely different, if the State of Israel were suddenly to vanish. This sense of danger of annihilation gave American Jewry a strength it had never before known or imagined, and which it brought to Israel's aid. It proved to the American government and the American people how strong the ties between American Jewry and Israel were. This force did its work in many ways, and was of priceless assistance to the struggling, warring state.

But this too we should remember well for the future: this concentrated "laser-beam" force did not (indeed, could not) transform the American government and make its attitude toward Israel and her war an unequivocal one. The Americans had no intention of embarking on direct military intervention in the area. They did not even seem to be thinking of indirect military intervention in the form of participation in a combined naval force which would either open the Straits of Tiran or threaten such action. The Americans did not intervene in the war to the extent of even a single soldier, one aircraft, or one ship (other than the unfortunate *Liberty*). The Six-Day War was fought by the Israeli army alone, with weapons that were mostly not of American but of French, British, or Israeli manufacture.

The results of the Six-Day War—the Arab defeat, the build-up of the Israeli and Arab armies, the closing of the Suez Canal, with its attendant effects on the world's economy (one of many examples being the revolutionizing of shipping and of tanker construction), the errors and failures of the heightening of the Soviet Union and her involvement in the Mediterranean region and the Middle East, far-reaching changes in the United States' status in the Middle East, a series of changes and revolutions in the Arab world which have only just begun—all have resulted in repercussions of enormous global significance.

THE UNITED STATES BALANCE SHEET

On the debit side of the United States' balance sheet in this part of the world after the Six-Day War must be entered, first of all, the undermining of her previously not-too-brilliant status among the Arabs. There was not an Arab country where hatred toward the U. S. did not deepen somewhat, as was formally expressed by the severance of diplomatic relations with the U. S. by many of the Arab States. Of course, this time around Nasser could not, as he had done in 1956 in the case of the English and the French, convince the Arab world that the United States had participated directly—with troops and aircraft—in the hostilities, and contributed to the Israeli victory. Evidence to the contrary was too strong. He did, however, manage to represent the United States as the greatest, and indeed the only, supporter of "Israel the aggressor," and as the power which, by reason of this unqualified support (in this neither Nasser nor his successors lacked proof—especially once the U. S. became Israel's great supplier of modern weapons and huge financial aid), was now the Arabs' chief enemy.

This simple theory went straight to the heart of the defeated Arabs. It did a great deal to ease their profound dejection after the 1967 rout. If all Israel's strength had been vested in her by mighty America, then the Arabs were not dealing with a mere three million Jews, but with the world's mightiest power "ruled by Jewish-Zionist interests."

Hence the blind belief that the disaster which had come upon the Arabs had been wrought by a malevolent imperialist world power. Its status in the Middle East having been undermined, the United States directly and indirectly lost influence and bases. With magnificent promptitude and skill the Soviets exploited this hostility toward the Americans. The Americans lost out not only to the Soviets, but also to the French, who made a "small fortune" out of their inimical attitude toward Israel and regained a little sympathy (not to mention a little oil) in the Arab states.

Also on the debit side of the balance sheet may be entered the United States' distress and embarrassment deriving from the feeling that Israel was exclusively her client. This distress existed in a segment of American public opinion and was also felt in American contacts with many countries in both the East and the West. This was even more obviously felt during and after the Yom Kippur War.

The United States was in a troubled and somber mood. At a time when American public opinion was screaming for no further intervention or involvement in little wars (now that American military involvement in Indochina was winding down) and clamored for the reduction or cessation of foreign aid; when poverty, unemployment, crime, the racial problem, the drug crisis, and other issues were crying out to be solved—at such a time it was not easy for American administration to explain their assistance to Israel. Had it not been for the close affinity of American Jewry to Israel, one wonders how the government could have "sold" the people its activities in behalf of Israel since the Six-Day War. The Jews of the United States were helping the government to explain acts which, while they did benefit Israel, were not all motivated by love of Israel and were in part clearly aimed at preserving the vested interests of American power.

Israel, by not conforming to every caprice of American policy, by conducting a policy of her own while at the same time accepting the aid from the United States, caused that country not a few headaches and not a little discomfort.

On the credit side of her balance sheet, as a result of the Israeli victory of 1967 the United States was able to enter some very impressive achievements. It is always pleasant to be on the winning side. If the United States was to be falsely accused of having made a favorite son of the "Israeli David," it was well for her not to have made a wrong choice. In this case she put her money on the winning horse and thereby made not a little psychological profit.

Unlike the situation in Vietnam, where the United States backed the weak side, or in Korea, where she barely managed to achieve a draw, American money was well invested in Israel. The arms she sold Israel were in the best of hands. The Israelis resembled North Vietnam in the sense that they absorbed the weaponry of their supporter, America, and used them with great skill; whereas the Egyptians received arms from the Soviets but had difficulty absorbing and making use of them, just as the South Vietnamese had trouble absorbing American arms.

Moreover—and this was far more important—the Arabs, with all their hostility toward the United States over its support for Israel, discovered that America alone held the principal, and perhaps the only, key to influence and pressure upon Israel. Hence, aware of their own weakness, they concluded that they had to try to reestablish contact with the United States, so that the latter would "persuade" or "force" Israel to retreat and restore the territories. Moreover, despite their frustration, despite (or perhaps because of) their hatred for America, the Arabs began to respect the United States for having succeeded in defeating them ("through Israel"): they admired American arms and American techniques, since it is psychologically easier to admire the Phantom jet as a sophisticated technical instrument than to acknowledge the superiority of the Israeli pilot who flies it.

Hence, paradoxically, American prestige in the Arab states

increased after 1967, and the Americans, who did not really deserve it, made excellent use of the fact. They played a brilliant game of poker with the Israeli cards in their hands—and this at an immeasurably smaller price than they paid in Korea or Vietnam.

Indirectly, the United States also gained in strength in those Arab states that have not repudiated her presence, such as Saudi Arabia, Jordan, and Morocco. The U.S. also tried, again by skillfully playing her Israeli cards, to regain admittance and influence in "socialist" and "progressive" Arab states, which discovered that the Soviets alone (who to date have neither presence in nor influence upon Israel) could not help them.

Also on the credit side of the Six-Day War balance sheet, the Americans recorded the closure of the Suez Canal, the isolation of the Soviet fleet in the Mediterranean from the fleet in the Red Sea and the Indian Ocean, and the difficulties experienced by the Soviets in shipping supplies to their allies in Vietnam.

Indirectly the credit side of the American global balance sheet also included the billions of rubles and the gigantic Soviet effort invested in the Arab states. These tremendous investments, at least in the economic sense, caused the Soviets what the Vietnam War caused the United States: the pouring of resources into a bottomless barrel, with an attendant weakening of the economy and deprivation of development projects within the Soviet Union itself.

A belief which the United States also exploited on all fronts —the Arab, the Soviet, the Chinese, the European, and the African—was that America held the key to the opening of the Suez Canal. If America waved a magic wand or policeman's truncheon over Israel, the latter would retreat from the canal, which would then be opened, to the benefit or detriment of the various interested parties with whom the United States had dealings.

And finally the Americans were also able to chalk up another asset: Israel served as an unparalleled testing ground for modern, sophisticated American weapons (just as Egypt and Syria served as a testing ground for Soviet weapons). These American weapons were in good hands. The price the United States paid for this testing ground was a low one, for prior to the Yom Kippur War the arms were not given to Israel but were sold for dollars.

The Yom Kippur War made Israel even much more dependent on the United States than before both for its weaponry and budget. On the other hand, the American administration, with Dr. Kissinger, very skillfully exploited all the old and new cards in her hand and enhanced even more than before its standing with all the Arab states, including Egypt and Syria. Dr. Kissinger has shown that only the United States can deliver some goods to the Arabs, and only the United States can act as an honest broker between the parties. Coming on top of the renewed U.S.–China relations and the detente with the Soviets, U.S. prestige throughout the entire world was considerably enhanced.

MUTUAL RELATIONS

It is important to understand that Israel's great dependence on the United States since the Yom Kippur War—and not for one moment should our dependence on American political support and aid in armaments and monies be derided—does not consist of favors being bestowed upon us, nor does it constitute an exclusive dependence. Between us and the United States there exist, and it is proper that there should exist, mutual relations, if not as between equals, then at least as between two sides neither of which is exclusively a donor or exclusively a recipient. The situation is complex and involved, since the interests at work are partly common to both and partly mutually contradictory.

Israel must not be caught up in or maneuver herself into a position of absolute dependence on the United States. She must not come to resemble other states that are American creations, which are so deeply dependent upon her that she accords them scant consideration when plotting what moves to make. Relations of this kind are bad for any people or state; they are utterly devoid of mutual respect and in the final analysis will arouse, on the part of the dependent, recipient state, an attitude of hatred toward the donor state. Dozens of examples can be cited of states in Europe, Latin America, Asia, and Africa that have received large-scale assistance of all kinds from the United States and have repaid her with enmity and hostility.

Complete vassaldom could prove calamitous for us: first, because it is not our true situation, and second, because if we begin to believe that we are becoming a mere satellite or a "colony" of Washington, or begin to wonder where we would be without her, then we shall lose some of our greatest assets, particularly our great pride in our distinctiveness and in the fact that all that has taken place here—the Zionist enterprise, the founding of the State of Israel—are independent, original Jewish-Zionist achievements.

Since the beginning of our undertaking, we have had recourse to the assistance of nations and world powers. We have always sought allies and supporters among the nations of the world. It was a very hard job, perhaps one of the hardest, that the founders of our enterprise had to tackle. Herzl, Weizmann, Ben-Gurion, and many other leaders were perpetually knocking at the gates of the world's powers, asking for understanding and help; but they never groveled. They never said, "Come and build us a state," or "Help us establish a Jewish society." Our pride, nourished by our unique achievements in this country, enabled us to stand up straight.

At different periods of our undertaking we had recourse to the assistance of world powers: the Turks, the British, the French. They responded favorably only as long as their interests coincided with ours. We are now being aided by the United States, and precisely because this aid is so massive and the political risks inherent in its acceptance are so great, we must constantly remind both ourselves and the Americans that it was not the United States that founded the Zionist enterprise and the State of Israel. American government aid to Israel (as distinct from the assistance of American Jewry) was for many long years quite marginal. Up to and including the 1948 War of Independence this aid was distinctly limited; and although from 1948 to the Six-Day War it was very important, it was still far from being extraordinary. Even today, after the Yom Kippur War, American aid to Israel is only a small fraction of what the U.S. has spent in Vietnam.

The social, economic, and political pattern of the Zionist undertaking was hardly influenced at all by American models. We ourselves cast every die, every mold. Israeli agricultural and industrial projects are our own original creation. We never asked for or received American "advisory" missions to tell us how and what to do in this or that sphere. We did seek to learn methods of implementation from many, including the Americans, but we imitated no one, and certainly not the Americans. We never accepted their dictates. At the most, we took only their advice.

The Americans did not give us plans for building a kibbutz or a moshav, a trade-unions federation, a cooperative movement, social or governmental institutions. Neither did the Americans have any part in the setting up of our national army. Our army was an absolutely original Israeli creation.

Now, when American weapons make up the backbone of the air force, the armored corps, and other Israeli army corps, our doctrine in no way resembles that of the arms suppliers. We absorb the weapons from them, learn how to operate them, and use them in our own way, in accordance with our own special needs.

These are truths that we must constantly reiterate to ourselves so that our national backbone is not injured. This does not mean that we, a small state and a small people, are not subject to the influence of other peoples, including the Americans. And indeed who in Western and even Eastern society is not affected by currents of thought, patterns of living, and behavioral norms deriving from America? We too have come under the influence of the American life-style, music, technology, and patterns of behavior, which have flowed out over almost the whole world.

Moreover, because of our unique ties with six million American Jews, who are themselves among the pacesetters and the fashion arbiters in their country, we are even more open to these influences. Many ties already exist between us and the Jews of America. There is today in Israel a colony (in the cultural and sociological sense) of some tens of thousands of American Jews, those who have immigrated to Israel and those who come to attend our universities.

This American group has no parallel to other groups of American settlers outside their own country. If it should continue to grow, as we hope and wish, this little land will in future generations incorporate an assemblage of hundreds of thousands of Jews from the United States, who will bring with them American cultural assets and behavior patterns. But this is to be entirely separated from any notion of our exclusive dependence on America.

FIELDS OF MANEUVER

We must make it clear, to ourselves and the Americans, just how far we will go along with them and from exactly what point we shall go it alone or with others. We must also be quite clear in our minds just how far the Americans are prepared to go along with us and from what point they will go it alone or with others.

It is within this fairly wide area that we must maneuver, and to this end we must tell ourselves and the Americans what we want, what our war objectives and our peace objectives are, what principles we would die for sooner than betray, and what sort of Israel we want.

Just as we scrutinize ourselves, it is fitting that we should scrutinize the Americans too, so as to learn within what bounds they are ready and willing to maneuver with us.

Israel's existence, as well as the granting of aid to her economic, social, military, and technological development, have been axiomatic for every American administration. The most active and influential factor in this commitment is the tremendous identification of American Jewry with Israel. This force is not measured in American politics solely in terms of the Jewish vote, although that is a factor not to be ignored. A population six million strong, of high social and economic standing, concentrated in a few key states, constitutes a fairly weighty factor at election time. There is a theory that there is no Jewish vote in the United States. Perhaps on many American issues the theory holds true, but as far as Israel's existence is concerned, the Jewish vote is very much a fact.

In any foreseeable future, every American president or potential president must lend an ear to the American Jewish constituency. If he abandons or appears to American Jewry to be abandoning Israel, he will be inflicting significant injury on a segment of American voters, and they will return hurt for hurt. Apart from the Jews, Israel enjoys the true sympathy of many non-Jewish citizens of the United States, and this factor too affects the deliberations of the American government.

Apart from public opinion and the electorate, American global interests also dictate that the administration guard the existence of a strong Israel. It can be said that if Israel had not existed, she would have had to be invented. The use the Americans are making of this asset has already been described. The Americans will therefore do a great deal for us, and will go a long way to help us preserve our existence. But this road has, from their standpoint, a boundary beyond which they will not pass. That frontier is—direct involvement in combat in the area and the danger of becoming involved in a conventional or nuclear war.

Subsequent to Vietnam, and for the foreseeable future, every

American president will operate under the supreme interdiction of not sending American troops to be killed over anything less than a threat to the very existence of the United States. Israel's existence, we should clearly understand, is less, very much less, than that. With all the importance that we, and the Americans, ascribe to our existence, Israel is not Hawaii, not Alaska, not even the Straits of Panama.

The Americans will help us fight, but they will not fight for us. They will not shed their blood for our existence. They will not engage the Soviet fleet on our account.

No American president will declare war in our behalf against any one of the Arab states, and certainly not against the Soviets. Even if he were to declare war, neither Congress nor the American people would support him.

The Americans will do a great deal to prevent war: they will warn the Arabs, the Soviets, and perhaps also the Chinese not to intervene; but they will not go beyond severe warnings and threats. We saw this in 1948, 1967, and 1973, and we must see it now too.

Any one of us who demands that the Americans give us a commitment for direct military intervention, or that they enter a military alliance with us, is asking something that for the Americans is psychologically impossible. This does not exclude American guarantees being given for our security within multinational or international great-power frameworks.

We must not try to draw the Americans beyond this line, first, because we will not succeed in the attempt, and second, because we would be placing American Jewry in an untenable position. As long as they are urging their government to do its utmost to help Israel in all spheres, they stand upon firm ground as American citizens, desiring the good of both their country and Israel. Even when they say that as Jewish American citizens they will volunteer to fight in person if Israel should go to war again, they are still on safe ground. But they cannot dissociate themselves from the general national American consensus which now says that never again will Americans shed their blood except in direct defense of their country, or over something that appears to the American people as a whole to be of supreme national interest. Direct war over Israel's existence does not fall within the framework of this consensus.

We and the Americans are in agreement that until viable arrangements leading to peace are attained our soldiers will not move from their positions on the cease-fire lines, wherever those lines may be. The Americans agree with us that certain changes will be made in the borderlines of a future map of Israel. In their thinking, such changes are meaningful. They agree, for example, that the Gaza Strip should not be returned to Egypt or have a common border with Egypt. They agree that there should be certain changes in our favor in the future borders between us and our eastern neighbor (Jordanian Palestine), and that there should be a change in the status of Jerusalem. They agree that a formula must be found to enable us to remain on the Golan Heights. They agree that any territory returned should be demilitarized and effectively inspected, and that we should enjoy special status in the Straits of Tiran.

Their outlook on this issue is not final or fully crystallized (indeed, is our own outlook final or fully crystallized?). Perhaps it is precisely because we have not hammered out our view or made it clear to them that they have arrived at a doctrine of their own. I well remember some talks I conducted on various occasions with members of President Johnson's administration after the Six-Day War. They implored us, "Tell us what you want," "Make some clear proposals," and added, not always cordially, "You are sensible, intelligent people; think of something that we would find reasonable and would be able to defend."

Our polemics with the Americans on this topic have lasted for over six years. It has sometimes been an arid discussion, but it still offers scope for maneuver. I believe that had we hammered out a clear doctrine concerning Israel's future borders, along the lines of what has been said in the foregoing chapters, we would have been able to explain it to the Americans—and others.

Another area that concerns the Americans is that of their vested interests in the Arab states. The Americans have not given them up. They are holding on to everything they can: oil interests first and foremost, but also any position that gains them political, cultural, and other influence in the Arab countries. They are doing and will do everything to expand those interests.

Despite a trend toward disengagement, the United States is neither willing nor able to become a second-class power in the near future. Her tremendous economic and physical weight dictates that she express an opinion and hold interests of her own in every region of the twentieth-century world and the world that succeeds it.

These interests have dictated, continue to dictate, and will in the future dictate the line of American policy. It has not always been the same as our own in the past, nor is it likely always to be so in the future. We must be fully aware of this fact. We must correctly assess our strength and our potential. Let us not regard every American step that is not precisely in accordance with our wishes and needs as "obstinacy," "foolishness," "shortsightedness," or even "anti-Israelism." We must proceed on the elementary supposition that the United States knows what is best for herself in the Middle East; that she has a policy which is first and foremost pro-American and only afterward pro or anti someone or something else (do not we ourselves act on the elementary consideration of what is good for the Jews?).

As to our side of it, the Americans too must realize that we are prepared to go along with them, but only within certain limits. They must clearly understand our "annihilation complex," and be aware that in the future we shall fight for our survival with the same ferocity as in the past. The minute we feel that the Arabs are about to set upon us and try to defeat us in battle—either alone, with the help of the Soviets, or with the help of any other party—we shall strike, perhaps even preemptively, with all our might. In this matter we shall not wait for directives or dictates from them or anyone else. We shall fight for the existence of the state within the cease-fire borders, and if necessary we will also fight beyond those borders. We shall fight with American and other weapons; we shall fight with all the deterrent force, striking power, element of surprise, and resourcefulness at our disposal. The Americans must understand that we shall not ask or wait for anyone to come over and save us.

The Americans should realize that in a war we shall not act with gentleness. We shall not play according to the interpower and global rules of the game. On the whole international chessboard we have only one piece—and that is ourselves and our state. Unlike the Arabs, the Americans, the Soviets, and others, we cannot afford to lose a piece and then expect to win the game. Once we have lost the piece named the State of Israel—we have lost all.

Our local tinderbox could set ablaze a furious regional and universal conflagration. Let the Americans realize this fact and draw the appropriate conclusions: if Israel possesses deterrent power and self-confidence, that dreadful day is less likely to arrive. It happened in 1967 and 1973 that we fought alone, and world peace was endangered; if such a situation should recur it could be far more menacing than ever to world peace. A strong Israel stands a fair chance of averting such an outcome.

The Americans must understand our "obstinacy" with the Arabs regarding peace maps. They already know we are prepared to restore territories but they must understand that such restoration (meaning not intermediate, partial, or temporary settlements, though these are good in themselves) can come about only after meaningful peace arrangements.

It is we, and not the Americans or anyone else, who must be convinced that we are talking with the Arabs about peace and not about substitutes for peace, and that they honestly intend to build a true peace and put an end to the conflict between us. The Arabs are still toying with the hope that all the United States needs to do is to "squeeze Israel like an orange," and stop rendering her aid and assistance, for Israel to hand them back the territories. There are also Americans who think the same way. This is a fundamental error. Any Israeli government that is prepared to restore territories must be ready to show itself to be tough as regards the way such a restoration is to be carried out and what Israel receives in exchange, and also as regards the shape of the peace that will come into being after such a restoration.

We must try very hard to find allies and partners in addition to the United States. If we are successful, our relations with the Americans will be considerably eased. In her relations with the United States, Israel must avoid becoming a one-dimensional object. This is not good for her, nor is it good for the United States. Israel must seek and find multidimensionalism in her relations with the nations of the world.

9

THE SOVIET UNION

TOWARD THE WARM WATERS

On the face of it our relations with the Soviet Union would appear to be devastatingly simple: we stand face to face with a superpower which is using the Arab-Israeli dispute as a battering ram with which to demolish the West's last remaining ramparts in the region. They are arming the Arabs to the teeth and instructing them on the use of these arms against us. This power, it would seem, sides wholeheartedly with the Arabs, supports their every stand against us, rigs every international forum everywhere in the world with obstacles against us, and incites the whole Soviet-aligned Communist camp against us. As a great power with an anti-Zionist tradition of several decades, and an anti-Semitic tradition of centuries, she harnesses both hates to the anti-Israeli chariot thundering head on against us.

If relations between the Soviets and ourselves were truly so simple, unequivocal, and final, we should be obliged to write them off. We would scratch out their name and say to ourselves, "This is a hopeless undertaking, a lost cause. This gigantic power is wholly malevolent and desires only to destroy us as a people and as a state. We have nothing to seek from her, because we shall find nothing but enmity."

But relations between the Soviet Union and Israel are far more complex and involved than they appear to be. As with American-Israeli relations, there are factors at work here, such as the regional aspects of Soviet global policy and the internal Jewish-Zionist aspects of the Soviet domestic scene, which are inextricably interconnected and intertwined.

"The Holy One, blessed be He, did Israel a kindness by dispersing them among the nations"—so said our sages. The adage contains a grain of contemporary truth. It so happens that the two greatest Jewish Diasporas are to be found within the two superpowers. Each of these Diasporas vastly complicates the life of its superpower on account of the Israel-Arab problem. The tableau of relations between the Soviet Union and ourselves, which at first glance appears starkly black, should be carefully scrutinized; it may be that an observant eye will detect certain other shades, certain grays, which in the future may well brighten.

In examining the relations of the Soviets with the Arabs, and the Soviet Union's trends in the Middle East, it should not be forgotten that these are identical with Russians and Russian trends. This is true not only because the Russian people is the dominant people in the Soviet Union, but also because—and this is the main point—the Middle East at present is inextricably bound up with Russian trends, traditions, and intentions of the past.

In a certain sense it may be said that these relations had their beginnings in the clash between the Byzantine Greek Orthodox Empire and the Arab Islamic Empire. When the former were defeated by the latter, the Russian czars and the Pravoslav Church regarded themselves as the true heirs to the Eastern Roman Empire; and indeed the influence of the Christian Byzantine civilization and religion upon Russia was very great.

Over the course of generations the Muslim Arab Empire became the Muslim Ottoman Empire. It conquered and totally razed Christian Byzantium and began to clash with the Russian Empire. Even before the clash with the Ottoman armies, the forces of Christian Russia had fought ceaseless wars with Mongol and Tatar tribes, who had accepted the religion of Islam and brandished the sword of Muhammad against the bearers of the Pravoslav cross.

These long wars—first against the khans of the "golden horde," and later, for many centuries, against the caliphs: the Muslim Ottoman sultans—had patently imperialistic motives deriving from a will-to-expansion: that of the Ottomans (northward, into European and Asiatic Russia); and that of the Russians (southward, to the territories of the former Byzantine Empire). These wars also had a religious motivation; they were Islamic holy wars against Christianity. As was usual in those days —and to some extent today as well—all these motifs interlocked and were mutually sustaining.

In the days of the great czars and czarinas—Peter, Catherine, and their heirs—war against the Ottoman Empire became a supreme imperative for the Russians. They aspired to expel the Ottomans from the whole of Europe and free the Slavic peoples struggling beneath the Ottoman Islamic yoke. They dreamed of reaching the warm waters of the Mediterranean and slashing through the noose of the Dardanelles. They aspired to conquer Istanbul, to restore the ancient glory of Christian Constantinople, and liberate the Christian holy places in Jerusalem and Palestine from the Muslims.

The wars between the Russian Empire and the Ottoman Empire continued for more than two hundred years. Now this side had the upper hand and now that; but at last the Russians edged the Ottomans farther and farther south. By these and additional conquests in the Caucasus and central Asia, the Russian Empire "absorbed" a large Muslim population, a factor which has influenced Russian policy.

Were it not for the conflict of imperialist interests in the Middle East between the Russians and the British, and also to a certain extent the French, the Russians could have changed the face of the Middle East beyond recognition by the eighteenth and nineteenth centuries. They might well have realized their dream and gained control of most parts of the Ottoman Empire, including the eastern Mediterranean basin and the Holy Land. Only strong British support of the Ottomans by political means and force of arms saved them from a Russian conquest. (It should not be forgotten that in the Crimean War, British and French Christians fought shoulder to shoulder with Ottoman and Egyptian Muslims against Russian Christians and that the casus belli was the holy places of Palestine.)

The Russian czars did not despair of the Middle East even at the beginning of the twentieth century. With the outbreak of World War I, when the Russians made common cause with the British and the French against the Germans, Austrians, and Ottomans, they regarded the occupation of Constantinople as one of their primary war objectives. They believed that this time, with the British on their side, they would be able to crush the declining Ottoman Empire and at long last divide it among three Christian empires: the Russian, British, and French. The Russians indeed contracted agreements in this matter with the British and French right at the beginning of the war.

But World War I ended in a way that had not been anticipated. The Ottoman Empire was vanquished, but an independent Turkey arose on part of its ruins, and the balance of the Middle East was divided between Britain and France. The Russian Empire became the Union of Soviet Socialist Republics. One of the first steps taken by the young Soviet Union was to expose the secret agreements about the sharing of the Ottoman Empire. Soviet Russia declared that she neither had nor would ever have any part in these "imperialist plots."

During the first years of its existence the USSR turned inward. It began to salve its wounds and build Communism in its own country and in its own way. But an age-old dream is not easily forgotten. The Georgian cobbler's son from the town of Gori, Joseph Vissarionovich Dzhugashvili—Stalin, who later became one of the greatest dictators in human history, was not the

246 / LAND OF THE HART

man to forget or allow others to forget these "oriental" dreams. As a native of the Caucasus, the borderland and battleground of the Christian north and the Muslim south and the area of encounter of Eastern and Western civilizations, Stalin continued to dream of Soviet penetration into the Middle East.

The method of penetration was different now, and during the 1920s the Soviets began to use it. They founded Communist underground parties in the states that arose on the ruins of the Ottoman Empire. This move was part of a global strategy of founding Communist parties everywhere, each connected by an umbilical cord to the Comintern in Moscow and blindly obeying Stalin's directives.

The Comintern set up a Middle East Department. Through its ties with the fledgling Communist parties in Egypt, Syria, Lebanon, Iraq, and Mandatory Palestine during the 1920s and 1930s, it began to penetrate into the Middle East.

Even in those early years the Soviet Communists understood that they could exploit the existence of a Jewish Zionist enterprise, under the imperialist British Mandate, in order to gain the support of the Arab world. They decided to turn the Communist parties into an anti-Zionist tool and thereby gain for themselves the affection of the Arab world, regardless of the fact that Communist atheism was in direct contradiction to Islam. Through their anti-Zionist stand these Communist parties succeeded in receiving Arab sanction. During the 1920s and 1930s Arab Communists were in the forefront of anti-Zionist activity. The Communist dialectic had no trouble finding an ideological sanction for cooperation between antireligious Arab Communists and other Arab nationalists, on whose banners were emblazoned extreme religious slogans. All was fair that would consecrate the objective: the liberation of the Arabs from the yoke of "British-French-Zionist imperialism."

With the German invasion of the Soviet Union in 1941, the Soviets entered into an alliance with the British, American, and French "imperialists." They discontinued their harassment of these allies in all arenas of the world, including the Middle East. When World War II ended in an Allied victory, it fell to the Soviet Union to make the great Russian dreams in Europe and the Far East come true. At a terrible cost in human life, the Soviet Union quite unceremoniously and with unadorned directness occupied and annexed hundreds of thousands of square miles of Eastern Europe and populations numbering in the tens of millions. She surrounded herself with a defensive belt of East European states, which she bound to herself with political, ideological, and military ties.

Stalin tried to take advantage of the world's postwar weakness and confusion to penetrate the Mediterranean Sea in the direction of the Persian Gulf. The Soviet army got a foothold in Persian Azerbaijan and "forgot" to leave. Only strong British and Western pressure moved it back within its bounds. Yugoslavia was seen by Stalin as a Soviet protégé, with an attractive Mediterranean coastline suited to his objectives. Only Tito's rebellion stopped the Soviets from keeping it for good. Resolute eleventh-hour Anglo-American intervention in Greece prevented a Communist takeover, which would have led to its being severed from the Western powers and being converted into a Soviet political and military base in the Mediterranean.

THE RED STAR AND THE SHIELD OF DAVID

Together with these attempts at penetration, the Soviets also directed their attention to the Arab nationalist liberation movements aimed against the British and French. They saw in them a potential instrument for Soviet ends and hoped that the support and encouragement they gave these movements would cause the British and French to abandon the Middle East, leaving a power vacuum which the Soviets would then proceed to penetrate. During those fateful years from 1945–48 the Soviets encountered what was for them a strange situation: the Zionists too were rebelling and fighting the British. The Soviet reaction to this singular phenomenon was itself strange and exceptional: at the most crucial hour in its history, Zionism was accorded Soviet aid.

The Soviets later tried, with characteristic facility but without complete success, to gloss over this "shameful" chapter in their Middle Eastern policy. But the Jews, the Zionists, and the State of Israel will never forget. We shall always remember, nor shall we let the world forget, that in 1947 the resolution for the founding of a Jewish and Arab state in western Palestine would not have been passed by the United Nations had not the Soviets given it their active support. We shall not forget that in 1948, when we were fighting a desperate war for Israel's independence, the Soviets, through the agency of Czechoslovakia (and at full purchase price, which detracts not one whit from the act itself), sent us a large quantity of arms which at the time weighted the campaign in our favor. We shall not forget that no sooner was the state founded than the Soviet Union was vying with the United States as to who would be the first to recognize the young state and who would send the first ambassador.

To understand the rapid cooling of Soviet-Israeli relations in 1949 and the early 1950s, we should first examine the Jewish domestic situation in the Soviet Union. For the present we shall simply note the fact that toward the end of Stalin's life, an icy wind began blowing in our direction from Moscow. During those years the Soviets were trying very hard to penetrate every crack and fissure in the Middle East. One such crack, which in the course of time became an open door, was the Arab-Israeli dispute. The resentment and frustration of the defeated Arab states grew after 1948. The Soviets took advantage of Egypt's keen desire to throw the British out of the country, and of the 1952 "officers' revolution," which shook the whole edifice of monarchical rule in Egypt and at once joined Egypt to the international nonaligned camp, with Nasser becoming one of its leaders.

Barely three years after the Nasserist revolution, Egypt was already prepared to sign her first arms deal with the Soviet bloc (ironically, through the agency of Czechoslovakia). Also at about that time the Soviet Union began courting and arming "revolutionary" Syria.

The Israeli victory in the Sinai in 1956 and the British-French failure in their invasion of Suez were further highly powerful catalysts in the Soviet penetration of Egypt. More arms shipments arrived from the Soviet Union; Soviet advisers and instructors began the rehabilitation of the Egyptian army. Nasser's policy, in both foreign and domestic spheres, took on a more marked Egyptian-style "socialistic" character. All these served to open wide the gates of Egypt to the Soviets. A similar constantly accelerating process occurred during the late 1950s in Syria and in other Arab states as well.

Some people—mainly Americans and West Europeans—claim that were it not for Israel's existence, the Soviets would not have expanded and penetrated the Middle East. This is a naive assertion at best, and at worst takes on a malicious anti-Semitic coloration. Russian penetration of the Middle East began long before the Zionist enterprise in Palestine.

In recent years the Soviets have, of course, exploited the Arab-Israeli dispute—but that was not all they exploited. They deepened their penetration of Egypt as a result of the arrogant and obstinate policy of John Foster Dulles, who refused to finance the Aswan Dam with American money. This shortsightedness on his part had nothing to do with the Arab-Israeli dispute. Had the Americans financed the construction of the dam and built it with their capital and know-how, things would have turned out very differently in the Middle East.

The Soviets took advantage of the Kassem revolution in Iraq, striking deep into that country with money, know-how, and arms. They made good use of the time prior to the British evacuation of Aden and of the vacuum created in this southern part of the Arabian Peninsula. Similar events occurred in Sudan, Algeria, Somalia, and other states that lie very remote from the arena of the Arab-Israeli dispute.

THE SIX-DAY AND THE YOM KIPPUR WARS

In the Middle East the Soviets have conducted themselves in the best tradition of the "classic" European empires, which sought spheres of influence, markets, bases, and colonies in this part of the world. One of their classic mistakes was their handling of the Israeli-Arab conflict prior to the Six-Day War.

If one assumes that in 1967 the Soviet Union was interested in helping to build up tension along the Israel-Syria border and to "inflame" the Arab governments just a little more against Israel so as to bind them more closely to herself; that she did not want to spark a tremendous blaze leading to all-out military confrontation between Israel and the Arabs—then she displayed a vast and dangerous lack of understanding both as regards "her" Arabs and as regards Israel.

As realistic and as cautious as they were, the Soviets apparently did not understand the psychology of the Arabs, did not realize what their boiling point was, and did not guess with what speed they could work themselves up to that point.

Neither did the Soviets correctly gauge the full force of the lust for revenge upon Israel that burned in Arab hearts. They did not recognize the special sense of pride which sometimes prevented the Arabs from "taking orders" from anyone and forced Arab leaders to take risks without giving consideration to the outcome, because they were anxious not to lose face.

If the Soviets are not to be suspected of having been fully confident from the outset that the Israelis would beat the Arabs (and their marks in Machiavellianism are probably not that high), then they made a very great mistake in their assessment of the Arab side.

In 1967 the Soviets also failed to understand the Israelis and their reactions. Chuvakhin, the last Soviet ambassador in Israel, was discharged after the Six-Day War and made the scapegoat, the man responsible for the error in assessing Israel's situation. The error was not attributable to just one man, however, but to the entire Soviet apparatus and system.

Although they had good espionage and intelligence in Israel, the Soviets did not grasp the nature or the quality of the Israeli army, or how much force it could mobilize for the fray. They undoubtedly knew the precise number of tanks, guns, and aircraft the Israeli army possessed, and its strength under total mobilization, but they did not ascribe the proper weight to this order of battle. They judged the Israeli army by routine and accepted yardsticks. They probably rated the regular army highly and the reserve army much lower. If they gave the regular brigades' mobility and striking power an X, then they would have assessed the reserve brigades at half-X. Indeed, any sensible Soviet intelligence officer, thinking in routine terms, could not but suppose that when an army very rapidly mobilizes "peasants" from kolkhoz- and sovkhoz-like villages (kibbutz and moshav members) and mixes them with industrial workers, shopkeepers, clerks, taxi drivers, and teachers to create a reserve brigade, such a brigade can hardly compare with a regular brigade. They assumed that it was vastly inferior to a regular brigade, especially when these reservists were carried into battle by buses, bread-delivery vans, and used civilian tenders. Who would not judge such a brigade to be very inferior on seeing that its troops were manning outdated World War II tanks?

This erroneous military assessment arose from a source far deeper than mere routine thinking. Very many echelons in the Soviet army, and therefore in military intelligence too, are staffed by three types of officers: those who have somewhat forgotten the object lessons of their own wars, including the war against the Germans; those who are too young to have taken part in any war at all and have been educated solely on maneuvers and textbook solutions; and those who think in terms of a global war, with the simultaneous participation of tens of thousands of tanks, thousands of aircraft, and hundreds of warships. Soviet army officers, of all people, should on the face of it have been very well aware (far more so than the Americans) of the strength of the Israeli army. They only needed to recall how the

Russians once used unconventional methods in their own wars; the surprise attacks and flanking movements by semiregular light cavalry (the cossacks); Kutuzov's surprise tactics in the 1812 war; and the partisan brigades and labor and peasant forces that were quickly trained and recruited to defend Stalingrad, Leningrad, and the suburbs of Moscow during World War II. They should have remembered that Russian strength derived from an awareness of having no alternative and from the knowledge of what they were fighting for and whom they were defending. Had the Soviet generals and statesmen compared us to themselves in their hardest and greatest days, they would have reached the conclusion that we would fight the way we did and advance as far as our armies advanced.

The Soviet error also derived from another factor, which it is important to dwell on because it is relevant both to the present and the future. Soviet understanding is defective not only on Zionism but also on the structure of Israeli democracy. According to reports received by them in 1967, our government was divided, vacillating, and stammering, slow to make decisions; and the country was also in a difficult social and economic situation. There was an economic slowdown, unemployment, and tension between ethnic communities. To the Soviets, trained in centralization and monolithism, it seemed that an Israeli regime which indulged in hairsplitting arguments, where everything was exposed and open, where "leakages" were legitimate, where all the dirty wash was laundered in broad daylight —that such a people and government were quite incapable of uniting and fighting for their lives.

In the Soviet Union the Six-Day War and its outcome produced stupefaction and a loss of prestige at home and abroad: their side had lost, the equipment they were so proud of had been destroyed, and their military advice in the planning of the war had turned out to be so much nonsense. This Soviet loss of prestige increased the ferment in the Communist countries and influenced Chinese anti-Soviet thinking.

After the Six-Day War the Soviets took a few hasty steps dictated only by great chagrin and not by cold logic. One of these was the severance of relations with Israel, which put them outside the circle of powers able to influence both Israel and the Arabs. They maneuvered themselves into a position in which they could play either themselves or the Arabs only on the Middle Eastern political chessboard. There is very good reason to believe that after the Yom Kippur War and even more so with the start of the Geneva talks, the Soviets regret this hasty decision and will try to correct it.

On the other hand, it is very important to note that even in the Arabs' hardest hours during the Six-Day War, when the magnitude of their defeat was already apparent, the Soviets did not enter the war directly. Neither did they threaten to enter and intervene directly, as Bulganin had done in the Sinai Campaign in 1956. The factors operating here were not only what was said on the hot line between Moscow and Washington, but also Soviet realism and the supreme imperative governing Soviet leaders, which dictates that they exert all their power and ability not to become directly involved in a war in which the blood of Soviet soldiers will be shed, and take no actual part in fighting unless it is vital to the homeland or in the very highest interests of the state. Important as the Middle East may be in their eyes, it is not so important as to warrant the shedding of Soviet blood. It is very probable that even their saber-rattling and threats during the pivotal phases of the Yom Kippur War, when the Israeli army was advancing toward Cairo and Damascus, were empty. But Israel could not afford to play this game of Russian roulette.

When the initial shock of the Six-Day War wore off, the Soviets understood that they must quickly rebuild the ruins of what had been the armies of Egypt and Syria to a point from which they would be able in the future to attempt another leap.

Within two years they had already resupplied their Arab armies with everything they had lost, plus various extras, especially guided missiles. What they had forfeited in prestige the Soviets tried to make up for by a campaign of anti-Israel propaganda of unsurpassed virulence.

The war of attrition on the Suez Canal restored to the Soviets some of their lost prestige. The fact that two years after their defeat the Egyptians were able, with the help of modern Soviet weapons and active Soviet instruction, to fire thousands of artillery pieces; the fact that the Soviets were able to position on the west bank of the canal and other places in Egypt a mighty and sophisticated array of missiles, and that they had strengthened and reinforced their fleet in the Mediterranean—these facts, in addition to what the Soviet army had perpetrated upon Czechoslovakia in 1968, showed the world that when the issue was one they cared about, the Soviets constituted a modern world power of awesome magnitude.

Soviet policy tried to convert the Arab defeat into still another opportunity for the consolidation of their position in the whole region as the only true defender of the Arabs. At the fairly cheap cost of anti-Israeli and anti-American propaganda, the Soviets gained more sympathy and more friends in the Middle East. In addition to direct military aid, the Soviets also increased their economic and technical assistance in an attempt to strengthen their ties with the Arab states sufficiently to form binding bilateral alliances.

THE SOVIET UNION'S BALANCE SHEET

After twenty years (taking the 1955 Soviet arms deal with Egypt as a starting point) of ever-increasing Soviet intervention in the Middle East, they can draw up an interim profit-and-loss account.

Heading the credit column is the triumphant fact of their having realized the age-old Russian dream: the Soviets, heirs to the builders of the Russian Empire, are in the Middle East. Their flag flies from the masts of modern ships that are very much at home in the waters of the Mediterranean. Their missile bases cover the face of Egypt and Syria. Their sailors, pilots, and soldiers are having their photographs taken beside the pyramids and acquiring a tan under the good sun on the sands of Port Said, Alexandria, and Latakia. Their engineers are building giant dams and railways, roads and industrial plants all over the Middle East. They are buying and selling in almost the whole region.

The Soviets have gone far beyond what the early Russians dreamed about regarding the Middle East. They have converted their bases into a many-sided and multidirectional springboard: westward—to the Maghreb; eastward—to the Persian Gulf countries; southward—to Yemen, the Indian Ocean and the African continent; and northward, threatening Turkey, which they hold in a pincerlike grip. They exploited their success in the Mediterranean Sea. As one of their moves in the chess game against NATO and the Americans, they positioned a few heavy pieces near their opponents' weak flank in southern Europe, thereby threatening NATO. Entrenched in these advantageous positions, the Soviets hope that Western Europe and America will have one more reason to come to terms with them in Europe as a whole. They are planning to use the Middle East as a springboard for more distant targets, and they regard their Middle Eastern bases as part of a large flanking movement in the direction of India, Southeast Asia, and the fringes of the soft belly of China.

On the credit side of the Soviet balance sheet may also be entered the fact that the Middle East is now serving as a major field exercise for Soviet arms, military methods, and tactics, as well as a first-rate testing ground for the behavior of thousands of their men who serve as advisers and engineers and in other capacities in regions far away from home. In all these, and especially in the military field, the Soviets made many mistakes. But there can be no doubt that they learned their lessons, changed their methods, tried innovations, and endeavored to examine what the causes of the failures were and how they could be avoided in the future. These new tactics, new weapons, and new methods were tested with no little surprise and some initial success in the Yom Kippur War.

The Soviet interim balance sheet in the Middle East also has a negative side. A man, or even a whole nation, may dream a glorious dream, but when it comes to pass he may find it has some nightmarish aspects. The Soviets did indeed reach the warm waters of the Mediterranean, but they suddenly found that those waters were too hot. They reached the Middle East because of the vacuum created by the British and French evacuation, and by exploiting the weakness of the Arabs and the mistakes of their American competitors. But once they had penetrated some Arab states in depth, the "white man's burden" (formerly borne by the English and the French), which the Soviets expected would give them a sense of satisfaction, turned out to be very heavy.

In Egypt the Soviets discovered that they were dealing with a great people in possession of a way of life all its own, and that that people did not accept them. After a lengthy national struggle with British "protectors," consuls general, high commissioners, and sirdars, the Egyptians were cool to the sudden presence of Russian *polkovniks* and instructors.

Moreover, it had taken the Egyptians one hundred and seventy years, since the Napoleonic occupation, to adapt themselves to the West European, basically Franco-British civilization, and to blend this culture with their own great Muslim-Arab tradition and culture. This slow and unique blending process was far from complete when the Soviets streamed into Egypt, bringing with them different values, different ideologies, a different mentality, and a different language—a culture that was at variance with everything the Egyptians had become accustomed to over the course of generations.

It is thus not surprising that at the very outset of the "Sovietization" of Egypt, various potential and actual causes of friction came into being between the Egyptians and the Soviets. It was

THE SOVIET UNION / 257

hardly to be expected that the Egyptians would absorb the Soviet model of socialist-Communist ideology and practice. They developed antibodies to Soviet indoctrination in all spheres: military, administrational, cultural, ideological, and social.

The Soviets have one characteristic that has increased the friction between them and the Egyptians: the Soviets came to Egypt from a tightly closed and suspicious society. Outside their country, Soviet personnel were required to live in closed colonies, and they suspected and informed upon one another. The Soviets did not "open up" as did the French, British, and other Europeans who came to Egypt in the past, but remained withdrawn. The Egyptians, a very open people, inevitably came to regard this Soviet introversion as an expression of scorn, of the arrogance of the strong toward the weak. It is said of the Americans that outside their own country they can appear very "ugly." The Soviets can appear a great deal "uglier."

Small wonder that a process began in Egypt by which the Soviets were shouldered out of every field they hoped to penetrate in depth. Even the army was not exempt from this process. Egyptian officer cadres did not want to swallow everything the Soviet advisers and instructors decided to feed them.

All this culminated in the ousting by Sadat of most of the Soviet advisers from Egypt in 1972. And although the Soviets continued to supply tremendous amounts of the most modern weaponry to Egypt before and after the Yom Kippur War, the relations between Egypt and the Soviet Union have not been on the same footing since the ousting.

Future Soviet-Syrian relations may follow basically the same lines as future relations between the Soviets and the Egyptians. Friction will take a different form in each of these countries and will be felt in different degrees, but the basic process will be the same. The Arabs will want in the future as in the past to obtain Soviet aid, but not at the cost of their independence. They will continue to be very difficult customers.

This does not mean that the Arabs will throw the Soviets out of their states, or that the Soviets will get tired of it all, take their suitcases, and return to Odessa. The Soviets came to the Middle East with the intention of remaining there for a long time, and the Arabs will be in need of them for a long time; but neither party will get much joy out of this match.

Also on the debit side of the balance sheet must be entered the vast monies and resources that the Soviet Union is siphoning from her own economy to pour into the Arab states of the Middle East. This is far from a simple matter. Even the United States, with a far wealthier economy than that of the Soviet Union, has learned that to drain one's economy of resources for the purpose of investing in wars, military assistance, and economic aid to outside countries does nothing to improve one's own health. This draining of funds is arousing the strongest criticism from the American public, the outcry being that the money ought to be devoted to the solution of domestic problems.

In the Soviet Union there is no public to raise an outcry; nevertheless in that country, too, there is a great deal of bitter grumbling among the people, whose standard of living is considerably lower than that of the people of Western Europe. The patient and taciturn Soviet citizen knows that only tremendous internal investments would ever enable him to achieve a decent apartment, a private car, and the hundred and one assorted trifles that he desires. He is well aware that the price of prestige in the Arab states and the realization of the "warm-water dream" in the Middle East cost tens of billions of rubles and is being achieved at the expense of his standard of living. Moreover, the Soviets are beginning to learn what the Americans discovered before them: that when one begins to render assistance to foreign countries in arms and equipment and technical and economic aid, one is pouring money into a bottomless pit.

The final irony (and this is also a subject in which the Soviets could take lessons from the Americans, who have experienced it) is that when the power rendering assistance either ceases to do so or reduces its scope, the recipient states become deeply resentful. Not only are they not grateful for what they have received in the past, but they actually bite the hand that has been feeding them.

THE ISSUE OF RUSSIAN JEWRY

We have dwelt on one aspect of the relations between us and the Soviet Union: our place in the Middle East and the USSR's attitude toward us against the backdrop of the Arab-Israeli conflict. We must now discuss the second aspect of these complex relations: the attitude of the Soviet Union (and previously of Russia) to Judaism and its Jews, to Zionism and its Zionists.

Within the borders of the present-day Soviet Union live more than three million Jews. A minority—those living in Georgia, the mountain-dwelling Jews of Daghestan, and the Buchari Jews—have lived in these same places for over a thousand years, a long time before the Russians arrived there. In Russia itself there were small Jewish communities even as far back as the Middle Ages, almost from the dawn of its existence as a kingdom. With the expansion of Russia in the eighteenth and nineteenth centuries, and with the occupation of large parts of Poland, Lithuania, and the Ukraine and their annexation to the empire of the czars, Russia also took possession of a large Jewish community, which by the end of the czarist era totaled more than three million people. Most of them lived in crowded conditions in the Pale of Settlement on the western border of the empire; a minority lived in the center and southeastern fringes.

In the long history of the Jews under czarist rule, there were only short periods of calm and tranquillity. Most of this history is shot through with anti-Semitism, ceaseless harassment, persecution, and pogroms. The authorities made the Jews the scapegoat for all the troubles that plagued the country.

In the nineteenth century their intolerable situation roused among the Jews of czarist Russia the desire to seek a cure for their ills. Hundreds of thousands of them fled from Russia, mainly to the United States. A small number formed the Love of Zion movement and departed for the Land of Israel. Others left Jewry and joined Russian revolutionary movements; still others entered the revolutionary process while preserving their Jewish national identity (the Bundists).

At first the authorities' attitude to the Zionist movement in Russia was ambivalent. On the one hand, the rise of a nationalist movement in the midst of one of their many minorities was seen by them as a factor operating against the Holy Russian Empire, sole ruler of all its folk groups. They therefore viewed Zionism with displeasure, and persecuted it. On the other hand, since the Jews were a foreign, inorganic body in the bosom of Mother Russia, there were some who thought, "Let these filthy *Zhids* go to their Palestine. Let them bang their heads against the wall, as long as we need no longer see them among us." In the second half of the nineteenth century a ramified, vital, and variegated Zionist movement developed among Russian Jewry, toward which the authorities' attitude was alternately one of scalding wrath and freezing contempt.

Whereas the Jews and Jewish activity elicited nothing but anger and contempt on the part of the czarist regime, there was a vastly different reaction on the part of the early revolutionaries, especially those in the socialist camp. Many of the leaders of the revolutionary movement were themselves Jews. The revolutionary underground was one of the channels in which young Jews could give vent to their passions, their talents, and their aspirations to bring about a fundamental change in their lives by means of revolutionizing their society. As Marxist-socialists who were creating a set of doctrines which would provide answers to all questions, Marx came up with a definitive answer to the Jewish problem too: Judaism is a by-product of capitalism, and when that disappears, Judaism too will disappear.

The Bundists believed that they had found a dialectical way of preserving a certain Jewish labor identity in the future socialist society. All these early revolutionaries, especially the Bundists, regarded Zionism as a tough ideological opponent for the souls of the youth within the Jewish Pale of Settlement, from which came many a talented revolutionary and ideologist.

With the outbreak of the Bolshevik Revolution and immediately after it, when the Pale of Settlement restrictions were annulled and anti-Semitism was outlawed by the young Soviet regime, hundreds of thousands of Jews erupted into the new Soviet life. There they began filling the void that had been created in government, administration, commerce, education, army, and other spheres of life.

At the same time, persecution of Zionism grew. Although the Soviet leadership included a number of non-Jews whose attitude toward it was exceptional, Zionism was mercilessly hounded and quickly went underground.

During the first years of the Soviet regime it became apparent to all concerned—to the rulers, the Russians, and the Jews themselves—that Marx's prescription was not working: the Jews were not a passing phenomenon and they were not assimilating within the new Soviet Communist society. The Jews' marked presence in high echelons of authority were their undoing.

Because of the distressing circumstances that prevailed in the USSR during the 1920s and the need to find scapegoats, Stalin once more began fanning the deep anti-Semitic sentiments embedded in the hearts of the Russian people. In the late 1920s and the 1930s he embarked on purges in which he eliminated his closest comrades-in-power—many of whom were Jews.

A theory which temporarily gained dominance during those years and was promulgated by Soviet ideologists, Jews and non-Jews alike, was that the Jews were not being assimilated and were not disappearing because they lacked a basic component for becoming a real people: a territory of their own in which the great majority of them would be concentrated. Let the Jews then be given a stretch of land, said these theorists, where they can found a Jewish republic as one of the entire complex of peoples' republics comprising the Soviet Union.

Thus arose the Birobidjan project. Jewish leaders, with the blessing of Soviet leadership, called upon their brothers throughout the Soviet Union and upon Jews the world over to go to Birobidjan, in Siberia, and there build a Soviet Jewish national home.

In Birobidjan an autonomous Jewish province was created. The tens of thousands of Jews who settled there toiled hard to make this unique colonization experiment successful.

The Jewish project in Birobidjan was choked within a number of years by the Soviet authorities. They regretted the whole business and also regarded it as a security risk. A Jewish republic on the Chinese border looked to Stalin, on second thought, like a nightmare.

During the 1920s and 1930s the Soviets succeeded, or thought they succeeded, in breaking the religious and national backbone of Jewry in the Soviet Union. They shut down thousands of synagogues and institutes of education and higher learning, prohibited religious and Zionist organizations, and almost succeeded in cutting Soviet Jewry off from the Jews in the rest of the world. It should, however, be emphasized that this severance was never complete and final. During the 1920s and 1930s thousands of Jews from the Soviet Union immigrated to Palestine legally, semilegally, or illegally. There probably existed even then a school of thought among the rulers that it was best to be rid of the Zionist "troublemakers" and deport them to Palestine; on the other hand, there may have been some who were pleased with the thought that a small number of Soviet Jews could arrive in Palestine and there found Communist cells. There were also officials, at all levels, who could be bribed into issuing exit visas.

In its own hideous way World War II led to a revival of the

Jewish problem in the Soviet Union and a renewal of contact between Soviet Jewry, world Jewry, and Zionism.

The holocaust did not bypass the Jews of the Soviet Union. About one and a half million Soviet Jews were caught up in the German occupation and were among the six million annihilated. As they pushed further eastward, the Germans found not a few willing collaborators in the murder of the Jews; dormant anti-Semitism among Ukrainians, Latvians, Lithuanians, and others suddenly flared up, and many members of these peoples helped the Germans liquidate the Jews.

The Soviet Union absorbed into her interior regions, where the invaders never reached, hundreds of thousands of Jewish refugees: citizens of the Soviet Union and also Polish, Lithuanian, Estonian, Latvian, and other Jews, who, in their flight before the oncoming Germans, reached European and Asiatic Russia. In this gigantic land, then under a war regimen, their lot was not an enviable one—but their lives were saved. The influence of these Jewish refugees upon Soviet Jewry was tremendous. Since virtually all of them were imbued with deep religious and Zionist values, they left their mark on a whole new generation of Russian Jewry.

Hundreds of thousands of Jews served in the Russian army. As the army eventually advanced westward they returned with it to their towns, now reduced to ashes, and to the common graves of their families. They came to Poland, opened the gates of the concentration and death camps, saw what the Nazis had done to their people, and tried to help their surviving Jewish brothers. Soviet Jewish soldiers encountered Jewish soldiers from America, Europe, and the volunteers of the Jewish Brigade in the British army. These encounters were to have a far-reaching effect years later on everything that took place within Soviet Jewry.

As the war raged on, Stalin decided to utilize universal Jewish national feelings and harness them to the Soviet anti-Nazi war chariot. Emissaries (among whom were some of the best Jewish writers) went out, as representatives of the anti-Fascist Jewish committee founded in the Soviet Union, to the Jewish Diaspora, there to recruit support for the Soviet struggle against the Nazis.

With the war over and the victory won, the Soviet attitude toward the Jews underwent two diametrically opposed and mutually contradictory processes. On the one hand, the anti-Semitism fanned by the Germans had not died down. Jews returning to their former places of domicile in the western part of the country were not received like homecoming citizens. The locals regarded them as outsiders and resented their having survived. During that period—the last years of Stalin's life —the five "black years" in the life of the Jews of the Soviet Union began. The victorious and aging dictator, crazed by his own suspiciousness, regarded the Jews as suspect. Had not the Jews conspired against him and against Communism when they had encountered their brothers in Europe? Had they not proved themselves rootless cosmopolitans? Would not the Jews now, after the greatest of Russia's wars and the most triumphant of her victories, cause unrest wherever they were? Stalin tried to allay his fears and suspicions by intensifying his campaign of persecution against the Jews.

At the same time, in 1947 the Soviet Union began giving its support to the founding of a Jewish state in Palestine. Ostensibly there is a distinct contradiction between these two diametrically opposed trends. A partial explanation may be that Soviet support for the founding of a Jewish state in Palestine arose from the desire to exploit the Jewish struggle against the British as a means to accelerate the expulsion of the British from Palestine and create a vacuum in the region. But their support for the Jewish fight for a state may be assumed to derive from other motives too: hundreds of thousands of Jews were then wandering, uprooted and dazed with shock, in Eastern Europe, in areas the Soviet Union had annexed or in which she was about to install regimes loyal to herself. These wandering Jews were liable to remain in those countries as a hostile element, resentful and embittered, fomenting unrest. Then why not enable them to leave Europe and reach a country they would be prepared to fight for, thereby reinforcing the Jews who were expelling the British?

Even under Stalin, Soviet policy had never been entirely monolithic. Over the issue of supporting the founding of a Jewish state various trends were at work in the Soviet Union; even then there may have been a tendency to regard an independent Israel as a potential refuge for the Jews of the Soviet Union. The Soviets may have hoped that the state that would arise would be a Jewish Communist, pro-Soviet republic.

Stalin is certainly not to be suspected of having acted, either during 1947 or at any other time, out of humanitarian motives. It is also obvious that the factor determining Soviet policy was her own interest. At the same time it may be assumed that among the group of people that surrounded Stalin in those years there were some who were deeply touched by the Jewish cause. It may have been a Molotov, who was married to a Jewish woman, or a Kaganovich, in whose heart a hidden Jewish spark may have been kindled; or perhaps it was a Mikoyan, member of an Armenian minority that had been persecuted for hundreds of years; or perhaps other men.

It may therefore be assumed that the Soviet decision to support a Jewish state arose from various interests—opportunistic, egotistical, Machiavellian, and perhaps even humanitarian.

This pro-Israeli policy was very short-lived. By 1949 it was over, and an icy wind began blowing over Israel from the direction of Moscow. This change too had its motives: Israel had won her War of Independence. She had helped get the British out of one Middle Eastern arena. From the Soviet point of view she had outlived her usefulness. Israel's appearance on the Middle East scene had thrown up around her a field full of bitterness and frustration and disillusionment. In Egypt, Syria, and Iraq the ground lay waiting for the Soviet plow. Ostentatious coolness toward Israel and the erasure of the memory of the brief romance with her were now part of the process of preparing the soil for Soviet seeding.

A no less important reason for the cooling of relations between the Soviet Union and Israel was the reaction of Soviet Jewry to the founding of the state. The insanely suspicious Stalin found that hundreds of thousands of Jews in the Soviet Union were exulting over the establishment of the State of Israel, and he did not like it. For him, this was conclusive evidence that the Jews were a dangerous element indeed; that their loyalty to the Soviet Union was questionable; that their hearts really belonged to a capitalist state in the Middle East.

The establishment of the State of Israel and Soviet Jewry's reaction to it whipped Stalin's hatred for the Jews to an even higher pitch, and in the last years of his life it may have driven him mad. The "doctors' plot" was the height of Stalin's insanity, invented in the last months of his life. Had he lived awhile longer, he would undoubtedly have brought about the exile and mass murder of Jews.

Stalin's heirs, first in the collective leadership and later when Khrushchev was sole ruler, were not similarly possessed by this madness. After his death they halted the process set in motion by the "father of the peoples," which was liable to have cost Soviet Jewry its physical existence. The policy they adopted toward the Jews was one of deliberate atrophy, its purpose being to debilitate them.

Khrushchev had good and sufficient reason, partly arising from his deep, irrational anti-Semitism and partly from pragmatic considerations, to leave his country's Jews a ghost nation, caught between hammer and sickle: "No" to contact with Jews abroad; "No" to links with Israel; "No" to emigration to Israel; "No" to the reopening of Jewish religious and secular institutions in the Soviet Union. But, at the same time, "Yes" to the preservation of Jewish identity in their passports—for purposes of surveillance; "Yes" to anti-Jewish discrimination in almost all spheres of life, especially in the government, the Communist party, and the army; "Yes" to a campaign of propaganda and denigration against Judaism and Zionism.

Khrushchev and, later, Brezhnev believed that with this treatment the Jewish problem would of itself go into decline and simply fade away. They adopted this "nonmethod" for lack of a more promising solution. The bothersome little problem did not rate their serious attention and they hoped it would solve itself.

Their expectations were not fulfilled. The problem refused to disappear. On my return from Moscow about ten years ago, I wrote that the Soviets were not succeeding in choking off and silencing the problem, that they were exacerbating it, and that out of the dead end they had driven the Jews into might burst forth a new Jewish national and Zionist resurgence movement.

Such a movement has in recent years been growing before our very eyes. It did not emerge spontaneously but was borne on the shoulders of proud, courageous Jews. The movement derived impetus and encouragement from the very fact of the existence of the State of Israel, from the presence of the Israeli Embassy in Moscow, from the Israeli emissaries, and from the steadily increasing identification of World Jewry with the fate of the Jews in the Soviet Union. At first the Soviets flatly denied the existence of a Jewish problem or of a Zionist-nationalist movement within their borders. But as this movement in the Soviet Union gathered momentum and the answering echoes became louder, it became a Soviet domestic issue of a magnitude quite disproportionate to the number of persons involved in it. The "let my people go" syndrome touches upon the very basis of the Soviet regime's ideology: here were thousands of Soviet citizens, one of the many peoples of the Soviet Union, getting to their feet and shouting, "This is not our homeland! This is not our regime! Let us leave and return to Israel."

Even had this manifestation not been bound up with the Middle East, even had Israel been situated on an island in the middle of the ocean, it would have been a very thorny and critical problem for the Soviet regime to handle, since that regime bases itself on the dogma that it is the most progressive and the best in the world. It was considerably more critical in view of the fact that many Soviet Jews wanted to emigrate to Israel, which lay at the hub of a sensitive area of the world where the USSR was deeply involved as supporter of the Arabs that were fighting Israel.

The Jews in the Soviet Union number not more than 1.5 percent of the population; but they are concentrated in the great cities and in the capitals of the national republics that make up the Soviet Union; there they constitute about 10 percent of the population. In these great political, social, and cultural centers the Jews constitute a real problem.

If the Soviets had been in need of evidence that there existed in their midst a Jewish-Zionist national movement, and that this was no mere peripheral movement but one that encompassed hundreds of thousands of adherents, that evidence was supplied by the reaction of Jews to the Six-Day and Yom Kippur Wars. Today the Soviet authorities understand that the problem of the Jews of the Soviet Union is inseparably bound up with the problem of Israel, and that every Soviet move as regards Israel and the Arabs has domestic repercussions upon Soviet Jewry.

The Soviets know that they have on their hands a problem of Jews—and it is quite immaterial whether this involves all the Jews of the Soviet Union or a large part of them—who feel themselves to be strangers within her. One might think of it as a problem of Jewish "refugees" living in the Soviet Union. If refugees are people who have been uprooted from their proper place, who feel themselves outsiders in the place where they are living, and who want to return home, then this definition applies to many Jews of the Soviet Union. Not only were these Jews uprooted from their land in the very distant past, but in the past generation many of them have been torn up and exiled again and again within the Soviet Union itself. Many of them feel themselves to be foreign, hated, suspect; with all their hearts they desire to return home—to the Land of Israel.

All echelons of the Soviet government are today aware that there does exist among them a Jewish-Zionist problem, and they no longer deny it. In recent years the government has been trying an odd assortment of solutions: their searing condemnation of Jewry and Zionism alternates with their freezing contempt for them; they try to exert pressure on the Jews and tighten the leash, but sometimes they simultaneously relax their pressure and throw the Jews a "bit of rope," allow them to grasp at a lifeline. They wage a massive smear campaign and do everything within their power to cut off their Jews from Israel; at the same time, they open the gates slightly, allowing Jews to leave for Israel in the hope that the foment will lessen; but when, as a result, the foment increases, tens of thousands of Jews are seen to have reached their goal, the Soviets again revert to threats, trials, and violence. In the face of the Jewish problem the mighty and powerful Soviet regime stands helpless and confused, torn by contradictions and opposing currents, vainly replacing one method of treatment with another, and simultaneously essaying diametrically opposed solutions.

The Soviet Union has no clear-cut, long-term policy regarding the Jewish problem; it is pursuing a pragmatic hand-to-mouth policy. Immigration from the Soviet Union to Israel is unplanned. No one in Israel knows who will immigrate, when, in what numbers, or from where.

In attempting to extract a little silver from the dross, the Soviets are exploiting the issue of Soviet Jewry as a psychological weapon in the Israeli-Arab dispute; we know that they hold the keys to the floodgates that would release hundreds of thousands of Jews from the Soviet Union to Israel. But this fact is known to the Arabs too. They also know that the Kremlin rulers alone—not the government of the United States or any other country—could double Israel's population within a short period of time.

It may be assumed that from their point of view the Soviets are making good use of this concealed weapon and that its presence is felt in every room where the Soviets conduct negotiations with the Arabs.

THE DANGER OF CONFRONTATION AND THE VITAL NEED TO MAINTAIN CONTACT

Soviet political acts regarding the Jews and Israel give rise to terrible dangers.

First, there are the military risks. The architects of Israel's policy, from Ben-Gurion onward, have held to a hard and fast rule not to run the risk of military confrontation with a world power. They realized that the Israeli army was an excellent one, should be prepared for war with its Arab enemies in the region, either one at a time or all together—an astounding achievement in itself. But they also understood that if modern military great-power forces should intervene in a direct war against Israel, they could be confronting the Israeli army with a task it could never perform. The potential outcome could be fraught with disaster. In 1948 Israel took great care not to entangle itself directly with the British army; from 1956 onward it has taken precautions not to become involved in a direct confrontation with the Soviet army.

There is no need to visit the Soviet Union to arrive at a correct assessment of its tremendous military strength. Her armored corps rides in some of the world's best tanks. Her excellent pilots fly thousands of highly modern, sophisticated aircraft. Her army has the capacity to fly many paratroop brigades over great distances. The young, very modern Soviet navy is developing helicopter combat. The Red army controls diversified systems of surface-to-air, air-to-surface, sea-to-sea, sea-to-air, and surface-to-surface missiles of all ranges. And Israel learned a very bitter lesson about Soviet weaponry in the Yom Kippur War. All this is without counting the nuclear and nonconventioanl weapons systems.

The Americans and the Chinese, not to mention the West Europeans, are very cautious about any showdown with the Red army. We had better realize the simple and terrible truth: within the foreseeable future the Arab armies cannot destroy Israel—but the Red army most certainly can. It would be at a cost of life and prestige, but if the Soviet leadership should decide to destroy Israel by force of arms, conventional or non-conventional, then we shall cease to exist. And let us not pin our hopes on the Americans automatically intervening in our favor in such an event.

This truth need not necessarily plunge us into fear. We are not a rabbit, to be hypnotized by a cobra. We must live and plan, while acknowledging this reality.

This coin—the risk of a war between Israeli and Soviet soldiers—also has its obverse, Soviet side. The leaders of the Soviet Union must also make their reckoning. For them, too, such a war would have its terrible aspects. They must take into consideration that should they impose upon us direct war with them (and it could happen as a result of a hundred and one psychological errors on the part of either side), and should their armies clash with the soldiers of the Israeli army and with armed Israeli civilians in the Sinai Desert, on landing coasts, on the Golan Heights, or anywhere else in our land, this would be nothing at all like the 1968 Czechoslovakian excursion or the suppression of the Hungarian uprising in 1956.

If anything could be said to resemble, even remotely, what is liable to happen in the event of hostilities between the Soviets and ourselves, then the Finnish example is as close as we can get. The Soviets well remember how a small brave people withstood them in defense of its country, and knew how to fight in every possible way with every weapon it could lay hands on.

A Soviet war against Israel could be bloody and protracted. It could tie up large Soviet forces: thousands of tanks and aircraft and hundreds of thousands of combatants.

Even without thinking in global terms (although we have seen what global significance attaches to a dispute in a small island named Cuba or to a "limited" war in Vietnam), a direct war of this kind could produce the gravest results inside the Soviet Union.

The Soviet Union is proud, and rightly so, of the fact that for a whole generation it has been able to avoid involving its men and its soldiers in bloodshed and war. Since World War II, when the blood of millions of its sons was shed and about a third of the state was sacked by the Germans, the Soviets have succeeded in rebuilding their land, increasing its influence, and entering new oceans and continents—without sacrificing one single Ivan. Not for nothing do they proudly point to their policy and its achievements as compared to the policy of the United States, which every few years has involved its troops in distant wars. Soviet youth, soldiers, and civilians are good patriots, but they hate wars. The wounds of two world wars and a civil war within the last three generations are still unhealed.

The Soviet authorities, who find it difficult enough to explain to their peoples why they are investing gigantic sums in the Arab Middle East, will be hard pressed to explain to them why they are shedding their sons' blood there, notwithstanding the virulent anti-Israeli and anti-Jewish propaganda being conducted by the Soviets.

The reaction of the peoples of Europe and America to a Soviet war on Israel may be one of great rage. They will not send their sons to war, but the whole delicate structure of détente, commercial ties, tourism, exchanges of knowledge—in short, the entire complex of relations that the Soviet Union has been building up so patiently over the course of many years could be severely damaged as a result. The Soviet Union paid a heavy price in prestige for the invasion of Czechoslovakia in 1968; her image, both at home and abroad, was badly damaged. A war against Israel could lead to the utter collapse of her whole web of relations with the West.

For all these reasons, and others which perhaps cannot be envisaged, a direct war against Israel by Soviet troops could trigger a terrible unforeseen chain reaction. Should we then take comfort in this apocalyptic vision? Of course not. We do not want to be a latter-day Samson, content to know that when we die the Philistines will die with us. The Soviets must be aware of the great dangers that dog their relations with us. Both sides must seek a path toward rapprochement and mutual understanding.

First and foremost, we should realize that the Soviets are in our region to stay. They have no intention of bowing out even when the Arab-Israeli conflict is resolved. And the Soviets must realize that we too shall always be here; they must reckon with us as a constant factor in the Middle East.

In view of the great dangers we have described, we and the Soviets must seek both conventional and unconventional ways of establishing contact. Such contact, even if informal at first, as in the Geneva talks, should be directed toward the renewal of diplomatic relations between our two states. The establishment of contacts and the renewal of diplomatic relations do not mean affection and friendship—that is a long way off—for they must be built on a basis of mutual benefit, understanding of the other side, and avoidance of fires being sparked by mistake and for want of communication.

Since the time when Jewish immigration from the Soviet Union was renewed in 1968, the Soviets have been using it as a device with which to signal to Israel. These signals say, "We are not interested in your destruction, and under certain conditions dialogue with you would become possible." The immigration of a few tens of thousands of Jews to Israel from the Soviet Union since the Six-Day War, while anti-Israeli defamation continues, while the rearming of the Arab states proceeds apace, and while there is no letup in the show trials and the pressures against Soviet Jewry, is a unique phenomenon. It should be remembered that this emigration—or controlled exodus—of tens of thousands of Soviet citizens from the Soviet Union and their immigration to another country is an extraordinary manifestation. It is without parallel in the Soviet Union: the Soviets permit no one but Jewish citizens to emigrate, and permit them to emigrate to Israel only.

The Soviets are doing this not for love of Israel but out of a realistic acknowledgment of the situation of the Jews in their country. The fact that the Soviets relate ambivalently to the phenomenon of "Jewish rebellion" (demonstrations, protests, sit-downs, the existence of underground groups for the study of Hebrew and Zionism) is most instructive. On the one hand, they threaten, arrest, imprison, and pass sentence; and on the other hand, the authorities peep at the Zionist phenomenon "through their fingers." The KGB and the militia are quite strong enough to prevent Jewish demonstrations if they wanted to. But it may be assumed that at least some of the top echelons of the security service and the government are prepared to exercise some tolerance toward an upsurge of Zionism in the Soviet Union.

The Soviet Union is not monolithic in her attitudes toward contemporary Israel, any more than she is monolithic in other matters. Arguments prevail in ruling circles on every foreign and domestic issue. The same applies with regard to their attitude toward the Jews and Israel: there are arguments, there are various schools of thought, mutually contradictory and opposing steps are being taken because of differences in basic outlook and methods of solving the problem.

"DINOSAURS" AGAINST REALISTS

In the matter of Israel, as in many other vital matters, Soviet ruling circles are divided into at least two schools of thought: one I call the "dinosaurs"; and the other, the realists.

The "dinosaurs"—neo-Stalinists—cling to the world of yesterday. They want to see in the Soviet Union (and indeed in the whole world) the yesterday that is so familiar to them: cold war with the West, rigid dogmatism in foreign affairs and even more rigid dogmatism in domestic affairs, economic centralism, and exclusive Communist party control over the whole state. The realist school, on the other hand, tries to maneuver in foreign relations, to assess situations not by old-fashioned, outdated yardsticks but by cold, realistic calculations. It may be that this school is also somewhat more open on the domestic front, at least in the field of economic affairs and technology.

In the matter of Jews and Israel too an ongoing controversy is being waged between these two schools of thought. The realist school in the Soviet Union may have come to realize that Israel is a stable and permanent political entity in the Middle East, with which they must parley. They may have reached the conclusion that in Israel, and only in Israel, will large parts of Soviet Jewry be able to find a solution to their problems, and thereby ease domestic pressure and unrest. We for our part must repeatedly explain to the Soviets that we have no interest in cold war in general, and certainly not in a cold war in our region. I believe that Israeli declarations with regard to the future of the territories and the open options regarding them will make it easier for the realists in the Soviet Union to enter into some contact with us. At least some Soviet leaders have understood, like the Americans, that what is under discussion are not unilateral retreat and waivers, but that in return for restoration of territories we shall demand meaningful peace.

It may be that in the future, in the post-Brezhnev era, the policy of the Soviet government will be determined by people whose way of thinking, as regards the outside world, their country, and their society, will be different from that of today's rulers. It is not to be assumed that change in the Soviet regime is just around the corner or that in the near future the country will be ruled by a humanitarian socialist democracy. But one should not ignore the fact that certain persistent far-reaching changes are at work in the structure of Soviet society, that part of the intelligentsia and the youth want changes in the direction of greater liberalization and do not want a return to "dinosaurism." It may be that these people, who will one day be in charge of the fate of the Soviet Jews and relations with Israel, will think of us and our problems in different terms.

Even today it is possible that some of the architects of Soviet policy no longer think of us and the Arabs in terms of black and white, and understand that in the long run a large-scale immigration of Soviet Jewry to Israel would be seen as a great achievement on the part of the Soviets in the Middle East, gaining them the kind of stable political credit they received from the erection of the Aswan and Euphrates Dams.

If hundreds of thousands of Jews brought up and educated in the Soviet Union should immigrate to Israel, they will by no means necessarily constitute an anti-Soviet factor. While it is not probable that they will constitute a pro-Soviet factor or entertain any great affection for the regime they fled, they can most certainly constitute in this country a very large community of Russian-speaking lovers of Russian culture; they will implant here the positive values—and such values do exist—of the country they came from, just as the Bilu generation and the members of the Second and Third Aliyas implanted here attitudes of appreciation and affection toward the great values of Russian culture.

In discussing the United States I said that in time there could come into being in Israel a community—in the positive sense of the word—of hundreds of thousands of Jews born in the United States. The same applies to Soviet Jewry. Israel will be able to benefit from whatever is good in these two great universal civilizations. Together with the native-born Israelis and those originating from the Islamic countries, they will form here a unique Jewish amalgam.

I believe that we have something to talk about with the Soviets. We must turn around and say to them, "We are not your foes. At critical moments in the recent past you have helped us, and together we may be able to build a bridge over the gulf that lies between us. We are not the military policemen of any power in the Middle East; we did not come here to guard the interests of any one nation in its global struggle against another. As a Jewish state whose two great Diasporas are to be found inside the two superpowers, as a Middle Eastern state desiring to live in peace with all its neighbors, near and far, we aspire to true neutrality."

The Americans, too, will probably be relieved to find that we are not tied to them alone but are seeking sympathy, support, understanding, and cooperation everywhere, including the Soviet Union. I believe that in the future not only the Americans but also the Soviets can help us build bridges between ourselves and the Arabs.

In May 1971 I appealed to the Soviets from the rostrum of the Socialist International in Helsinki, which I attended in my capacity as secretary-general of the Labor party: "We are expecting signals from the Soviet Union and we want to respond to them. We are asking the socialists of the world to help us in this. We are listening attentively and with open hearts."

Those words are still valid today.

10

THE COUNTRIES OF EUROPE

CURRENT ACCOUNT

In discussing our relations with Europe, we refer not only to the Common Market countries, but to all countries of both Western and Eastern Europe.

Western Europe now stands at the beginning of federalization. The first triumphant milestone in this process is the emergence of the Common Market. It is a highly complicated process, with severe birth pangs; nevertheless it possesses a strong dynamic force of its own. The Common Market countries constitute a very powerful magnetic field to which additional European states are constantly being attracted. There will be many ups and downs and many years will pass before the founding of the United States of Europe.

Western Europe is not a superpower in the political sense of the term. It is still divided into a dozen and a half states, each with a different past, tradition, and language, and each with its own vested interests. In the economic sense, Western Europe is already marching toward superpower status. In terms of population, gross national product, and standard of technological development the Common Market countries today compete on an even footing with both the United States and the Soviet

Union. If the Common Market expands to encompass all the countries of Western Europe, they will become the greatest and strongest superpower in the world, both economically and technologically. In terms of population, too, it will have caught up with the Soviet Union and the United States, and will take third place after China and India.

Unlike the two superpowers, the United States and the Soviet Union, which in one way or another are militarily involved in the Middle Eastern dispute and with whom our relations are highly complex, the states of Europe do not now maintain any military presence in the region. Nevertheless, Europe has a tremendous influence on the area and maintains strong economic, cultural, and political ties to it.

Europe, with its more than three hundred million inhabitants, most of whom enjoy one of the world's highest standards of living, is a gigantic market that depends very heavily on the products of the Middle East, the most important of which is oil, the greatest mover of the wheels of European industry. The vital importance of Middle Eastern oil to Europe has been dramatically emphasized during and after the Yom Kippur War. Europe is also the greatest supplier of goods and products to the countries of the Middle East, where many political, social, and cultural traces of European colonialism remain.

We—Jewry, Zionism, and Israel—also have an ancient and weighty "account" with Europe. In the past our relations were somber; in the present they are crucial; in the future they could prove to be splendid.

European interest in the Middle East in general and in the Jews in particular goes back to the changing relations and clashes between the ancient civilizations of the Mediterranean basin. The Philistines may have been one of the European tribes that came over the sea to the Land of Israel and clashed with the ancient Israelites for centuries. The Greeks conquered Palestine under Alexander the Great and left an indelible stamp on the whole region and also upon us and our civilization.

Against the Greco-Europeans we fought liberation and guerrilla wars during the Hasmonean period, to protect our religious and cultural values against their encroaching civilization.

After them, we came under the yoke of the European Romans. We tried to break this yoke through rebellion, and we went into exile. In the course of our contacts with the civilizations of Greece and Rome, and while our strength as an independent state was being broken, in Judea and the Galilee the historic and fateful encounter took place between the Hellenist-Roman pagan world and Jewish monotheism. This encounter gave rise to Jesus and Christianity, which sprang from Judaism. Christianity conveyed some of the content and values of its parent religion to what then constituted the whole European world—the Roman Empire—and within three hundred years Christianity dominated Rome.

In a certain sense this could be regarded as Jewish revenge upon the pagan world that now found itself "Christianized" by emissaries who were themselves Jews or of Jewish descent. Early Christian Europe took a sevenfold revenge upon us, and began to victimize the Jews who did not allow themselves to be swept along in the mighty current of Christianity, but instead preserved their originality and distinctiveness. Since the first centuries of the Christian Era the Jews have been homeless wanderers in Christian Europe. They were regarded as the crucifiers of Christ; the young Christian Church persecuted them ruthlessly; over the centuries Christian governors, kings, and princes expelled them from one country after another.

Jewish history in Europe is the history of Christian anti-Semitism and Jewish martyrdom. There is not a single people, not a single state, in Europe that at one time or another has not maltreated the Jews, from the Crusades and the Spanish Inquisition to the Nazi ovens at Auschwitz.

The Jews in Europe had temporary places of refuge, without which they would have been utterly wiped out. Fleeing the Roman sword, the Jews arrived in the south of France and the

lands of the Rhine; from the sword of the kings of England they
fled to France; from the terrors of the Spanish Inquisition, to
England, Holland, and Italy; to escape the German sword they
went eastward to Poland; to escape the Polish sword, to Lithuania and Russia; to escape the latters' swords they fled westward again to Germany, France, England, and the United
States. In these places of refuge, between this nation's sword
and that, European Jewry lived. It guarded the glowing embers
of its being, created religious and cultural values, came to know
that education is the greatest asset of the hunted fugitive,
created poetry and literature, and finally founded a national
renaissance movement—Zionism.

This, then, is the dreadful side of our European "account."
But there is also a brighter side. At various periods the Europeans have regarded us as the great bearers of culture, as a
bridge between civilizations. The Jews in Spain mediated between the great Islamic culture and Christianity; the Jews were
among the torchbearers of civilization in Germany, France, and
Poland. A glance at a European *Who's Who* in philosophy,
literature, the humanities, or the social and natural sciences will
reveal how great was the Jewish contribution to European civilization. But the Jews paid a price for their contributions.

We in Israel carry with us the heritage of European civilization. We appreciate and participate in its beauty, and we de-
spise and are unable to forget its bestiality.

BIRD'S-EYE VIEW

The European attitude to the Jewish national renaissance
movement differed from place to place and from time to time.
We shall, without any pretense of presenting an exhaustive
study of the subject, give a brief account of our relations with
the peoples of Europe.

We have had the warm understanding of non-Jewish sympa-
thizers in England, France, Holland, Belgium, Scandinavia,

Italy, and other countries, while at the same time in those countries we have had opponents and foes. We have had a very special relationship with Britain. The English helped get us Zionists on our feet. Without them we might not have come into existence. Yet because of the English we were almost stillborn. After thirty years of deep love-hate relations, they bequeathed us their language, culture, and methods of government. We live with them at present in a stable and sometimes excellent relationship.

Of our account with the Germans it is hard to speak, since one cannot measure the holocaust. As long as there are Jews whose arms are tattooed with German numbers and whose flesh still bears the marks of the fangs of the Gestapo dogs, Jews who relive the atrocities and the slaughter in their dreams, we cannot achieve normalization of our relations with Germany. A generation after the holocaust a unique type of relationship was established between the sons of the murderers, seeking forgiveness, and the sons of the murdered, prepared to forgive but not to forget.

Our account with France has been one of fluctuations, from deep sympathy toward our enterprise before and immediately after the State of Israel was established; through massive political and military aid during the 1950s and the early 1960s; to the present very low ebb in our relationship. This account is full of contradictions and apparent conflicts of interest. It is to be hoped that our relations may one day take a turn for the better.

We have an account with Italy too. During the black era of Fascism the Italian people were barely infected with the disease of anti-Semitism. We may record to the credit of the Italians the fact that during the holocaust they saved as many Jews as they could, helped our refugees in their wanderings, and assisted us in getting those people aboard immigrant ships headed for the Land of Israel. Throughout modern times, during the whole history of Zionism, the Italians have evinced a true and deep sympathy for the *resurgiammento* of the ancient Jewish people.

The Benelux countries, too, served for centuries as an asylum and shelter for the Jews. During the holocaust they worked to save Jews. Zionism and Israel have almost always been regarded by them with sympathy and even affection. Holland offered a radiant and courageous example to Israel during and after the Yom Kippur War by not yielding to Arab oil blackmail.

Our relationship with the Scandinavian countries includes many shining episodes: the rescue of the Jews of Denmark, the Swedes' treatment of the refugees of the holocaust, and the Norwegians' and Finns' defense of their few Jewish countrymen. An occasional icy wind blows in our direction from Scandinavia, but we have many friends and supporters there, and their generally positive relation to our enterprise is a source of encouragement to us.

Our account with Austria contains the very blackest of black pages, from the time when it was part of the Nazi Empire; but it also contains some golden pages from various periods of the Austro-Hungarian Empire, within which the Jews were allowed to live in relative security. It was Austria where in modern times they first received civil rights and where they were able to develop a full cultural life. Recently Austria has helped us by serving as a transit station and a temporary shelter for tens of thousands of immigrants on their way from Eastern Europe to Israel.

Our relations with neutral Switzerland are unique and longstanding. Switzerland was the site of the early Zionist Congresses, and was often a haven for Jews in flight from Fascist hate.

We have a long account with Spain and Portugal, starting with the Jewish golden age in the tenth century and continuing through the period of the Inquisition, the conversos, and the expulsions. Both these countries deported their Jews. Our relations with them at present are deadlocked because of the nature of their regimes. We should not forget, however, that these regimes had no hand in the slaughter of the Jews in World War II, and that thousands of Jews found shelter and temporary refuge there. Whenever a change occurs in the incumbent regimes in Spain and Portugal there is every prospect for the establishment of good relations between the Iberian Peninsula and the State of Israel.

Our account with Greece is as long as the Exile. In recent centuries, both when Greece was under the yoke of the Ottomans and after it received independence, Jewish communities there have flourished, led by the Jewish community of Salonika. During and after World War II the Greeks helped us save many refugees and bring them to Israel. When Greece reverts to democracy we may have a good neighbor in the eastern Mediterranean.

We also have an account with countries which politically are not West European but East European, and are governed by Communist regimes. Romania has for several years exemplified the possibility of coexistence and cooperation between Communist countries and the State of Israel. By not having severed her relations with Israel, Romania secured advantages in both the West and the East, as well as among the Arabs.

There is no good reason why Yugoslavia, also a Mediterranean neighbor of ours, should not renew her relations with Israel. Her Jews have always been accorded fair and tolerant treatment, and no burden of resentment exists between us and the Yugoslav peoples.

Whenever relations between us and the Soviet Union improve, there will also be good relations between Bulgaria and ourselves, just as there were up to the Six-Day War. This would accord with the gratitude we bear the Bulgarians, who protected their country's Jews and helped the great majority of them to make their way to Israel as soon as the state was established.

A détente between us and the Soviet Union would also bring about a renewal of relations between us and Poland, Hungary, and Czechoslovakia. We need not dwell on the role played by those three countries in the chronicles of our people; but the State of Israel did have ties with them until the Six-Day War.

EUROPE'S ROLE IN THE MIDDLE EAST

Western Europe's near-total dependence on Arab oil makes it extremely sensitive to events in the Middle East. However, this dependence is by no means entirely one-sided, as one might superficially conclude from the Arab oil embargo of 1973. It is true that modern industrialized Europe depends on the Arab states as its main source of energy. But it is no less true that the oil-exporting Arab states are in the last resort dependent upon Europe, whose purchase of oil enriches them enormously.

With all their braggadocio Arab statesmen and economists are gazing with no little concern on the energy-supply situation of Europe. The development of nuclear energy is making only slow progress, much slower than was expected. Still, its use is constantly increasing. In coming decades atomic energy will be a weighty factor in the European energy picture. Feverish prospecting in all parts of Europe has already led to the discovery of large gas fields in the North Sea. It may well be that further such discoveries will free Europe of her almost exclusive dependence on Arab oil. The Arab oil embargo and blackmail will no doubt act as a tremendous catalyst in Europe's efforts to find other sources of energy.

This is the future for which the Arab states must prepare. They must establish modern light and heavy industry, which will itself consume ever-increasing quantities of the oil they produce. One of the most important sources of capital and know-how for setting up a modern industrial infrastructure in the Arab states is Western Europe. For this reason the European states have a tremendous and growing influence on the Arabs. Aside from this, Western Europe is the biggest buyer of the Arab states' agricultural exports. In the future the Middle East could become the main supplier of vegetables and other foodstuffs to Europe.

European cultural impact on the Arab states is also still very strong. The Arabs have driven out the British and French, but they cannot efface their influence. This influence is far stronger and more genuine than that of Soviet culture, which is itself the fruit of European culture.

Europe's importance to Israel is also very great. Today Israel sends most of her agricultural and industrial exports to Western Europe. Europe, with her hundreds of millions of consumers, is the largest market for Israeli products at present and will continue to be in the future. We export most of our products to Europe and purchase most of our import goods from her. It would not be an exaggeration to say that the future development of our national economy and technology depends on the future of the relations between us and the Common Market countries.

Europe is also important to us on the scientific, cultural, and social planes. Israel is developing scientific ties with the whole world. Israel, as a leading state in some scientific fields, has developed very close ties with the United States. In the future, cooperation will also develop between the European and the Israeli scientific communities.

The multiparty governments of Europe are very similar to ours. The structure of Israel's political and social institutions is based on British and European models, less on American traditions of government, and even less on those found in the countries of Eastern Europe. The large political parties in Israel are affiliated with international centers in Europe (the Socialist International, the Liberal International, and the like). We do not want our lives to become mere imitations of the European life-style. But Europe can continue to be a major source of inspiration to us in many areas of our life.

Europe maintains a special attitude to the Arab states, as well as unique relations with us, and it may one day help effect a compromise and rapprochement between us and the Arabs. In the conflict between us and the Arabs some European states appear to both the Arabs and ourselves as less motivated by self-interest than are the superpowers. A unique kind of role could be filled in the Arab-Israeli dispute by the Mediterranean European states. Italy, for example, is regarded as a country that likes and is liked by both sides. She does not allow herself to be unduly pressured by her interests in the Arab states and is very eager to maintain peace in the Mediterranean region.

When France regains an even balance in her stand in the Arab-Israeli dispute, she too will be able to resume her status as a potential mediator.

West Germany is today the strongest of the West European states; in terms of population, economic power, energy, and industriousness she leads all her neighbors. She will have a leading role to play in the economy and technology of the European Common Market. She will seek markets outside of Europe for her products. The Middle East could become a major market for German know-how, capital, and resources. We must approach the Germans with the demand that they continue to discharge the huge debt they owe us. It is their duty not only to continue to assist in the constant strengthening and development of the Jewish state, as they are now doing, but also to be a factor in the financing of great regional projects, such as finding a solution to the Palestinian Arab refugee problem. By doing so Germany will be able to help close the historic and tragic circle of World War II: the holocaust—Jewish refugees; the founding of the State of Israel—Palestinian Arab refugees. Major participation in regional development and rehabilitation projects in the Middle East should be regarded by the new Germany as a national challenge. In this way not only will justice be done to the Arab refugees, but a great German contribution will have been made to the restoration of calm in the region and to the well-being of Israel. Only with the coming of peace between the Arabs and Jews will the Jews be cured of the holocaust complex that the Nazis stamped in blood on the Jewish consciousness.

11

THE THIRD WORLD

The Middle East, Europe, the Soviet Union, and the United States are the four geohistoric regions with which the fate of the Jewish people and the fate of Israel are directly connected. The Middle East is where the Jewish people was born, where its land is situated. In Middle Eastern states large creative Jewish Diaspora communities once existed, and it is over this region that the Israel-Arab conflict rages today. The State of Israel has many special ties with the countries of Europe, the Soviet Union, and the United States. But these four great regions, however important, account for only about one-third of the human race.

Israel's relations with the other two-thirds of the world, known as the "Third World," do not unfold against a background of that world's past ties with Judaism and Jewry. There are no significant Jewish Diaspora communities in the countries of the Third World, and there never have been. Most of these countries, especially those in the Far East, are remote from the Judeo-Christian heritage.

THE FAR EAST

The history of the people of the Third World did not involve the Land of Israel. This country is not a holy land to the peoples of China, India, and Japan—or to their religions. Jerusalem is not sacred to them; they have neither dreamed of nor fought over Palestine. The names of Israel's kings and prophets, its traditions, songs, and literature mean little or nothing to these peoples. They have rich ancient traditions of their own in which we play no part, either as a "chosen people" or an "accursed race." We did not appear on the stage of their history; we never entered their field of vision.

Israel's relations with the Third World can and must be founded on a basis of mutual benefit, of give-and-take, in the most positive sense of the term.

With Japan, farthest east of all the great states of the Far East, Israel has stable relations. Japan has become the third greatest world power in terms of her economy and industry. She is heavily dependent on Middle Eastern oil. This is the basic reason for the guarded relations that exist between her and Israel.

In certain respects the two states, situated as they are at the two extreme poles of the Asian continent, have some common denominators. Both maintain a very high standard of technology and science; both concentrate their efforts on specialized, sophisticated exports; both lack raw materials and must make up for the deficiency in initiative, improvization, education, manual skill, and persistence. There is thus room for cooperation on a far broader basis than exists today, in the exchange of know-how, in the increase of mutual commerce, the expansion of tourism, and in joint Japanese-Israeli projects in scientific research and development.

Our relations with India are cold to the point of iciness and have been so ever since India gained her independence, almost at the same time that the State of Israel was founded. Her large Muslim minority is often thought to be the reason that India has not developed closer ties with Israel. But the true reason is the desire of Nehru and his heirs to win unqualified support in the Arab world. India is well aware that there are Muslim states—Iran, Turkey, and others—that maintain relations with Israel and yet are by no means hampered in their relations with the Arab countries. The establishment of ties between India and Israel would seem to be mainly conditional upon the improvement of relations between Israel and the Arabs. Such ties could be of considerable value to both countries, especially in the implementation of irrigation and agricultural projects.

China is closed to us. We have not been able to make the Chinese understand what we are. They compete with the Soviets in denouncing Israel as "an imperialist and American agent in the Middle East." They support the most radical Arab extremists and depict the Soviets as traitors to the Arab cause.

China has been trying for more than a decade to gain footholds in other parts of the Third World and to compete with the Soviet Union for leadership. She has penetrated some states in Asia and black Africa by means of development projects and economic, technological, and military assistance; and she is also trying to penetrate the Middle East. For the present China is no match for the Soviet Union in those countries. Not only is the Soviet Union closer geographically to most of these states, she is also richer, she possesses more sophisticated techniques, and she has more to offer. In lieu of this material and technical wherewithal, China sometimes offers extreme revolutionary ideology and Little Red Books by Chairman Mao. Without making light of China as a world force, one may reasonably assume that in the near future she will not be able to intervene directly in the Middle Eastern arena.

It may be that if international tensions are relaxed and Communist China becomes more open to Europe and the United States, Israel too will be able to establish some contacts with her. And if the Chinese get to know us as we are, they may come to recognize that mutually beneficial bonds could be established between them and us. Toning down the Arab-Israeli conflict and arriving at a state of peace in the future might bring swift Chinese recognition of Israel and the creation of fruitful relations with us. But even before that, there could be unexpected developments on the rapidly changing international scene. We must be prepared for this and alert for whatever opportunities might arise. We must repeatedly declare that we desire to reach an understanding and establish ties with the People's Republic of China.

Our cordial relations with Singapore, the Philippines, and Thailand indicate that there is a prospect of expanding our contacts with the world of Southeast Asia. This is a world unto itself, encompassing a population of hundreds of millions, rich in raw materials, thirsty for technology, an area whose markets are only now beginning to open up.

THE HELPFUL ISRAELI

While the balance sheet of our contacts with the peoples of the Far East is somewhat scanty, our relations with the continent of black Africa went along well for a long time because of an energetic Israeli initiative during the 1950s. These efforts met with impressive success from the outset, especially in the fields of agriculture, water projects, medicine, the armed forces, and the police. The Israeli presence in most of the independent countries of black Africa was a great achievement for Israel. The Arabs' massive efforts to persuade the rulers of the African states to cease their dealings with us were finally successful just prior to and in the wake of the Yom Kippur War. Still, black Africa is not entirely closed to us. Many thousands of its people have studied and toured in Israel; thousands of our people have been active in its lands. It is to be hoped that in the foreseeable future the African states will once again resume diplomatic relations with Israel.

Our relations with the states of Latin America are generally good. Many of them have been and remain consistent supporters of Israel. Tens of thousands of Latin Americans have toured and studied in Israel. Hundreds of Israelis are active in those countries in scientific and technical fields, particularly in the planning and execution of agriculture and irrigation projects.

The countries of Latin America are in need of socioeconomic

change; if these do not come about by rapid development, they will be achieved by revolution. The governments of these states are well aware of this fact; hence the constantly growing demand for technological advice. The prospects are fair for a constant growth of economic, technological, and scientific cooperation between Israel and these states during the 1970s.

A unique phenomenon is the web of relations existing between us and three of our neighbors: Iran, Turkey, and Cyprus. We have different relationships with each of them. But it should be emphasized that although these states border upon and are closely involved with the Arab states, we have been able to establish warm and stable relations with them. Although Islam is practiced in Iran and Turkey, this has not been an obstacle to their maintaining relations with us in all fields; nor have our good relations with Cyprus prevented her from maintaining completely normal relations with the Arab countries.

The vested interests inherent in geographical proximity, recognition of Israel's ability to render significant and large-scale assistance in several fields, the mutual advantages to be derived from economic and commercial relations, the value of investments, and the exchange of know-how and culture—all these factors were far more important to these countries than any possible repercussions arising from the Arab-Israel conflict.

Her relations and ties with these countries lead Israel to hope that the day will come when the Arabs will be guided by their true interests to recognize us, negotiate with us, and live with us in peace.

As a result of these stable relations with the non-Arab Middle Eastern states, Israelis have reached the Turkish Euphrates and the Blue Nile of Ethiopia. They have come there, not in the aftermath of war, but as geologists, electrical engineers, hydrologists, hydraulic engineers, agronomists, and farming instructors. They were invited by the governments of those states, who knew that their countries could be helped by Israel, which is situated in the same region, has the same climate, has similar types of soil: a land whose landscape and skies resemble their own.

After peace is established, it is in this way—and only in this way—that we shall also reach the Syrian and Iraqi Euphrates and the Sudanese and Egyptian Nile.

12

THE FACE OF SOCIETY

Zionism, the national renaissance movement of the Jewish people, set itself two basic aims: the founding of a safe refuge in the Land of Israel for any Jew wishing or forced to immigrate there, and the creation of a new Jewish society in the Land of Israel, based on justice, equality, and human freedom.

We shall now examine how close Zionism has come to achieving its objectives, and what the goals are that it still faces.

The first objective was reached with the founding of the State of Israel. Since its establishment, the state has admitted over one and a half million Jewish immigrants from all parts of the Diaspora, many of them coming because they wanted to, others because hardship and persecution forced them to flee their countries, and still others because of a combination of volition and duress.

The Jewish state is not only a refuge but an open refuge—open both ways: to the entry as well as the departure of Jews. About 10 percent of her immigrants have regarded Israel as a temporary haven only and have left, for various reasons, and emigrated to other lands. This percentage is relatively very small, compared to other countries where migration has been open both ways. The vast majority of immigrants have remained in Israel, despite the very hard conditions of life in a small country surrounded by enemies.

The refuge we have created here will continue to be an open one; but it is not a safe one. Surrounded by Arab peoples who desire the destruction of our enterprise, we have been obliged to concentrate our best efforts on establishing a people's army, so as to be able to defend ourselves and enable other Jews to find a haven in Israel. As long as there is no peace between us and the Arabs, this army is our best guarantee that we may continue to realize the first objective of Zionism.

Until the state was founded the Jews of Palestine constituted only a small percentage of the entire Jewish people. About a hundred years ago we started almost from zero. On the eve of independence we had about 5 percent of world Jewry; 25 years after the state was founded and its gates were opened, more than 20 percent of the Jewish people live within its borders.

We cannot deny that over half the Jewish people live in countries whose gates are open to emigration, and yet only a thin trickle of immigrants make their way to Israel from those countries. We believe that a widespread immigration campaign in the Diaspora will yield results, and that young Jews will be drawn to Israel and will come to build their homes here. If our belief is borne out, and millions of Jews do immigrate to Israel, if the great majority of the Jewish people does come to be centered in Israel, then we must find a basic answer to the question that the Jewish people, the Arabs, and the world will ask: Where will these additional millions of Jews live?

The haziness and the nebulousness that has surrounded this vital question, especially since the Six-Day War, has been injurious to our cause. This is not to say that detailed maps should be drawn, or that the specific security and strategic needs of our country should be enumerated. But an answer must be given to the basic question we are being asked and are asking ourselves: In order to settle the majority of the Jewish people in our state, do we need additional territories?

My answer to this is—no! This is what we said to ourselves, the

Arabs, and the world throughout the years of our existence
prior to the Six-Day War. This is what our generation was
brought up on, and this is what it educated its children to
believe.

Of course, for the security of the State of Israel we need
additional security guarantees in the form of focal territories,
about which we shall come to an agreement with the Arabs in
peace negotiations. But we must reiterate our truth: that we are
not an expansionist state. It is not the lust for expansion that
drives us.

We must answer the question, not only of where millions of
Jews are going to live in Israel, but of how they will gain their
livelihood. Will they live dignified, interesting, worthwhile
lives? Will they have a reasonable standard of living? The answer to these questions is important to us, as Jews and as Zionists.

In other words, we must come up with an answer regarding
the realization of the second aim of Zionism; we will have to
decide what kind of society we want to build in Israel, and
examine whether or not we have progressed in the direction of
creating a new Jewish society based on the values of justice,
equality, and human freedom.

In order to be able to answer this question we must realize
that the social values we aspire to are now inextricably bound
up with the Palestinian Arab problem and the issue of the territories—all of which we have already dealt with.

Assuming that Israel and the Zionist enterprise can come to
terms with the Arabs, and that Israel should continue to be a
state in which Jews constitute the great majority, we ought to
discuss the social objectives of Zionism and examine what values of human equality and freedom we hold; what we have
achieved and what remains to be done; what actions we have
taken; and how our faults can be corrected.

The Jews of the nineteenth century who began dreaming
about a state of their own envisioned a just and unique state,

unlike those they knew. Such were Rabbi Kalischer, Rabbi Alkalai, Rabbi Mohilever, Moses Hess, Ahad Ha-am, and that
greatest of visionaries: Herzl.

It is no surprise that after two thousand years of subjugation,
injustice, and inequality the founders of the Zionist movement
should have dreamed of a utopian state. Some dreamed of a
state in the likeness of the ancient kingdom of Israel; others
thought of the biblical "good old days," when every man sat
under his vine and fig tree, when peace, justice, and law
reigned.

Among these men were some who wanted to pour the new
wine of universal doctrines of justice into the old beaker of
Jewish morality and justice. How wonderful it was in the darkness of exile to revel in golden dreams of a Jewish state which
would be a light to the nations, where the wolf would dwell with
the sheep, a nation which would not lift up its sword against any
nation, whose governors would be as wise as Solomon, whose
laws would be legislated by a Sanhedrin of eminent Torah scholars, where there would be no more poverty, whose citizens,
equal before the law, would always abide by that law.

The small groups of First Aliya idealists (1882–1903) who
began putting their Zionism into practice were, as is natural
among pioneers, egalitarian to a degree. The first members of
Bilu and Hovevei Zion resembled each other in the spiritual
motives that impelled them to immigrate to the Land of Israel,
and also in age, country of origin, aptitudes (or, more precisely,
ineptitudes!), and material circumstances; in short, the socioeconomic differences between these intimate groups were very
small. Although they brought with them no fixed doctrine of
total equality, they did practice maximal equality among themselves from the outset.

Similarly, the beginnings of settlement in Palestine were
characterized by a large degree of relative egalitarianism, because of the small number of settlers, the common dangers they
faced, the difficulties that beset them all equally, intimate ac-

quaintanceship with one another, and the impossibility of getting rich quickly in a small, impoverished country under Turkish rule.

The pioneers of the Second Aliya (1904–14) brought with them from the Diaspora, and established in this country, a doctrine and ideology of social justice and maximal equality. They dreamed that their doctrine would become a guiding light, not only to the small Jewish society they found in Palestine on their arrival, but also to the great Jewish society that would arise there in the future. They brought with them the best socialist doctrines and utopias, and wanted to build in the land of their forefathers not only a society and state that would be open to all Jews, but also a society of workers living in dignity, a society in which there would be no place for degrading poverty or exploitation by the wealthy.

The marvelous thing is that they not only preached a fine sermon but also practiced what they preached. They tried to implement their doctrine themselves. They did not want to wait for the succeeding generation to carry out their doctrines. They were impatient to create an egalitarian society, or at least the kernel of it, in their own lifetimes.

Youthful, freed of family burdens, divested of the yoke of convention, enthusiastic, and full of faith in their goal, these people made a daring leap toward the realization of a new Zionist and egalitarian way of life. They created the *kevutzah* and the kibbutz (voluntary collective farming villages), the moshav (cooperative small holding village), and the *moshav shitufi* (cooperative village); they forged the first producer and consumer cooperatives; they created the Sick Fund. The crowning glory of their work was the General Workers' Federation (the Histadrut), which was not only a trade union but also a comprehensive framework encompassing the lives of Jewish workers in Palestine, as hired laborers in town and country, as independent farmers, and as owners of their own means of production in building and in industry.

The men of the Second Aliya created the Labor movement and socialist-Zionism. The ideology of the Labor movement, based on the supremacy of work, the value of equality, the exaltedness of the laborer in general and the tiller of the soil in particular, was like an electric plug, which, fitted into the socket of the Zionist enterprise, set up a high-tension electric current and drew to itself young people who were prepared to dedicate themselves to it.

There was yet another factor that contributed to the promotion of new ways of life in pre-Israel Jewish society. Prior to the establishment of the state the Zionist enterprise was not a complete society; it was not responsible for all the needs of its members. The Zionist enterprise was sheltered beneath the wings of another authority, first the Turkish and later the British; this freed the Zionist enterprise of responsibility for society as a whole. It was the foreign authorities, not the Jews or the Arabs, who were responsible (or were supposed to be responsible) for the safety of life and property. They maintained an army and a police force in the country and established a judiciary and a prison system; it was their law that the citizenry obeyed. It was they who laid the budgetary and administrative foundations for the creation of an economic infrastructure in the country: roads, waterworks, public works, ports, airfields, and railroads. Within the protected environment the Jewish community generally, and the Labor movement especially, were able to create unique life-styles characterized by very strong elements of equality.

The existence of a social gap, inequality, rich and poor, exploiters and exploited in the prestatehood period cannot be ignored. All these were very much in evidence. But Zionism could rightly point out that it was working not only for the establishment of Jewish sovereignty but also for the creation of a new, more just society.

At the time the State of Israel was founded the Zionist enterprise was built upon a well-defined social ideology whose foun-

dations were a democratic way of life, parliamentary government, creation of a pluralistic economy, and aspiration toward
a more egalitarian society. All these were axiomatic truths for
most of the Yishuv. Upon the sovereign State of Israel devolved
the responsibility for society as a whole, for Jews and non-Jews,
for its physical safety, its law, its economy—everything. In the
new reality that came to obtain with the founding of the state,
the Zionist enterprise underwent rapid "institutionalization."
This change would have occurred even had the young state's
population been more or less static; but it was felt far more
acutely in a state which immediately upon its creation had to
face problems of immigration, absorption, and demographic
changes of overpowering dimensions.

Very rapid demographic changes, under stress of ceaseless
war or war tension, have brought every country of immigration
in the world to a condition of severe social crises. A similar crisis
took place in Israel. But a number of factors operated to enable
Israel to hold her own. The Jewish community had a longstanding social and political awareness that immigration and
absorption took top priority in its life—indeed, were the purpose of its existence. Thus without any need for much preaching, people showed a readiness to "crowd in," to make room for
the next arrivals.

For decades the Yishuv had been educated in voluntarism,
because it had no laws or means of enforcement. Therefore it
was not difficult, at least during the early years of the state, to
demand the continuation of the volunteer tradition.

Strong egalitarian trends were at work in the Israel of the
early 1950s, without which it could not have withstood the
strain of the absorption of hundreds of thousands of destitute
Jewish immigrants from Islamic countries, as well as survivors
of the European holocaust. The state could not at one and the
same time give the arrivals good food, good housing, good jobs,
and good education; even the veterans themselves were for the
most part then living at a pretty modest standard in housing,

nutrition, dress, and so forth. Moreover, state and society succeeded in those days—mainly on the psychological level—in making austerity not only a necessity but a veritable virtue. While the new immigrants did find an established society of "old-timers," they could not say that that society was rich or arrogant or ostentatious. Without idealizing life in the 1950s, which was so difficult and bitter both to immigrants and to those in charge of immigration, one cannot doubt that the values of the volunteer spirit, equality, and austerity prevented crises far worse than those that actually took place.

THE ETHNIC COMMUNITY PROBLEM

By the middle 1950s we already faced the great new social problem that we are still grappling with to this very day—the ethnic community problem. At the time the state was founded, the Jewish Yishuv in Israel was largely homogeneous. Over the course of about eighty years it had been slowly built up from layer upon layer of small immigrant groups that gradually merged with one another, in spite of a certain amount of friction. Into this "merging of the exiles" brew, the values of equality and social justice were constantly being poured.

Some social polarization existed even then, against the background of countries of origin. Jews coming to the Land of Israel from Europe (Ashkenazis) a hundred years ago found here a Jewish population, the relatively well-established strata of which were mostly Sephardic Jews, who had been living in the country for many generations. The various waves of immigration arriving from that time until the founding of the State of Israel came from many countries, mostly East European; virtually the only elements they had in common were that they were all relatively youthful, poor, and equal.

During the 1950s and 1960s a demographic revolution occurred among the Jews of Israel. The Jewish people in the Diaspora can be classed many different ways. One is the division into Ashkenazis and Sephardis. The Ashkenazis lived generation upon generation among Christians and within a Christian civilization, mainly in Europe and later in America as well. The Sephardis lived generation upon generation among Muslims and within a Muslim society, mainly in the Arab countries, but also in Persia, Turkey, and other non-Arab Muslim countries. For all that, the Jewish people preserved its unity and distinctiveness. But differences naturally came into being between these two great groups in the course of the centuries. If proof is needed that environment, climate, and culture exert an influence on man over the generations, the Jews have amply demonstrated this truth.

Thus the Jews of today are not only different from their early ancestors, they are also different from one another, in complexion, physical build, spoken language, as a result of the environment and conditions under which they lived. But even these are not the only differences. The Jews also absorbed much of the culture and civilization of the peoples among whom they lived. They had different ways of life, different customs, a different standard of education, and were brought up on different poetry and literature.

The Jews also rose and fell with the fortunes of the countries and peoples with whom they "lodged." When the state, the empire, or the civilization in which they were living enjoyed a cultural, economic, or commercial boom, the Jews too were borne aloft on the crest of the rising wave; and they sank with their neighbors during periods of recession and disintegration.

At the end of the nineteenth century and the beginning of the twentieth, about three-quarters of the Jewish people were living in Christian lands, and about one-quarter in Islamic countries. During that period, so fateful for the Zionist enterprise, most of the Islamic countries (especially the ones dominated by the disintegrating Turkish Empire) were sunk in profound and protracted political, economic, cultural, and social torpor—which also left its mark on their Jewish populations.

The Christian world, on the other hand, was at that time witness to strong cultural and social ferment, which gave rise to the industrial revolution, modern technology, modern nationalism, new social doctrines, and, later, to two world wars. The Jews in the Christian world took part in these processes. Frequently they were its driving force; even more frequently they were its victims.

During the long chronicles of the Jewish people there were periods of ups and downs among both Sephardic and Ashkenazic Jews. The strange pride that many Ashkenazic Jews take in their European origin is groundless. Basically we are a Mediterranean people. Our true cause for pride is in our having preserved our distinctiveness among Europeans and Christians, among Arabs and Muslims.

It was in the Middle East, not in Europe, that we created the best of our unique cultural and religious values. It was from here that our Law went forth. From here its basic precepts spread, through the agency of Christianity and Islam, throughout the world. Here, upon the Israelite foundations, arose the glorious edifice of the oral law, the Mishnah, and the Talmud. Here gaonism, piyut (poetry), Hebrew grammar, Jewish philosophy, and the Kabbalah (Jewish mysticism) were created and developed.

The countries of the Middle East provided a refuge for the Jews who fled before the sword of "civilization" and the Catholic Spanish Inquisition about five hundred years ago. Great as the Christian European civilization was, it was one in which we were always being put to death. In recent generations European civilization has proved to be one of unparalleled savagery and barbarism, and we began escaping from it to the Middle East, there to build ourselves a home and a refuge in our own land. It was men raised by the standards of Christian Europe who sent the Jews to the gas chambers and the death camps. The latter-day Amalekite who rose up to destroy us was a typical European. This is something we should not forget.

MASS IMMIGRATION

Prior to Israeli independence the structure of the Yishuv, in terms of the countries of origin of its members, reflected more or less faithfully the structure of the Jewish people as a whole. Out of the approximately six hundred thousand Jews who lived in Israel in early 1948, about three-quarters originated from the lands of Europe and Christianity, and about one-quarter from the lands of Islam.

The Nazi holocaust wrought a horrendous change in the Jewish demographic balance. It did away with the great reserves of immigration that had existed among the Jews of Europe. The great wave of immigration to Israel of the Jews of the Islamic countries during the 1950s brought about a revolution in the structure of the Israeli population, which was followed by far-reaching changes also in the age, occupation, social, and normative structure of the Jewish population in Israel.

Prior to the establishment of the state there had been no immigration of whole tribes, whole communities, or whole societies. Every Diaspora sent some of its sons to Israel. Beginning in the 1950s entire communities began arriving in Israel, mainly from Islamic countries. This brought with it a plethora of new problems.

The immigration of the remnants of the European holocaust after the establishment of the state was a selective one. The selection had been made by the Nazis. Those who survived were generally the strongest and the youngest. Broken and worn though they were, they nevertheless found in themselves the strength for relatively swift regeneration in Israel.

The Jewry of the Islamic countries, on the other hand, immigrated virtually en masse—men, women, and children; the strong and healthy, the feeble and sick. Thus there arrived in Israel, within a very short time and almost simultaneously, the Yemeni Jewish exile, the vast majority of the Babylonian (Iraqi) Jewish exile, about half of the Persian Jewish exile, most of the

Moroccan Jewish exile, and large parts of the Syrian, Egyptian, Tunisian, Algerian, Libyan, and various other Jewish exiles from Islamic countries.

This huge, almost messianic aliya of entire communities was not prepared for the shock of encounter with Israeli reality in the early 1950s. The small Yishuv was hardly in a state of readiness for this mass immigration. The Israeli did not recognize his brothers and did not know what he was going to do with them in their new homeland. Thus both the Yishuv and the immigrants groped their way toward one another, through tentative overtures, through trial and error.

It was my privilege to be among those who stood at the center of this activity. I can testify that we had no experience, no "textbook solution" to tell us how to act and what to do. What experiment did we not perform with these new immigrants? We founded heterogeneous settlements and housing developments and neighborhoods in which we artificially "blended" one community with another, one village with another, townspeople with ex-villagers; we created all sorts of small social groups—which divided and disintegrated with great rapidity while we watched. We tried founding homogeneous settlements, housing developments, and neighborhoods, and again encountered unexpected misunderstandings and difficulties. We tried to administer communities, and we tried letting the communities administer themselves. We tried, arbitrarily and at top speed, to implant democratically elected institutions into the patriarchal family structures of Islamic Jewry. We pulverized the human, familial, social, and traditional cement and tried to replace it with another kind, but this did not work.

All that we did in our race against time was done with great haste, with no previous planning, with shoestring budgets, without coordination among the various agencies, with incessant friction between the settlement institutions and the settlers.

Today we are paying the full price of those experiments, with compound interest. One thing should be made clear to the younger generation that grew up on our acts and our mistakes: our intentions were good and they were pure. We sought the good of the immigrants. To this end we dedicated all our time, our strength, our hearts. The targets we set ourselves—though they were probably somewhat utopian and naive—were those of equality for all and a generally high living standard.

We made many, sometimes irreparable, mistakes. Yet we must not forget the great work that the veteran Yishuv accomplished during the 1950s and 1960s. There they lie before us, the hundreds of new villages and dozens of new towns that were founded. When we publicly castigate ourselves for our deficiencies in absorbing the mass immigration, let us do so uprightly, with mercy and justice. This Yishuv—its governing bodies, its institutions—tried, and is still trying, to repair the errors of the past; and of course this corrective action is accompanied by new mistakes.

DIFFERENT STARTING LINES

A single generation after the absorption of the mass immigration we are faced by vast problems of social polarization in our midst. Much of the whitewash hastily slapped onto our work is peeling away, and we are left face to face with stark reality.

The Jewish population of Israel today consists of one-half originating from Islamic countries and one-half originating from Christian countries. From this point of view, Jewry in Israel is therefore by no means representative of the contemporary Jewish people. For whereas Ashkenazic Jews make up the great majority of the people, the situation in Israel is different.

The situation can be analyzed and explained; shortcomings and errors can be pointed at. But there is one thing that none of us must ignore or fail to perceive properly. The established Jewish Yishuv, the great majority of which was Ashkenazic, had a better starting line, a higher springboard, and greater initial acceleration for its race. It was quickly augmented by the

majority of Ashkenazic immigrants arriving after the establishment of the state. Most immigrants from the Islamic countries
did not have such a good starting line, and their initial acceleration in the race was far slower. One of the major factors causing
the difference was the size of the family. Most Jews coming
from Christian countries either brought with them from the
Diaspora, or created here, a small, nuclear family (father,
mother, two to four children). A family such as this had a tremendous initial advantage in helping its sons and daughters to
progress in all areas of life: education, housing, health, and
vocational training.

Most of the Jews from the Islamic countries, on the other
hand, brought with them large families. Veteran leaders
(mostly Ashkenazis with small families) encouraged them to
continue to maintain these norms in Israel. They were
prompted in this by religious, national, and even dubious
security motives. Also at work here was the reaction to the
catastrophe suffered by the Jewish people and the desire to fill
up the terrible demographic gap as quickly as possible. At this
stage we need not stop to assess this past encouragement. What
is clear is that there came into existence in Israel whole sectors
with families having large numbers of children, the great
majority of which originated from Islamic countries.

It does not take an expert sociologist to understand that this
combination of large families who are new to the country, taken
with the fact that they arrived completely destitute, was instru-
mental in causing entire sectors of the Israeli population to
"run" much more slowly, and sometimes even to fail to get
beyond the starting post in almost all areas of life.

Another factor making for polarization is the abandonment
of maximum possible equality as a goal. During the past generation we began to scorn this value. There were reasons for this.
We discovered that the value of absolute equality, which the
founders of the Labor movement had so fervently preached, no
longer conformed to life as we knew it and was opposed to

man's impulses and aptitudes. We saw that it did not fit in with life on the kibbutz, was not well suited to life on the moshav, and was not at all suited to urban life. Those who preached equality began to be regarded as naive.

Urbanization, industrialization, specialization, and professionalization militated against the doctrine of equality and against its realization in practice. By adopting a life-style imported from Europe and America, we came to admire technological and industrial hierarchies which do not tolerate equality.

Disillusionment with Communism, which had preached equality and justice yet had been transformed into tyranny and inequality, fed our growing scepticism of equality as a supreme value. The pomp that accompanied the establishment of the state: the ceremonies, the dress uniforms, the glamour of high positions, the rank of ministries and ministers—all militated powerfully against equality. It is one thing to live in a small, intimate pioneering community, when the president of the National Committee is personally acquainted with almost all the citizens of the state-to-be and the mayor of the first Hebrew town is on a friendly footing with almost all his town's inhabitants; it is another thing to be a prime minister or minister, with thousands of subordinate employees under one's direction. It is one thing to be a company commander in the Palmach, where officers and men are all volunteers, where no one wears a uniform and authority is bestowed by the force of one's personality; it is another thing to be the commander of a modern army brigade and in charge of a sophisticated, complex war machine that by its very nature is hierarchical.

When we became institutionalized, when we divided up into our various hierarchies in conformity with the best modern ideas, it was no wonder that in the lowest stratum of each of them we found those people whose prospects for advancement were minute. It is no surprise that as a result a vicious circle was formed, in which people originating from Islamic countries found themselves trapped and imprisoned in a nonegalitarian system which could, unless corrected, continue for decades.

Just as we abandoned our aspirations to equality, we also lost another quality that had accompanied our enterprise from its inception and was bound up with the aspiration to equality: that of simplicity and folksiness.

The leaders of the Zionist enterprise knew themselves to be the emissaries of a poor people, and they behaved accordingly. Their life-style was simple and unpretentious: their dress, accommodations, hospitality, and general living standards. They wore the *rubashka*—the blue shirt with the open collar—or khaki clothes; they traveled by bus; those among them who were kibbutz members would serve in the dining room. These were accepted and binding norms. It was this simplicity of style that produced the cordiality between the leadership and the people.

The simplicity and the folksiness did not, of course, prevent the emergence of certain social gaps, or even splits and quarrels; but they helped to strengthen the mortar that held the Jewish Yishuv together while the country was being built.

With the establishment of the state, our sense of simplicity became warped. The trappings of pomp and circumstance, self-importance, arrogance, the ostentatiousness that came with statehood—all conspired to make simplicity appear odd and ridiculous. The leaders were growing old and wanted to taste, at the end of their long road, something of the ceremonial delicacies; they ceased to exemplify simplicity and folksiness.

Israel's great materialist race was on. The pursuit was under way for an ever-rising living standard in all walks of life: food, dress, housing. People began to outdo each other in ostentatiousness and snobbism. This race necessarily left most of those originating from the Islamic countries far behind.

Israel is a small country, with a high population density. Jews are an inquisitive people, and the individual cannot escape his neighbor's watchful eye. Life is all the more open to inspection because of the mass media, which light up every corner of our public and private lives.

We belong to a society formed by the expectation of egalitarianism; when before our very eyes chasms begin to yawn in this society, we stand dumbfounded, reproachfully berating each other. The social expectation coefficient in our society is the highest in the world, and one of its consequences is envy. When this envy assumes the guise of ethnic differences ("you"—the European-born—"have," and "we"—the Asian- and African-born—"have not"), it turns into a monster quite capable of destroying the entire structure of the "merging of the exiles."

Even were our security situation stable, our economy normal, and peace knocking at our door, we would still be obliged to correct the social wrong that has come about in Israel, and regard the necessity for a better-regulated and more just society as a goal that must be reached if we are to continue to exist. But when we are under incessant external siege, when our economy relies on grants from world Jewry on the one hand and the productivity and competitiveness of the home front on the other hand, the obligation becomes much more urgent. In such a situation, it is at our mortal peril that we perpetuate the great social gaps that have emerged in our midst.

REINSTATEMENT OF DISCARDED VALUES

There are many paths leading to the realization of Zionism's social aims. But to follow them we must revolutionize our thinking, our way of life, and our actions. First of all we must return our aspiration for maximal equality to its original position of honor.

It is a fact that the leaders of the free Western societies, including the materialistic American society, have now fully realized that they must take seriously the human aspiration to optimal social equality. The American race for a high standard of living at all costs, the worship of the dollar, the establishment of a social system geared solely to the consumption of an endless array of new products has almost brought the United States to the brink of the abyss. Much of American youth has revolted against this inegalitarian, patently materialistic society, with its lack of substantive values and its burden of social rifts and injustice inherited from the past.

The future of the United States and of Europe, which is undergoing a similar process, will be more secure if these young people, most of whom are well intentioned, can find a positive way of realizing their yearnings for justice, equality, and human freedom within their various societies and can achieve an influence on the power levers of their countries—before they themselves are debilitated by drugs, apathy, and violence.

Our own Israeli society, originally erected on foundations of social justice and equality, must rapidly reinstate these values and come to regard them as a central aim in the upbuilding of the state and of Zionism. These values should be discussed at length and imparted to the younger generation.

But fine talk and polished phrases are not enough. Justice must actually be done.

One of the things we must do is stop the mad race for an even higher standard of living. The men to set an example in calling a halt to this race should be the Israeli social and political leadership.

It is essential for us to reintroduce simplicity, unpretentiousness, and austerity in all walks of life. The issue is not one of our bread and butter or of the roof over our heads; nor will anything be done at the expense of our cultural and artistic needs. The simplicity of "walk humbly" should replace ostentatious standards of living, excessive gluttony, ugly architecture, snobbish and flashy dress, superficial and trashy literature and art. This does not mean some form of artificial and hypocritical puritanism. A gay, laughter-loving life of healthy vitality, filled with free culture, can be quite compatible with simplicity, unpretentiousness, and austerity. If the mad race for an impressive living standard is stopped, or at least slowed, Israeli society will be able to allocate more of its resources to raising the living standards of those who are really in need and free them and their children from the chains of poverty and affliction.

It is incumbent upon our leadership to signal the end of the race. The very first to heed that signal must be the leadership itself. The next generation to whom the social, political, and cultural leadership of the state is relayed must take on the kind of simplicity and unpretentiousness suited to the present day. The leadership of a people under siege and in social distress must show a personal example of simplicity and austerity in everything: plain clothing, simple accessories, inexpensive cars, unostentatious manners, simple forms of hospitality, modest apartments.

I do not call for monasticism or asceticism, but for simplicity, in all the enchanting and captivating significance of the word.

One who talks about equality should first take upon himself a number of "do's" and "don't's" regarding his own way of life. Personal examples of simplicity set by prominent leaders of the state will give Israeli society and the Israeli government a powerful tool with which to slow the race for an ever-higher standard of living. But this alone will not fill the social gaps, or of itself arrest negative social processes or initiate positive ones. If progress is to be made toward closing the gap and toward greater equalization, there must be long-term socioeconomic planning. This depends on education, housing, health, welfare, and many other factors; they in turn depend on tremendous financial resources. But only a leadership advocating social equality and daily setting a personal example of simplicity will be able to cope with this social task and help Israeli society progress in the direction of equality.

REPRESENTATION

Inequality begins with the size of the family; from there it spreads to housing conditions, education, training, and other spheres of life. It also manifests itself in the sphere of leadership and representation. In the areas of family, housing, and education the situation can be corrected only by long-term planning and implementation, but in the sphere of representation it is possible to take deliberate and rapid steps that will entail no expenditure of funds and have immediate positive results.

In 1948 the leadership of the State of Israel and almost all the people in her representative institutions were of European origin. This exclusivity did not reflect the true structure of the Jewish community even in prestatehood Palestine, where Jews from Islamic countries accounted for about a quarter of the population. During the years of the state's existence the situation has been excruciatingly slow to change. The absence of any rotation system in our public lives, blocked channels of advancement to higher political echelons, the existing electoral system, which links the elected leaders of institutions to their party centers rather than to their constituencies—all these have delayed the rate of growth of new cadres from Islamic countries of origin and their entry into the upper echelons of leadership and representation in Israel. The meager increase in their representation over the years has sometimes come about as the result of a favor or an act of charity on the part of the veteran leadership.

We have thus reached an absurd situation: about 50 percent of the Jewish population in Israel originates from Islamic countries; yet in the government, the Knesset, the foremost institutions of the Zionist Federation, the Histadrut, the political parties, and the civil, administrative, economic, and governing institutions, the percentage of persons originating from Islamic countries is between 10 and 20.

It will be generally acknowledged that such a situation is intolerable. The claim that elections to representational institutions should be made on the basis of achievement and ability only, and not on the basis of ethnic origin, seems to be right on the face of it, but this would be possible only under certain fair and equal conditions which simply do not exist. To argue that such conditions *do* exist is tantamount to saying that persons originating from Islamic countries are neither suitable nor worthy of occupying more than 10 to 20 percent of places in the

314 / LAND OF THE HART

state leadership. To argue thus is either nonsensical or wicked or both. Among the new immigrants, especially the generation that grew up in Israel, there are many people originating from Iraq and Morocco, Yemen and Syria, Egypt and Lebanon, Tunisia and Algeria, Iran, Turkey, and India who are capable of serving honorably and well at any administrative level. The situation obtaining today in this sphere is an artificial one, the result of circumstances engendered by time. It must be corrected as decisively and as rapidly as time allows. It is vital that the political leadership undertake to correct distortions, even at the risk of appearing to establish quotas. While we should not ignore the great risks inherent in perpetuating representation-by-community, we must acknowledge that in practice semi-overt and humiliating quotas have existed for years. The first presidents of the State of Israel were of European origin; it is only right that this office should also be open to persons from Islamic countries as well as Israel-born citizens. Members of the Knesset ought not to be chosen according to countries of origin, but meaningful progress should be made toward closing the great gulf between 50 percent and 20 percent; this also applies to all other governmental institutions.

If I were forced to believe that in order to close the ethnic gap it would be necessary to perpetuate the community-representation method for several generations (and thereby also the sinecures and "reserved positions" secured by ethnic origin) I would be in despair. But I believe that by concentrated effort the problem can be solved within a generation—if not altogether solved, then at least it can be deprived of its worst aspects. The closing of the representational gap by quotas is a quick but temporary cure, which in the future will not be necessary. During the present period of explosive growth in our heterogeneous society it is vital that we use it.

At the beginning of the history of the world's democratic institutions "No taxation without representation" was a slogan. If we want the Jewish population as a whole to do its part in "taxation"—that is, in the overall national effort in all fields—then it is quite unthinkable to leave it without suitable representation.

At the same time we are repairing representational distortion, we must get down to finding basic, long-term solutions whose end result will be to render the ethnic community problem a subject for future historic and ethnological research, rather than a cause of sociopolitical unrest, as it is today. One process that is unfolding before our eyes, which offers the beginning of a true solution of the problem, is intercommunity marriage. Marriages between members of different European communities are a matter of course, and marriages between members of various oriental communities hardly present any problem. A heartwarming and important manifestation in our lives is the marriages between people of Western and Eastern communities. This phenomenon is slowly spreading. It can be encouraged by a steady rise in the standards of living, education, and housing of all communities. A life of constantly increasing general equality will accelerate this most welcome process, which within a single generation could effect the marvelous balance we are looking forward to—a merging of the exiles in its literal, physical, and biological sense.

CONCENTRATED EFFORT FOR SOCIAL AMENDMENT

It is a fact that the vast majority of those originating in Islamic countries brought with them life-styles that not only promote but actually necessitate large families. Anchored in the Jewish religion, this life-style was also influenced by the life of the environment and society in which these Jews lived.

Most Jewish families from Christian countries that came about the same time had much smaller families, except for a few Orthodox Jews of European origin who also tended to have large families. The first generations of native-born Israelis, irrespective of their parents' origins, had small and medium-size families (three or four children). Only a small minority of the Israel-born established very large families, and these were mainly people who had had an extreme Orthodox upbringing.

With the great waves of immigration from the Islamic countries, Israel found itself faced with a problem of tens of thousands of families with large numbers of children. These families needed no encouragement whatever to continue reproducing; some had ten or more children. Families of this size, even when given government support in the form of grants and welfare, will have a difficult time competing in the race for education, training, and standard of living.

I believe that the problem of families with numerous children will probably disappear within a single generation. The children of these families will not themselves establish families of comparable size, whether or not they are encouraged to do so. Within a single generation the average Israel-born family will have three or four children, irrespective of the country of origin of the parents. In one more generation native-born Israelis will constitute the great majority of the population in Israel. Even if large numbers of immigrants arrive, they will be coming from countries in which family size is similar to that of the Israel-born: an average of three or four children. About 90 percent of Jews originating from Islamic countries are already in Israel, with only about 10 percent remaining in the Diaspora. For Jews in Christian countries, the ratio is reversed: about 10 percent of them are in Israel and 90 percent still in the Diaspora.

The problem of large families is a temporary one. In my opinion the government should not meddle too much in this matter. We must realize that our spiritual, physical, and cultural strength will be derived from healthy and happy families.

We have dwelt on the great national effort required of us to advance toward equality and the closing of our ethnic gaps. We have discussed various means to this end: representation, intercommunity marriage, improvement in the living conditions, and reduction in size of large families. We have not gone into detail about solutions that ought to be self-evident: incessant efforts to improve housing conditions and liquidate slums and substandard housing, to construct low-cost housing for young couples, and to provide all levels of education, from kindergarten to university. In higher education we must set ourselves the target of doubling and tripling the percentage of students from oriental communities over the next few years.

Matters of housing, education, and health have been under extensive public discussion; everything pertaining to these fields has been researched and studied. What is now needed is budgetary priority, good planning, and rapid and efficient implementation.

The ethnic community problem that exists in Israel today can be solved. If the Jewish people had a million more Jews in the Islamic countries and they were to immigrate to Israel, one might say that the problem would only be solved in the course of generations. But as things stand we have the entire problem right here with us. The concentrated and deliberate efforts of a single generation will bring the solution into sight. Only when things improve in this area will we honestly be able to say that we have made progress toward maximal equality. Only by constantly advancing toward a solution of the ethnic problems in our society will we be able in good conscience to call upon more Jews to immigrate to Israel and live here with us.

13

RESERVOIRS OF IMMIGRATION

CHALLENGE—A MAJORITY ASSEMBLED IN ISRAEL

About one hundred years after the new return to Zion began, and twenty-five years after the founding of the State of Israel, less than one-quarter of the Jewish people lives in Israel. Out of approximately fifteen million Jews in the world, less than three million are in Israel. Six million live in North America, more than three million in the Soviet Union, over a million in Europe, about three-fourths of a million in Latin America, and less than half a million in other countries.

By simply existing Israel provides a sense of security for all the Jewish people. Jews know that if their situation in their countries of domicile should deteriorate, the State of Israel is open to them as a haven. This awareness exists among Jews who live in countries with gates that are open to those wishing to depart who do not immigrate to Israel. For them the State of Israel is an insurance policy for a possible time of crisis. It also exists among Jews living in countries whose gates are closed. To them the State of Israel is a source of strength in their struggle to break out.

Moreover, by its very existence the State of Israel serves as a basis for Jewish self-identification and as a source of Jewish pride. There are now virtually no Jews in the Diaspora—and this is something we discovered during the Six-Day and Yom Kippur Wars—who are not concerned with Israel's existence. She also serves as a source and inspiration for Jewish upbringing, culture, and education for all Diaspora Jewry. The dream of Ahad Ha-am appears to have come true: Israel has become a spiritual center of sorts for the Jewish people.

These achievements, although great, are by no means complete. The Zionist doctrine held that in order to fulfill its destiny the Jewish state would not only have to serve as a symbol and a source of pride, but would also have to contain within its borders the majority of the Jewish people; nothing but the people's physical presence inside such a state would provide a comprehensive solution to the Jewish problem.

We must now examine the truth of this doctrine and the extent to which it is being implemented. The centrality of Israel today in the life of world Jewry does not have the dimensions Ahad Ha-am once thought it would have. We must ask ourselves what kind of culture and ideals we are offering world Jewry, and in how many Diaspora Jews we arouse something more than constant concern for our existence.

As to the notion of the majority of the Jewish people being assembled in the State of Israel, we must answer these two fundamental questions: How many members of the Jewish people today either want or are being forced to immigrate to Israel, and how many of them may want or be forced to in the future? There are other questions we must try to answer: If there are many potential immigrants, what will millions of additional Jews do in Israel; how and where will they live; what will be the face of a Jewish state which contains the majority of the world's Jews?

These are questions that we shall be able to answer only after having briefly reviewed the situation of the Jews in each of their great places of concentration in the Diaspora, because the answers are as different as the Jewish situation in each individual dispersion.

THE DIASPORA OF THE SOVIET UNION

About ten years ago I returned from the Soviet Union after having completed my stint at the Israeli Embassy in Moscow— a task which my colleagues and I regarded as a mission to the Jews of the Soviet Union. After my return I wrote my first book, *Between Hammer and Sickle.* In the section called "How Many Would Immigrate to Israel?" I wrote:

In Israel, when I related my experiences, the question always put to me was: "What will happen when the gates are opened?" I would reply that this is a highly involved question, but that I had the impression that many would emigrate. Pressed to give an exact number, I would say that no one could possibly give such a number; the situation is dependent upon factors that are constantly in flux. Despite this, however, it might still be possible to give some sort of approximate number. To do this, it is necessary to discuss separately the Jews of the western borderlands, the eastern borderlands, and those of the center.

As stated, some three hundred thousand Jews live in the western borderlands—in the Baltic countries, the Galician areas annexed to the Soviet Union, and in Bukovina and Moldavia. Given only a chink in the wall, the Jews of Riga, Vilna, Chernovtsy, Kishinev, and other towns in these areas would burst forth and emigrate. We have already mentioned the special motives that would impel them, namely their many relatives in Israel, their Jewish upbringing, and their strong sense of alienation from the society in which they live.

Many if not most of the Oriental Jews of the Soviet Union—the Bukharan, Georgian, and Mountain Jews, who number about two hundred thousand—would go to Israel if given the chance. They would be motivated by a profoundly religious and near messianic longing to return to Zion and Jerusalem, as well as by close family ties and the obedience of all members of the family to their leaders and elders. They would emigrate, I think, just as the Jews of Kurdistan and Yemen did: entire clans with their rabbis, teachers, and Scrolls of the Law.

The picture of the Jews in central Russia, who constitute the majority of Soviet Jews, is less clear. It is difficult to say how many of the synagogue Jews would have the courage to go, despite all their yearning for Jewish life and all their courage and devotion to Jewry. They are now in their declining years, old, feeble, weary. Some would go; others would be fearful and would choose to stay.

Some middle-aged people would undoubtedly decide to leave their homes and jobs and emigrate to Israel. Many would find the decision a hard one to make. There would also be young Jews, students and those who had just started out in life, who would be prepared to go. There is no doubt at all about that. As a matter of fact, it is possible that younger people might find it easier to decide to emigrate and build a new life in a new country. The young are generally braver, more inclined to adventure and to making long-range decisions. But it is difficult to say how many of them would go if they were given a chance, though I believe there would be many more than we think.

In sum, we are dealing with between half a million to a million Jews who, I believe, are now ready to emigrate to Israel. And I do not mean to say that this is all there will be. I am referring only to the first wave of emigration.

What of the other Jews, those still hesitant, fearful, indecisive, who will wait to see how things turn out? This will be answered only when the first phase is completed and the first wave has left.

The nature of the second wave is contingent upon a hundred and one factors: How will the first wave be absorbed? What sort of letters will they send back to the Soviet Union? What will be the fate of the tens of thousands of uncircumcised Russian Jews who will come to Israel? What will be the attitude in Israel to those Russian Jews who have gentile wives? How will the professional and skilled workers find employment? What will happen to the thousands of doctors, engineers, and technicians? What will be the economic situation of the first wave? And so on.

When these words were written over a decade ago there were normal diplomatic relations between us and the Soviet Union, but the exit gates from there to Israel were sealed. No one was coming out. During the past decade two important processes have taken place with regard to Soviet Jewry. The first is the heightening of national and Zionist ferment among the Jews. The second is the reluctant recognition on the part of some of the Soviet leadership that no instrument of oppression against the Jews would work.

Even as early as the 1950s the Soviets, under repatriation agreements with Communist Poland, permitted tens of thousands of Jews who were citizens of Poland to leave the Soviet Union for their country. The Soviets were well aware that Polish authorities were then permitting these Jews to continue on their way to Israel.

In 1966–67, the Soviet authorities began permitting a small number of Jews to immigrate directly from the Soviet Union to Israel. During those two years about four thousand Jews came to Israel—a significant increase over the almost negligible figures of the previous years.

This wave of immigration had certain characteristic traits: it all came from Latvia, Lithuania, Bukovina, areas where the Zionist reawakening had come sooner and was stronger. From the Caucasus and Middle Asia hardly any Jews arrived, and from the center of Russia, only a few. The Jews arriving prior to the Six-Day War were middle-aged or old; many were in need of welfare; many were retired and unskilled; many received their exit visas after stubbornly holding out and repeatedly applying for "family reunion" permits.

The authorities' decision to permit Jewish emigration was accompanied by a strong anti-Israel and anti-Zionist campaign, both in the Soviet Union and in the Middle East. This strange dichotomy was to be repeated a few years later. The emigration of those four thousand Jews was clearly made possible by a decision in the highest echelons of the Soviet government. It was neither a casual decision, nor one that could be made on a low or intermediate echelon.

With the severance of relations between the Soviet Union and Israel as a result of the Six-Day War, the gates of immigration were again closed. It seemed that for the foreseeable future they would not be reopened. And yet toward the close of 1968, while the USSR was in the very throes of a vicious propaganda war against Israel and Zionism and while airlifts of military aid from the Soviet Union to Egypt and Syria were reaching vast proportions, the Soviet Union again opened her doors, and Jews began to emigrate to Israel. Immigration from the Soviet Union to Israel has continued ever since.

This wave of immigration includes diverse elements and all age brackets. They are coming from everywhere in the Soviet Union. Their age distribution is more normal. Their professional spectrum is also more representative of the occupations of the Jews of the Soviet Union.

The diversity among the thousands of Jews who have arrived here in recent years from the Soviet Union constitutes a fairly good indicator of the type of immigration we may expect from that country in the future. Among the arrivals are simple folks: artisans, carpenters, metal-workers, tailors, cobblers, furriers, and the like. There are Jews who have been officials at all levels of government commerce, bookkeepers of every conceivable sort, brokers, storekeepers, supply managers, warehouse managers, and so forth. There are engineers and other technicians in a wide range of professions. There are many who are engaged in all levels of the teaching profession. There are doctors and others engaged in paramedical professions. There are scientists engaged in the pure and applied sciences and in research.

One outstanding phenomenon, which will become more marked as the immigration continues, is the large and increasing number of professionals among the new arrivals. In certain areas, such as teaching, medicine, and engineering, it will be out of all proportion to the occupational breakdown of past immigrations. The arrival of tens or hundreds of thousands of Jews from the Soviet Union will bring Israel thousands of teachers, doctors, and engineers. This could prove to be a blessing or a burden to Israel, depending very much on how these people are absorbed. Ideally, their absorption should be guided by the special goals that Israel must set for herself regarding the future structure of her economy.

These Soviet Jews have created for themselves a world of

hopes and dreams which on the whole does not, indeed cannot, bear any resemblance to the actual reality of Israel. Many of them have built messianic castles in the air. The shock they sustain on encountering the reality of Israel is a profound one that sometimes overwhelms them.

With no Israeli emissaries, no Jewish Agency in the Soviet Union, no Israeli Embassy or Consulate, no wonder their opinions on daily life in Israel, on Israel's problems, or their problems in Israel are strange and sometimes even distorted. Moreover, all these Jews were raised in a regime in which a social and economic system of values that is totally different from our own operates. The strangeness and alienation generated by their contact with Israeli society can be very acute. Since they undergo no preparation for immigration, their transition to Israel is extremely abrupt and often bitterly traumatic.

There are and will be problems of ideology. Among those arriving from the Soviet Union there are some who, out of abhorrence for the Soviet regime and in reaction against its attitude toward them, toward Zionism and Israel, have become infected with chauvinism. Some of them will probably favor the use of force to "get things moving" and to "settle matters," whether in behalf of Soviet Jewry or in arranging their own private affairs in Israel. Some of them will use the ideological, religious, and national intolerance of which they were once the victims against national and religious minorities in Israel. There will be some who, in their natural disappointment over the encounter with Israel, will revert to the worship of Soviet Communism and will remember their lives in the Soviet Union with nostalgia; and because Israeli-style parliamentary democracy will be foreign to them, some of them may misunderstand and come to hate our way of life.

There are and will be problems of physical absorption. The Jews of the Soviet Union are almost all city-dwellers, who have been in a process of moving from small and medium-sized towns to large cities. To disperse them in Israel—in development areas, in small towns, and in villages—will be a formidable undertaking. Their expectations as regards housing, after having had to live for many years in densely packed "communal" apartments (three or four families to an apartment), are very great. It is very difficult (and with the increase of immigration will be quite impossible) to satisfy the appetites of people who all their lives have waited for an apartment of their own. As regards population distribution and housing, the Soviet immigrants and our absorption institutions are in for large helpings of mutual resentment and disappointment.

There are and will be severe problems of professional absorption. In many professions Soviet standards are very different from those in Israel. However painful it may be, people trained in these professions will have to go through retraining. The problem is particularly acute in the fields of medicine and engineering. Doctors, engineers, and people in allied professions who come to Israel will have to adapt to the norms practiced in Israel, which are derived from Western Europe and the United States.

There are and will be immigrants trained in professions that are either not recognized or not needed in Israel; they will have to acquire a new profession, a process which will damage their status and their pride.

There are, and will be, religious problems. We are already witnessing some of them: mixed couples, various proselytes, uncircumcised Jews, and so forth, plus the absorption problems posed by religious communities that observe the commandments in their own peculiar style, such as the Jews of Georgia.

All these problems are added to the ones so familiar to us from all our previous waves of immigration: "veterans" as against "newcomers," the "when I first arrived" set as against the new arrivals, the pangs attendant upon learning a new language, the loneliness common to every individual and family uprooted from their surroundings and their culture and groping their way in the new environment. These are all factors

with which both the newcomers and we already here will have
to grapple. The pangs of absorption will be severe and protracted. Only a great deal of warmth and patience on the part
of Israeli society can alleviate the difficulty and frequent anguish of this process.

The greater the waves of immigration that arrive, the easier
will be the collective absorption processes, the less poignant the
sense of strangeness, alienation, and frustration, the greater the
cooperation between the immigrants and the existing Yishuv,
and the greater the influence of the immigrants upon us and of
us upon them. We must bear in mind that the immigration of
hundreds of thousands of Jews from the Soviet Union will cause
a revolution in Israel, just as every large wave of immigration
in the past has revolutionized the structure of our society. Hundreds of thousands of Jews from the Soviet Union will bring with
them a tremendous variety of occupations, a rich culture, and
a creative dynamism that can only serve to enrich our land.

I believe that the Zionist reawakening among the Jews of the
Soviet Union will continue, and that in the future it will be
possible to come to some arrangement with the Soviets for the
emigration of those who wish to come to Israel. I believed ten
years ago, and I still believe, that the first waves of immigration
from the Soviet Union will bring to our shores (perhaps not all
at once but within the foreseeable future) between half a million and one million Jews.

We must prepare ourselves and our society for this immigration. As of now, we must think and plan where to absorb these
Jews—physically and economically, in what places and in what
occupations. We must draw up plans for the absorption of tens
of thousands of immigrants and also be prepared for the possibility of an immigration numbering hundreds of thousands
within short periods of time.

If a vast reservoir of Russian-speaking Jews should be formed
in Israel, lovers of Russian culture who grew up in one of the
greatest civilizations in the world, we all stand to benefit from

it. It would also be a great achievement for the Soviet Union. In a world in which interpower competition will take the form, not of war and violence but of mutual cultural, economic, and social influence, Soviet Jewry in Israel will be a real bridge for the Soviets in the Middle East.

Some tens of thousands of Soviet advisers and experts in the Arab countries are today of supreme importance to the Soviet Union. In the long run their importance is likely to prove of lesser significance than that of the hundreds of thousands of Soviet Jews who will live in Israel and who, when peace arrives, will constitute an organic, natural, stable, and permanent link between the Soviet Union and this part of the world.

IMMIGRATION FROM THE NORTH AMERICAN DIASPORA

About six million Jews live in the United States and Canada. Just as the immigration of between half a million and one million Jews from the Soviet Union to Israel is an attainable target in our time, so must we also aspire to an equally large Jewish immigration from North America. This goal poses a tremendous challenge to Zionism and Israel.

From its inception, immigration to Israel derived sustenance from two main sources. The first was the recognition by Jewish individuals and groups of the objective and practicability of the Zionist solution to the problem of the Jewish people in the Diaspora. Tens of thousands of Jews understood this and came willingly to this land as individuals or in groups. In this instance the land itself exerts a gravitational pull that attracts immigration. An example of this kind of immigration is that of Golda Meir and her comrades from the United States in the early 1920s.

The second source of immigration is sometimes designated "catastrophe Zionism"—immigration under duress as a result of persecution or the expulsion of Jews and their need to come to

Israel to find a haven and an escape from death. In such instances the gravitational pull of this country is of no initial
significance.

But very many immigrants coming to Israel are influenced by
both the "pull" and the "push." Even in the case of the present-
day immigration from the Soviet Union, the "push" (anti-Semitism and the desire to escape) operates together with the "pull"
(yearning for Israel) in such a way that the two can hardly be
separated.

Until the Six-Day War there was no significant immigration
to this land from the United States. A number of American Jews
who volunteered for the Jewish Battalion of the British army
that occupied Palestine during World War I remained in the
country and helped establish some villages and towns. A very
thin trickle of Zionist pioneer youth arrived between the two
world wars. Some American Jewish volunteers who served on
the illegal immigrant ships and who fought in our armed services during the War of Independence settled in Israel. Before
the Six-Day War, immigrants from the United States probably
did not amount to 1 percent of the Jewish population of Israel.
Indeed, the number of Israelis who emigrated to North America exceeded the number of immigrants arriving from there by
several tens of thousands.

North America was then a great Jewish exile, in which "push"
forces hardly operated. The "pull" of Israel attracted only a few.

Immigration from America to Israel has grown since the Six-
Day War; tens of thousands of Jews have arrived from there,
more than twice as many as came during the previous decades.
It is an impressive fact that in these recent years North American immigration has constituted a significant factor among total
immigration to Israel. This welcome phenomenon should be
reviewed, so as to pinpoint its motives, causes, probable continuation, and future, and the likelihood of its being increased.

The motives for this immigration are an inextricable compound of both "push" and "pull" factors. The Six-Day War and

the waiting period that preceded it served as a powerful "pull" force, especially for young people. Thousands of young Jews in America volunteered to help Israel. Most were sent to kibbutzim. Many returned to America, disappointed at not having had a chance to fight. Many others stayed in Israel, or returned to America for a while and then immigrated to this country.

The thousands of immigrants arriving after the war came to Israel gradually and in more organized fashion. What attracted them was post–Six-Day War Israel, exultant in its victory and intensifying its economic, scientific, and cultural activity. They were drawn by an Israel whose youth appeared to them to be healthy and uncorrupted, to have national and social values, a youth uncorrupted by drugs and crime. They were attracted by an Israel in which their teenage daughters could go out with boys and girls like herself without the parents having to fear that she would be beaten, robbed, or raped. They were attracted by a Jewish society in which there was, so they thought, no violence, robbery, or drunkenness.

Among the strongest "pull" forces must also be counted the religious factor. From one-quarter to one-third of the American immigrants came from religious Jewish environments; many religious young people reached the conclusion that their religion obliges them to immigrate and live in the Zion to which they have always prayed.

The new forms of social living in Israel, especially in the kibbutz, also constituted an attraction for young Jews, although not in large numbers.

Our universities, scientific institutions, yeshivas, and academies were additional "pull" factors, because of both their high academic standards and the peace that reigned on their campuses. Also, not a few Jewish parents want their sons and daughters to live and study in a Jewish society where prospects of finding a Jewish partner and not becoming involved in a mixed marriage are rather good.

Another "pull" factor is the new idea of a second home in

Israel. Many successful American Jews have built a second home here and spend part of their time in Israel every year. Here, among Jews, they feel that they can rest and recharge their batteries.

The "push" factors operating upon American Jews are known to us all by now: the effect of the Vietnam War upon American society; the partially violent struggle of the blacks for their rightful place in the sun; the rot of American urban ghetto life; the violence, crime, and drugs; Jewish participation in the American New Left and the angry "Wasp" reaction to this participation; campus violence; black anti-Semitism—all of these have effected a changed view of America on the part of many American Jews. Today there are American Jews who no longer claim, "It can't happen here." Some of these Jews have decided to bind up their fate with that of Israel. They are now arriving here, some as immigrants, others for a trial period, to see how things will develop in America and how successfully they can establish roots in Israel.

Let Zionism not plan immigration from the United States solely in terms of the "push" situation now prevailing in that country. It would be tragic for Jewry and for Israel if the United States proves unable to find the wisdom and strength to resolve its present problems. The bridgehead that Zionism must construct for the immigration of American Jewry is that of Jewish and Zionist education.

Throughout all the years of the Exile, Judaism was always Zionism in potential. An educated Jew—be it any one of the various shades of religious education or secular-national education—is a potential Zionist.

Confronted by processes of assimilation, of flight in all directions, of estrangement between Jewish youth and their parents, Zionism must fight back by deepening and broadening Jewish-Zionist education. Zionism in America today can be defined as an educational movement. It must be the main task of American Zionism to get through to Jewish youth in any way possible.

This can be done through the American Jewish establishment, with its thousands of organizations and communities, through the synagogues of the three major religious bodies, or through the unconventional, "antiestablishment" groups.

Today there is a rare opportunity to establish an identity of interests between Zionism and American Jewry's need to preserve and perpetuate itself. Zionism has an opportunity to penetrate into all areas of American Jewish life and to create an educational bridge between American and Israeli Jews. Over this bridge there will come thousands of students of all ages to study in Israel and take advanced training in all professions and at all levels. Some will remain in Israel; some will return to America imbued with Jewishness and Zionism and will impart to others whatever good they have experienced here. Over this bridge there will come to Israel tens of thousands of Jewish tourists from the United States. Some will stay; some will leave their children here; some will return, richer in Jewish and Zionist spiritual assets.

The important question is: Can Israel today serve as a magnet that will attract a great number of Jews from America to come and live here? I believe that the Jews of America will come in ever-increasing numbers to a Jewish state. I do not believe that they will be drawn here merely because we are larger now than we were before the Six-Day War. A "great," "medium," or "small" Israel is meaningless to Jews coming from a country that covers half a continent. American Jews will want to come to Israel in order to live among Jews and help us solve our great problems, including that of the Arab minority in our midst. But the founding of mixed Jewish-Arab communities and societies will not be regarded by most of American Jewry as a challenge, nor is the idea one they would find captivating. The prospect of ceaseless friction between two peoples in one land would hold no charm for them. A Jewish state and a unique society might attract Jews from America. A binational state is liable to deter them.

Another question is whether we will make it possible for American Jewry to continue freely to develop the main spiritual currents they have created and in which they were brought up in their country. American Orthodox Jewry is a vital wellspring of immigration, and we have something to offer it. But if we fail to give complete freedom to Conservative and Reform Jews to proceed in accordance with their own way of life, we will be closing off two great sources of immigration. Let us not dam the flow of any current whatsoever—religious, social, or ideological—that exists among American Jewry and that would seek a channel of its own in Israel.

We must also answer the question: What will be the face of Israeli society? Is the society we are building to be based on justice and equality, or will it be a materialistic society torn by class, ethnic, and social distinctions?

Anyone who believes that only a high standard of living, conspicuous consumption, and the pursuit of the dollar will bring young Jews from America to Israel is very much mistaken. Many of them have rejected these values in their own country. I am not referring to the beatniks or the hippies, but to those level-headed young people who would like something better in their own lives and in the lives of their children than what they see all around them in the United States today.

American Jews can help us solve the problem of ethnic and social injustice in Israel. They can bring with them tremendous energy and expertise. But they will be deterred from immigrating to an Israel which is not engaged in a serious effort to correct its social injustices.

And a final question: What will American Jews do in Israel? Considering the present professional stratification of American Jewry, Israel today can make a plausible offer to no more than some tens of thousands of them. We shall have to institute a professional revolution in the various branches of our economy if they are to be open to hundreds of thousands of American Jews. We must develop completely new channels and expand the existing ones if American Jews are to find here not only a livelihood but also a field of action for their energy and talents.

If we fulfill these expectations, then I believe that immigration from America will increase and that tens of thousands of American Jews will come to us every year.

In recent years many thousands of American Jews have immigrated to Israel. Simply by being here they are making a great contribution. Properly absorbed, they will be the ones to absorb those who follow in their footsteps. The immigration within a single generation of hundreds of thousands of Jews from the United States may now appear to be a daydream, but I believe that it is a goal attainable by Zionism.

IMMIGRATION FROM THE OTHER COUNTRIES OF THE DIASPORA

The other Diaspora countries have about two and a half million Jews. They are heterogeneous and scattered all over the world, and cannot be discussed in general terms. Viewed as a source of immigration, they can be said to have a potential of about half a million to a million Jews who might immigrate to Israel within a single generation.

Among these various exilic communities a few groups that have certain common denominators can be distinguished. About a quarter of a million Jews live in distress in the Arab states or in East European Soviet satellite countries. The fate of the latter community has virtually been sealed. They are small, oppressed, and cut off from the mainstream of Jewish life. They are not even given the opportunity to assimilate. Their only hope is in leaving. We must continually direct our efforts toward insuring that they will leave those countries and immigrate to Israel.

The same is true of the tens of thousands of Jews still remaining in the Arab states—over half of them in Morocco and the others (a few thousand or less) in Algeria, Tunisia, Libya, Egypt,

Syria, Lebanon, Yemen, and Iraq. Their lives are in danger. In some Arab states, such as Syria and Iraq, the Jews serve as hostages and in effect are no more than prisoners.

The Romanian exilic community numbers about one hundred thousand Jews. These are the remnants of a once-great Jewish community. Most of this community has immigrated to Israel and been satisfactorily absorbed here. The Jews remaining in Romania are connected, by ties of family and emotion, to Israel. They live out of their suitcases, facing in our direction, their fate hanging on the world of the authorities.

Another exilic Jewish community, the majority of whose members have already immigrated to Israel, is that of India. Within a few years it will cease to exist.

Iran, where about eighty thousand Jews still live, has treated the Jews at times with toleration, permitting them to develop cultural and communal institutions of their own; at other times she has persecuted and even annihilated her Jews. Under the present royalist regime, the Jewish situation in Iran is relatively good, both economically and culturally. The authorities permit Jewish and Zionist education. This is a direct result of the unique relations that have developed in the past decade between Israel and Iran.

The rapid development which their country is undergoing has improved the situation of Iranian Jews, who are in no hurry to immigrate to Israel. During the past years about half the Jews of Iran have immigrated to Israel. Thousands of Jews now travel from Israel to Iran and back on business and to visit relatives. In the future the balance will presumably be weighted in favor of Israel, and most Iranian Jews will immigrate to this country. Some of them will no doubt establish a second home in Israel.

The Turkish exile, with its long and glorious past, numbers about thirty thousand Jews. It is too small to maintain an independent cultural and social existence forever. Most of its members are now in Israel, where they are securely rooted. The authorities will not, presumably, make it difficult for the remainder to emigrate to Israel.

Israel will have to turn its attention to the tragedy of the Falasha Jewish community in Ethiopia. If there is any truth in the Zionist doctrine that Israel is a haven for all Jewish exilic communities, including those that have developed deviant forms of Judaism, then we cannot deny the Falashas their right to settle in Israel, especially since over the course of a generation the Jewish people and the Zionist movement have made a significant educational, religious, and nationalist investment in them. The problem is a very complicated one, and our handling of it has been woefully inept. The Falashas themselves are now thoroughly confused as a result of our failure to reach conclusions and take decisions regarding them.

The Western European exilic communities consist of over a million Jews. Most of them are today concentrated in France and Britain, and a minority in a dozen other countries.

The largest of these communities is France, where about half a million Jews live, including the quarter of a million Jews from Algeria, Tunisia, and Morocco who have been absorbed there in recent years. The French community has been undergoing certain demographic and cultural changes, and the "new Jews" —the Jews of the North African Maghreb—have been infusing it with vitality and youth. This exilic community constitutes an intercommunal melting pot, and the heat generated causes considerable tension and inevitable friction between the "veterans" and the "newcomers." The arrival in France of the Maghreb Jews is having the short-term effect of staving off the rampant assimilation of the veteran Jewish community in France.

French Jewry is a reservoir for a considerable immigration in coming years. It too is affected by "push" and "pull" factors. Free, democratic, and tolerant France is not entirely without residual anti-Semitism (indeed, what country with a Jewish population is without anti-Semitism?). If we add to this also current French anti-Israelism, we shall understand the nature of the "push" factors that are operating among the Jews of France. But what is far more important is the possible "pull" factor: most of the relatives and friends of the Jews of France are now in Israel. If the bitterness presently gnawing at the hearts of the North African Jews now in Israel were to be slightly lifted, if they were to make some progress in our society, the immigration of their relatives from France would be encouraged (and if their sense of frustration grows, immigration will be blocked). The French Jewish community constitutes a diversified reservoir of youth, students, professionals, and investors, and offers a broad field for Zionist educational activity. Some French Jews will come to Israel via the second home they will build here, and in the course of time thousands of them will in this way be able to maintain links with this country.

The more than four hundred thousand Jews of Britain are living in a democratic, free, and progressive society. Britain was among the first countries to give Jews a chance to live a decent and honorable life.

The rule of the British Empire for about thirty years in Palestine, the ups and downs in the relations between us, from the honeymoon to the beginning of the divorce proceedings, enhanced the national and Zionist consciousness of the Jews of Britain. They proved their Zionist loyalty during times that were very hard for them and us. Their having sided with us throughout our struggle with the British Empire was no small test of the strength of their Jewish-Zionist feeling. British Jewry developed a culturally rich Jewish and Zionist educational network. In relative terms a considerable number of their sons have immigrated to Israel. Of all the English-speaking countries, the percentage of British immigrants (proportionate to the size of the Anglo-Jewish community) is the highest. Unless unanticipated crises develop in Britain, hardly any strong "push" factors can be foreseen.

On the other hand, the field of Jewish-Zionist education is wide open in Britain, and the deeper the furrow the Zionist movement plows, the more bountiful will be the yields produced. One element of "pull" could prove to be the British tradition that we Israelis inherited from the British who ruled here and left their imprint on the country. Whether we like it or not it is a fact that we have absorbed a great deal of the British tradition (and who among us regrets it?). A significant part of our life-style in government, administration, the judiciary, the military, the police, and so forth is based on what we learned from the British. Our generation handed down this tradition to the next generation, which did not know the Mandatory regime; this facilitates the absorption of British Jews, who find something of the atmosphere of "home" in this country.

Other "pull" factors have been enumerated in our discussion of American Jewry. What was said there about the future structure of Israel's society and economy holds good for the Jews of Britain. And the second home may well become an immigration route for British Jewry too.

The other small exilic communities of Western Europe today live in greater or lesser physical and economic security. We might think that the miniature proportions of these communities would make it easier for them to assimilate. But surprisingly they are not vanishing even in the freest of these countries (the identification of Finland's one thousand Jews with Israel is an extraordinary thing to behold). All these countries offer an open field for Zionist work, for ties with Israel, for a second home, for youth immigration, for the education in Israel of members of the younger generation.

The Jewish exilic community of Latin America is a complex, heterogeneous world, with significant differences between one country and another. About half a million Jews live in Argentina; about a hundred and fifty thousand in Brazil, and about a hundred and fifty thousand more in the other two dozen Latin American countries. Almost all of these Jewish communities have a common denominator—they are found in countries that are going through explosive social change. The South American population, with the highest growth rate in the world, is experiencing severe growing pains.

South America is a continent of limitless possibilities, but it suffers from the sickness of class distinctions, social gaps, discrimination, and deprivation. It threw off the oppressive yoke of Spanish-Portuguese colonialism, perhaps the cruelest in modern history, but has not yet succeeded in establishing a stable life of its own. It is caught between military-conservative revolutions and Communist or quasi-Communist revolutions. Here live people fired by burning nationalist or Catholic or left-wing passions. Here everything runs to extremes: wealth and poverty; nationalist pride and apathy.

In the middle of all this live the Jews. In Argentina, Brazil, Chile, Uruguay, and other countries, Jews became part of the big cities; they became active in commercial firms, finance, trades, large and small shopkeeping. They do not belong to the wealthiest classes or to the landed gentry. But their economic situation is good. Many are now breaking into academic professions: medicine, engineering, and the like.

Except for the Argentinian community, the Jews of South America, because they are few in number, find it difficult to maintain a meaningful communal life. Assimilation gnaws at them. Not a few of the Jewish youth would like to march under the flag of the social revolution that is expected to redeem the peoples among whom they live, but so far they are not being absorbed into the ranks of the revolutionaries.

The Jews of Latin America, almost without exception, are Zionists and lovers of Israel. Their leaders and public personalities grasp at Zionism and Israel as spiritual lifebuoys which justify their communal life and Jewish educational system. They cling to Israel as a refuge in case of disaster. To many Jews disaster seems just around the corner. But they are not yet ready to move. Only a thin trickle has been flowing in the direction of Israel, although it too has gathered volume in recent years. Latin American Jews in Israel now number some tens of thousands. In spite of disillusionments, absorption pangs, and returnees, a solid bridgehead of South American Jewry does at present exist in Israel. They have infused the kibbutz movement with renewed vitality, thereby proving that the educational system offered to pioneer youth movements is still capable of yielding results. They are also to be found in the technological and medical professions, in industry and commerce. Immigration from Latin America may continue at the present rate of a few thousand a year. But it could, particularly if given a "push," be transformed into an immigration of tens of thousands within a short time.

The Jews of Australia and New Zealand are few in number —not more than about fifty thousand. They live in free and democratic countries of British tradition and culture. Their economic status is good. They are sympathetic to Israel. Even in these distant countries Zionist education can influence some of the best of Jewish youth to come to Israel.

Finally, there is the South African Jewish exilic community. For many years it has been customary to say that the approximately one hundred twenty thousand Jews of South Africa live on top of a volcano that is likely to erupt at any minute. But for the time being the volcano seems to be nothing more than a mountain of fat. These good Jews and good Zionists live a life of luxury within a great, wealthy, and tragic country. Economically secure, involved in the life of their country, these Jews are not about to be frightened by a cry of "Wolf!" They are aware that racist nations such as South Africa can continue to exist in our world only by the power of an armed minority that is capable of subjugating a powerless majority. But there are among them Jews who believe that someday the blacks will have their inevitable vengeance; these are the Jews who are now leaving South Africa.

The real incentive for immigration from South Africa is not so much the "push" of the erupting volcano as it is the desire many South African Jews have to live in a homogeneous, more civilized, and egalitarian Jewish society. It is these motives that have already brought Israel several thousands of the best of these Jews.

*   *   *

If the problems of immigration become central to our own lives, if we succeed in involving our younger generation with the concerns of the Jewish people, if we regard immigration as a fundamental goal, one that will continue to make possible Israel's existence as a spiritual center for the Jewish people as a whole, then I believe that in our generation we may attain a vast wave of immigration, which, combined with the natural increase of the Jews of Israel, will bring us very close to our goal of having most of the Jews of the world living within the borders of the Jewish state.

14

A VISION OF THE FUTURE

THE ECONOMY

What Constitutes a Normal Pyramid?

We envision a Jewish state which within a generation will approach the realization of the Zionist dream: it will have assembled within it the majority of the Jewish people and will number about eight million inhabitants, of whom about seven million will be Jews. To achieve this, the present Jewish population of Israel must more than double itself. Growth will result both from natural increase and from immigration.

There are those who claim that we need immigration only for the purpose of increasing our numerical strength. For years we have been pursued by this oversimplified claim. It was strongly reinforced when, after the Six-Day War, the territories and their one million Palestinian Arabs fell into our hands, and we began to fear a demographic imbalance. This argument is neither true nor wise; nor is it particularly helpful for the Jewish people, for Zionism, for immigrants to Israel, or for our relations with the Arabs. It implies that numerical increase in and of itself constitutes a value for us; its proponents claim that if there were twice as many Jews in Israel as there are now we would be so strong that a hundred million Arabs could never successfully oppose us. Such a line of reasoning would seem to imply that if true peace were suddenly to be established between us and the Arabs, we would no longer be in need of many more immigrants.

In 1948 six hundred thousand Jews overcame the armies of seven Arab states. In 1967 two and a half million Jews defeated the armies of Egypt, Syria, and Jordan. And if our enemies should again rise in an attempt to destroy us, as they did on Yom Kippur of 1973, we will again defeat them.

The true motive for immigration to Israel, the one which is right and proper in time of war as in time of peace, is not the local Jewish head count but immigration itself. We must regard immigration to Israel as a central theme in the life of the Jewish people. We must be aware, and prove to ourselves and to others, that the ingathering of the majority of the Jewish people in Israel is not connected with expansion. We must not lend ourselves to the outworn formula whereby immigrants come to a new country, drive out and supplant the original inhabitants, and are themselves followed by more immigrants, who supplant them, and so on ad infinitum. This formula is inappropriate and unnecessary to Zionism.

We must acknowledge this and prove that Jewish immigration to Israel is vital for the entire Jewish people of this generation. This is because there are very many Jews in the world whose lives and whose longings, whose abilities and whose genius will find a home only in Israel. We must prove that their coming here will not result in further territorial expansion. Socially, economically, and geographically their lives can be diverted into channels that will not adversely affect any individual or state in our area of the world.

Zionism has from the outset advocated the normalization of the life of the Jewish people, to be achieved by the return to its own land, and the reversal of the abnormal socioeconomic pyramid imposed upon it by life in exile. Zionism called for the creation of the normal pyramid of a healthy people. In the nineteenth century and the beginning of the twentieth a normal pyramid was one constructed on a broad base of tillers of the soil and food producers, overlaid by another broad base of unskilled, semiskilled, and skilled urban workers engaging in creative industry (the urban proletariat), themselves overlaid by row upon row of "nonproductive" service employees, while at the apex of the pyramid were a small number of various creative thinkers and intellectuals.

The early Zionists, especially the founders of the Labor movement, understood that they would virtually have to engage in an act of *creatio ex nihilo* if they were ever to develop in this country a class of Jewish tillers of the soil and manual laborers. To create the basis of this pyramid, they chose the path of self-realization. Manual labor became to them most praiseworthy, almost sacrosanct, and toil in the field and workshop was invested by them with the greatest prestige. This change of values was accomplished boldly out of a superb sense of mission.

Since agriculture was the basis of the pyramid, the Zionist movement for three to four generations focused its strength, energy, initiative, and resources on the creation of a flourishing modern Jewish agricultural economy in Israel. At the beginning of the Zionist movement a very strong emphasis was placed on laborious areas of work that were essential to the building of a normal pyramid—construction work, stonecutting, quarrying, road laying, stevedoring and so forth. As the years passed Zionist efforts were also directed toward the creation of an infrastructure for manufacture and industry. Once the state was established and hundreds of thousands of new immigrants were being absorbed, emphasis shifted to the development of the various branches of industry, making them the basis of Israel's economic pyramid.

In the early generations, and for motives that were justifiable at the time, no attention was paid to services which were defined as nonproductive, or as typical Jewish *Luftgescheften,* such as commerce and finance. Indeed, the reverse was true: they were sometimes treated with scorn and contempt.

While all this was happening, as a result of ceaseless technological and scientific revolution the outside world was undergoing far-reaching sociological and economic changes. In the highly developed and industrialized countries there arose, as a result of these changes, a socioeconomic pyramid quite different from the one that had existed a generation or two before. The classic pyramid, in which most of the population are peasants or unskilled proletariat, still exists in the populous Third World and acts as a very heavy brake on the development of those parts of the world. The agro-technical revolution led to a reduction in the number of farm workers. For example, only about 5 percent of the labor force in the United States consists of farm workers. They produce not only all the food required by their country's population but also tremendous surpluses. The technological revolution in industry has led to a reduction in the percentage of industrial workers, and their constantly growing specialization, while the unskilled workers in the industrialized countries are disappearing; where they do exist they merely act as a brake. This revolution has led to the creation of new branches in the economy, and consequently to changes in society—in modern administration, commerce, and marketing, and the enhancement of the value of science and research in all branches. It has intensified the need for a superior technical education and general education at all levels. This revolution has also begun to lend increasing value to the various services and branches which used to be considered nonproductive, such as mass communications, leisure industries, tourism, and so forth. In the most highly developed countries the classic pyramid has been turned almost upside down.

Israel is alive to these changes. During its twenty-five years of existence Israel has entered heavily into the modern industrial era. But a unique situation, somewhat paradoxical and of fateful import for our future and the future of immigration, obtains in the Jewish world. Most Jews in the Diaspora are to be found in spheres of endeavour which up to one generation ago were considered nonproductive but are now becoming increasingly important and essential to every developing country that wants to advance to the goal of a modern economy by the end of the twentieth century.

Israel attaches great importance and prestige to manual labor. At the same time, she desires to absorb as many Jewish immigrants as possible, tens of thousands of whom are doctors, engineers, teachers, scientists, businessmen, administrators, and social scientists. Will a modern, industrialized Israel be able to establish a socioeconomic structure which must necessarily be the most "abnormal" in the whole world, and absorb these immigrants? I am confident that she will. To this end her leaders must undergo another revolution in their thinking and values. They must set up a new scale of priorities for the planning of Israel's future economic, social, and professional structure.

I shall try to indicate some of the directions this revolution should take.

In discussing Israel's future economic endeavors and their development we must not cling to notions such as productive and nonproductive branches, because the significance of this distinction is dwindling. In contemporary society one cannot establish what is more and what less productive. Is the person who makes horseshoes more productive than the one who handles tourism? To take the yardstick of foreign currency profit and couple it with productivity is no longer valid. Foreign currency can be made out of education and medicine, exactly as it can be made out of oranges and cotton. Moreover, the yardstick of manual labor coupled with the notion of productivity is also being rapidly reevaluated. Is not the skilled worker feeding a computer with programing tapes so that it can operate lathes that will manufacture scalpels a manual laborer? And is not the surgeon who uses these scalpels to cut open a patient's heart and cure him also a manual laborer?

True enough, we are not yet living in an age of this kind. Our society, like even the most modern, is still stratified in accordance with the trades of the past. Tanners are still tanners and perfume merchants are still perfume merchants. Between the sewer cleaner and the nuclear scientist there still exist numerous rungs of the socioeconomic ladder. We must nevertheless begin even now to think of possible directions for the future, because the outer edge, if not the whole, of that future is already discernible.

For the purposes of this discussion I shall not use the terms agriculture, industry, or services, but shall speak of five fundamental branches in Israel's future economy. The purpose of these branches is that of "making" for man and society—"making" and not "industry," because "industry" carries a connotation restricting it to the manufacture of materials, tools, and instruments.

The five branches I should like to discuss, which in combination will constitute the entire structure of the future economy of Israel, are the making of food and water, the making of health and medicine, the making of education and information, the making of tools and instruments, and the making of recreation and leisure.

Food and Water

About ten years ago Israel began selling her know-how and technology in the manufacture of food and water to other countries, especially developing ones. We had our successes and our failures until we began selling combined know-how and integrated systems of survey, research, planning, technology, instruction, and implementation, and supplying Israel-manufactured tools and instruments. Thousands of experts and others engaged in the food and water industry were sent from Israel and in recent years have deployed throughout the developing world. Many thousands of students and experts in these fields have come to us from many countries to learn our methods of working with food and water. We are still at the beginning of this road. There is no reason why this movement of experts should not grow from thousands into tens of thousands and make Israel an international crossroads of research, study, and guidance in the making of food and water for the world.

We cooperate not only with the developing countries that are eager for enterprise, but also with the world's most highly developed countries. We are already working in close cooperation with American and European science and research in these fields, and there is no reason why, if peace arrives, we should not cooperate closely with the Soviets, the Chinese, the Japanese, and the Indians.

Completely new roads for the manufacture of food and water are now opening up before the world. Science is on the threshold of stepping over ancient boundaries and moving toward the manufacture of food without soil. Hydroponics and crop-growing in gravel are only the first indications of the future possibilities that science holds out in the field of food manufacture. There are the possibilities of making food from chemical substances and from brine.

I believe that Israel, limited in area but situated on the shores of two great seas and having at her disposal some of the finest scientific minds, could be among the initiators of these unconventional enterprises. We can be among the first to provide humanity with an answer to the problem of its physical survival —its twenty-first century bread and water. Food- and water-making can be among the five most important branches of our economy and our society. It can and must attract people of talent, know-how, resourcefulness, and initiative. It can continue to serve as a challenge for the coming generations that will be born in, and immigrate to, Israel.

Health and Medicine

In support of the thesis that the making of health and medicine can become one of Israel's main economic branches, the nature of this endeavor must first be defined. I refer not just to

medicine in its strict sense of the curing of patients but to all
activity, in both research and its application, in the very broad
field of the medical sciences.

This complex of endeavor will encompass everything pertaining to man's bodily and mental health, the spectrum of
theories whose subject is biology, microbiology, biochemistry,
organic chemistry, anatomy, physiology, pathology, histology,
and of course curative medicine. This branch will also include
pharmacology, virology, immunology, and research into the
various states of man: in infancy, childhood, adolescence, adult-
hood, middle age, and senescence. This branch will embrace all
the paramedical trades—nursing, first aid, roentgenology and
so on—and the dozens of auxiliary health and medicine trades,
including hospital administration (contemporary hospitals being some of the most complex of modern plants), administration
of clinics, convalescent homes, nursing homes, recreational centers, and the like. Also to be included in this branch are the
medical instruments industry, including everything from band-
ages to artificial hearts, and also all fields of rehabilitation.

This branch also comprises everything pertaining to sanita-
tion, environmental health, and individual and social hygiene.
Here may also be included veterinary medicine and all its sub-
divisions.

Jews participate heavily in these various branches of medicine. We must, therefore, ask ourselves what Israel can offer,
now and in the future, to tens and thousands of talented men
and women who have invested the best years of their lives and
a considerable amount of money in the study of medicine and
its allied professions; and what we shall do if there should simultaneously arrive from one of the great Diasporas some thousands or tens of thousands of researchers and practitioners in
the field of the human body. Furthermore, what shall we do in
Israel with our hundreds and thousands of young people who
annually seek admittance to our medical and allied faculties?
Shall we suggest that they undergo requalification, like the doc-

tors who arrived in the early 1930s and became poultry farmers? (We have, incidentally, a sufficient number of first-rate poultry farmers.) Shall we tell them that we have no room for them here, that because their professions are regarded as a service and are not productive they must undergo "productivization"? Surely today it is sheer nonsense to argue that these medical professions are less creative and productive than any other trade.

Shall we then regard the very high concentration of Jews in this branch as a heavy burden on Israel and a brake on immigration? This would be a conventional response. What we must do is institute a theoretical and practical revolution in our approach to medicine and health.

First of all we must stop treating this enterprise as a service. It is a creative enterprise, and those who engage in it create health and prevent illnesses. Moreover, we must regard it as fundamental to Israel's economy. We once regarded tourism as a service, but when we invested tremendous resources in it and handled it properly for a few years it became a vastly productive branch of our export economy. Health and medicine too can become a similar export.

The great goal we must set for ourselves is to turn Israel into a world center for the making of health and medicine. Israel must be a place of study, research, teaching, cure, and convalescence, able to serve millions of peoples. Then and then only will it have the capacity to absorb tens of thousands who practice in these fields, and at the same time open to its own sons all the broad horizons of this sphere of human endeavor.

How is this to be implemented? The answer is that this vision is based on two fundamentals; the need of hundreds of millions of people for many practitioners and much enterprise in health and medicine, and the tremendous concentration of such practitioners among the Jewish people and among future immigrants to Israel. There is, of course, the problem of distance for those millions do not live in Israel. But geographical distance is becoming less and less of a problem. Again, tourism is the most outstanding example: just as tens of millions of people now annually wander from one country to another in search of recreation and entertainment, it may be assumed that many thousands of people in need of medical treatment will eventually travel to wherever there is a concentration of the best institutions and personnel to supply them with this "commodity."

If the idea still appears unreal, we should remember that even today, without any special planning, thousands of people from abroad come here to be cured and to regain their health, including hundreds of Scandinavians seeking relief for their ills in the waters of the Dead Sea. Citizens of the Arab states also come here, regardless of the state of war, to ask the advice of our doctors. Hundreds of patients, mostly the eminent and wellto-do, come to us from Iran, Turkey, Ethiopia, and Cyprus.

If we are to advance in the direction of developing health and medicine we must jettison the outworn formula of "doctors per head of population." To plan along such lines would be to block the path I propose to take. The research and scientific institutions and treatment facilities in these fields must be cultivated on the basis of criteria other than those generally accepted for a country of our size.

If we take for example the number of medical faculties in Israel today (four) and the number of graduates they produce every year (two to three hundred), we shall see that these figures are by no means appropriate to the enterprise of health and medicine as it is due to develop in another decade or two. Many more medical facilities must be opened in Israel; there must be more university faculties to train doctors, more schools of dentistry and pharmacy, more schools for laboratory, technical, and other trades connected with medicine.

Israel can take the lead in founding great schools where thousands will teach and tens of thousands will learn, which will create and train a new-old type of healer. Although these healers will not have the academic qualifications of the doctor, they will have more medical knowledge than the medical orderly.

It is already obvious that in many parts of the world it will be physically, economically, and educationally impossible to close, by the end of this century, the tremendous gap between the size of the population and the optimal (or even minimal) number of doctors of medicine. One of the solutions that man might come up with to meet this problem is the creation of a class of healers, who have graduated from special schools awarding a degree in the medical sciences. These healers can deploy over needful populations, in the most difficult cases consulting doctors of medicine who will serve as team heads to several sections of healers. These teams will also include nurses, orderlies, technical workers, and medical administrators. All these will be trained in appropriate schools.

Israel could be among the first countries to found colleges and schools of this type, eventually graduating professionals from all over the world, particularly the developing world. Moreover, Israel, as a great center of research and teaching in the biological sciences, will be able to sell the world entire units of information, planning, and implementation in these fields. In other words, it will be able to export not only individual experts and doctors but also whole teams, which, beginning with the preliminary survey and planning and going on to the implementation and staffing stage, will found hospitals, various types of clinics, field hospitals, convalescent homes, and the like.

Also to be included in this branch is the making of medicine: pharmaceutics. Israel already has a relative advantage in this industry, whose development possibilities as regards diversification and innovation of its products, are almost unlimited. In this field Israel has first-rate researchers and also many of the raw materials (from the Dead Sea) needed in the industry. In the future this will necessitate a large addition of research forces and efficient marketing methods. Israel can acquire new markets for the products of this industry, which in many respects is still in its infancy.

Another field of endeavor still in its infancy is that of the research and application of medical engineering, the making of medical tools and instruments, and medical electronics. This too can be developed, streamlined, and enlarged.

Some people will say that this is all very fine as a vision of the future, but meanwhile we haven't enough beds for our own patients. Is it reasonable to dream of "importing" patients from abroad and "exporting" curative units? By the same logic one could argue that we should not branch out into organizing international tourism and founding tourist hotels until we have solved our housing problem.

By developing health and medicine along international lines, in anticipation of the future, we will incidentally sweep away all the obstacles barring the progress of medicine in Israel today. Moreover, I believe that a great deal of international public and private capital would be poured into Israel to be invested in this branch. The founding of several dozen hospitals, convalescent homes, research institutions, or combinations of these involves tremendous basic investments. We must regard these as development projects in all respects, like plants for foodstuffs and electronics.

If Israel has the vision to take up this challenge, it will be the first state in the world to transform the science and study of life, and the care of the human body, into a basic branch of its economy.

Education and Information

There is no better criterion for measuring a society or a state than the proportion of its entire resources that it allocates to education. The history of human civilization is the history of education—the transmission of information from one generation to the next.

From the outset the Zionist enterprise placed a high value on education. The Hebrew teacher lived alongside the first pioneer settlers, was one of them, and went with them wherever they went. The first Zionists, ardently desirous though they were of reversing the Jewish people's pyramid and establishing a class of Jewish farmers and industrial workers in Israel, did not want their sons to become ignorant peasants or unskilled industrial workers. The integration of manual labor with book learning was seen by them as essential. With the help of the Jewish people, the Zionists founded, even prior to the establishment of the state, a highly ramified network of educational institutions of their own in which the classes were taught in Hebrew. The revival of the Hebrew language was one of the miracles achieved by the Zionist enterprise through the labors of teachers and educators of vision, courage, and persistence.

The Jewish Yishuv brought the state great assets in the field of elementary and secondary education and the beginning of higher education—the Hebrew University in Jerusalem and the Technion in Haifa.

Once the State of Israel was founded hundreds of thousands of immigrants arrived whose standard of education in their countries of origin was completely different from that of Israel. A small part could speak Hebrew, but most could neither read nor write modern Hebrew, and indeed many were completely illiterate. The educational system of the young state faced tasks that seemed insurmountable. And some of the problems have yet to be solved.

We applaud what exists and what is being done—compulsory education, building projects, the training of thousands of teachers; the Hebrew seminars for adults and immigrants which have reached tens of thousands, the anti-illiteracy campaign, the many experiments in special and accelerated education, the educational reform and the introduction of more modern teaching methods, various breakthroughs in the field of higher education, and the founding of additional universities. Of all these we are proud.

We castigate ourselves over our deficiencies and shortcomings—the excessively high dropout rate in elementary and high schools, and the link between this and the ethnic, social, and economic gaps in our society; certain outdated methods of education and teaching; the lack of sufficient modern instruction for many teachers; the thousands of youngsters still drifting around outside the educational system and entering into a life of violence, crime, and ignorance; the fact that the percentage of students in our colleges originating from the Islamic countries is by no means the same as their percentage in the population; the fact that thousands of Israeli students are forced to go abroad every year because of the shortage of places in our universities, and that we still cannot welcome the thousands of Jewish students from abroad who otherwise would and could come to study here.

These and many other deficiencies prove that we are still at the beginning of the road of the making of education for the existing population, and that a great human and financial effort must be made if we are to solve our problems in this area.

Just as with medicine, the branch of education and information in the future State of Israel, with its eight million inhabitants, must be assigned its proper place. What will we say to the many teachers among our future immigrants? What are we going to do with them? What can we offer them? Can we absorb tens of thousands of educators and teachers from the Diaspora?

We must begin to look upon education with fresh eyes and see it as a productive rather than a service branch of our economy. We must act to make education an enterprise of major value.

Let us consider the real possibility that the educational enterprise we are discussing will direct itself not only toward a future State of Israel with a population of eight million people, but also toward a world Jewry numbering fifteen million people. I envision Israel as a laboratory and center for numerous educational endeavors and products—teacher-training for the schools of the Diaspora; a Torah center for yeshiva students and rabbis from all over the world; a network of schools at all levels with boarding facilities to which Diaspora Jewry can send its sons and

daughters; summer courses and camps; a vast language laboratory for the translation and dissemination of scientific material
(ponder how many languages will be at the disposal of an Israel
of eight million people); a center for the teaching of spoken and
literary Arabic.

As in the making of food and medicine, Israel can also sell in
outside countries whole educational and teaching systems, such
as planning and school engineering accessories and instruments, and also supply teachers at the request of various countries. Israel has first-rate teaching forces, great experience in
imparting knowledge to children and adults, initiative and experience with new educational methods (the various ulpans),
and a significant advantage in the field of language. She could
be among the pathfinders in the future enterprise of education.

The world is in need of new answers to problems of education. International capital will stream into centers from which
the world expects to receive unconventional answers to these
problems. I believe that Israel can be such a center.

Tools and Instruments

This is a vast enterprise. The tools and instruments serving
mankind are too numerous to be discussed here. We shall
briefly mention only the more important of them.

I envisage an Israel that will be capable of participating in the
imaginative production and distribution of some of the major
tools of the modern world: tools for housing, architecture, construction engineering, transportation, communication, the
building of airports and aircraft, components for space vehicles,
the energy industry, fashions, and the like. In many of these
tool-making areas we have already shown our expertise far
beyond what might be expected of a nation our size. An Israel
of eight million people can become a significant participant and
pioneer in man's tool-making efforts.

Recreation and Leisure

The day may not be far off when the five-day week will become part of Israeli life. Then our society, like any other modern society, will have to consider what its people will do in the spare fourth or third of their time. This activity has a very important social aspect: how will Israeli society utilize its leisure time? How will it avoid the dangers of degeneracy, loafing, and apathy? How will it fill leisure hours with pleasures that will not be detrimental to the entire fabric of society?

The making of leisure and recreation also has an economic aspect. Without detracting from their cultural and educational value, it may be said that literature and press, television and radio, cinema and theater, music and the plastic arts, sports and dancing are of economic value in terms of leisure, as factors designed to fill a person's time spent away from his work.

In addition to all this there are branches entirely devoted to the solution of the problem of leisure time—inland tourism, convalescence, recreational holidays. No less than other peoples (and perhaps even more because of their ingrained wanderlust and curiosity), the Jews like to travel, to observe, to move from place to place, and to visit one another. In their own country they do the same. There are few countries in the world where the population is so addicted to roaming its highways and byways. The country is full of convalescent and guest homes. And we have only in recent years begun to taste the pleasures of motorized and mechanized camping.

A separate branch in its own right is our foreign tourism. It is needless to stress Israel's great advantages in this field: the Land of Israel has been a land of Jewish and gentile pilgrimage for almost as long as it has existed.

I see an Israel increasingly preoccupied with the need to discover imaginative leisure-time activities for herself and her guests—a preoccupation that will in the future make such activities a major element of her economic and creative development.

POPULATING THE COUNTRY

We must prove to ourselves that the State of Israel can contain eight million inhabitants (and in time perhaps many more) within her borders, enabling them to live there in dignity, without the need for expansion in any direction. If we ourselves believe this with perfect faith, (and up to the Six-Day War this was what we were constantly reiterating, to ourselves, the Arabs, and the world) and if we can prove, by word, thought, planning, and deed, that our greatest settlement possibilities are to be found in our very midst, we shall also be able to convince the Arabs and the world that we are not out for expansion.

In recent years some Israelis have ceased to believe that there is room in Israel for a population of many more millions. They are of the opinion that we must absorb new territories, and hold on to them, not only for security reasons but also as potential locations for future large-scale settlement by the Jewish people. But they are gravely in error.

It is my intention to try to outline briefly Israel's future population map (not her political map, because political amendments and border alterations will be the result of negotiations between us and the Arabs, and of peace agreements).

Out of Israel's approximately eight million future inhabitants, some four million will live on the Mediterranean coast, about two million in the Negev, about a million in the Galilee, and over half a million in Jerusalem and its surroundings. These proportions dictate the direction of the main thrust of our future endeavor. In the coastal area and Jerusalem the number of inhabitants is to be doubled; in the Galilee it is to be increased fourfold; in the Negev, sixfold.

The Coastal Plain

The region stretching from Rosh Hanikra as far as Acre will accommodate a population of about a quarter of a million persons. Here will arise institutions of medicine—hospitals and convalescent homes—and also great concentrations of the leisure and recreation-making branch—sports, entertainment, innkeeping, excursions, and tourism. Here too will be concentrated food-processing and fishing and various other industries.

In Greater Haifa—the northern gate of Israel—about three-quarters of a million people will live. Here the chemical, the petrochemical, and the energy industries will be concentrated. There will be great concentrations of education and information institutions here. The economy will be based on the tourist and holiday-making trade, and there will also be medical and health institutions. Haifa will be the great transport and communications-making center.

Along the coast, between Zichron Yaakov and Herzliya, about half a million people will live. There will be various industries and great health- and holiday-making centers here, as well as education and information institutions.

The Dan region—from Herzliya to Yavneh—will be Israel's greatest city. In practice it will consist of Greater Tel Aviv. In this megalopolis about two million inhabitants will live, and they will engage in making various tools and instruments. Also a great center of education and information and medical institutions will be founded. The megalopolis will be the country-wide center for the making of leisure—entertainment, mass communications, and so forth.

In the region between Yavneh and Ashkelon, including Lakhish, there will be a population of about half a million. The twin cities of Ashdod-Ashkelon will be the naval gateway to the south of the country and the overland bridgehead to the Negev and the Red Sea. Here the making of energy and chemicals, and a diversified industry of tools and instruments, transportation vehicles, and communications will be concentrated. This area will also be one of the most important centers for the making and processing of food and water, and also a center of education and science, tourism and hotels, holiday-making and recreation.

East of Greater Tel Aviv, in the Ramleh-Lod region, there will be a population of about a quarter of a million, whose main occupation will be transport and communications, the making of tools and instruments, science and information.

There is no fundamental difficulty—either in terms of planning or of implementation—in having a population of about four million people in the coastal area. Over two million people are living there today, with great ports, airfields, well-developed industry, major institutions of education and information, as well as vast entertainment, recreation, and leisure-time facilities. The existing infrastructure could, with careful planning, absorb a population twice its present size.

The planners will have to build this future megalopolis in such a way as to provide it with "lungs" of green parks and seasides, to eliminate the existing slums in the towns in this area and not add new ones, to prevent the area from being choked by vehicles and general pollution—in short, to try to solve all the difficult, intricate, and complicated problems that face the planners of towns and megalopolises in every highly developed and very densely populated country in the modern world.

The Capital

Jerusalem, which will have over half a million inhabitants, is a particularly complex problem because of its uniqueness as a sacred city, with its peculiarities of landscape, climate, historic sites, the polar diversity of its population, and its topography. For all of these reasons it presents a worthy challenge for creative thinking and planning.

Of Jerusalem we expect everything—we want to build her rapidly as a modern city, but at the same time guard every vestige of her glorious past. We want the city to offer "all modern conveniences," but zealously cherish her sacred character and tradition. We want many new immigrants to settle in Jerusalem, but without prejudice to her Jewish and non-Jewish old-timers. We expect her to preserve her tranquil air as a place of spiritual elevation, but we also want millions of noisy tourists to visit her. We want Jerusalem to remain the Beautiful City, but we also want her to have modern roads and be a center of commerce and tourism. In short, we want a Celestial Jerusalem that is also a Terrestrial Jerusalem.

In all matters pertaining to Jerusalem we must proceed reverentially, with the sense of Jerusalem's belonging to us but without a trace of disdain for its sacredness to others, and above all with great humility. In Jerusalem, Israel's every act must be performed with generosity but without any self-abnegation; with originality but without risking the city's oneness; and always out of a desire to make her a city of peace for the peoples living in and around her.

The Galilee

The main effort of Israel in the future must be directed toward the settlement of the Galilee and the Negev. We must expand the existing towns in the Galilee and the Jordan and Beisan Valleys into cities of fifty to a hundred thousand inhabitants each. We must plan and establish the first research institutes and colleges, begin laying the foundations for the construction of special hospitals and medical research institutes, and expand the existing network of convalescent and guest homes. These ten cities of the Galilee and the valleys could then contain a population of about three-quarters of a million, with another quarter of a million living in the villages.

When peace arrives, the Galilee and the valleys could cooperate with their neighbors. The inhabitants of the Jordan Valley and the Beisan Valley could establish advisory and marketing cooperative projects with the Palestinian Arab food producers to the south and east; the inhabitants of the Galilean mountains could cooperate with their Lebanese neighbors in tourism, holiday-making, amusement, and sports.

The Negev

Half of Israel lies south of the coordinate connecting Ein-Gedi, Arad, Beersheba, and the Besor region. This region has something of everything: mountains and plateaus, plains and valleys, arable land, desert, and wilderness. It has seas, lakes, quarries, and mines. It has variegated climates and landscapes. Almost the only element held in common by all these areas is emptiness. In the recent past, desolation was almost total, and even today, after more than two decades of laborious Jewish development, the situation has changed only a little.

Israel's greatest, most daring, most attractive, and most hopeful settlement challenge is to be found in this region. This "Zionistic" pronouncement is in itself nothing new. At various periods the Negev has been fertile and densely populated compared to what it was at the beginning of the Zionist enterprise. History books and archeological excavations point to ancient rural and urban forms of settlement in the Negev. Here there were special civilizations like that of the Nabateans; the ports of Etzion-Geber and Eilat served the Israelites and other peoples as an outlet to the Red Sea and the distant and enchanted lands of Africa and Asia (the lands of Sheba and Ophir). But in the main, the Negev has always been a buffer area, a region of strongholds between the desert and the town. There the kings of Israel and their predecessors built bastions of defense on the trade routes; and the Romans erected their limes Palaestinae fortresses. Of course the Negev has always had a nomad population, living on robbery and fighting the civilizations of the north and south. Civilizations came and went, states rose and fell, but the nomadic bedouin population always remained.

If top priority is given to the research and study of the Arava and Negev settlement plans by the world's foremost experts, and if these studies show these plans to be feasible, and if we evince the audacity and drive to obtain the manpower and the financing to make a start on planning and implementation, I believe that within a generation we shall have progressed toward the realization of the dream of populating the Negev and the Arava with about two million Jews. About three-quarters of a million of them will live in the Arava, on the shores of the Dead Sea and the Red Sea; about half a million in Beersheba and its surroundings; about a quarter of a million in the central Negev, and a quarter of a million in the southwest Negev.

Built in this way, by the end of the century Israel will have achieved a healthy balance in population distribution and geography, and will be able to take her place at the head of the league of states of limited area but large population in their march toward the twenty-first century.

Large-Scale Plans Attract Generous Resources

At this stage we should ask ourselves how the present-day State of Israel, with its three million inhabitants, can grapple with and carry through the tasks it is going to set itself. We are saying that even while incessantly battling for survival, Israel will double its population in a single generation (mainly through immigration), will revolutionize its economic structure by founding new, unconventional branches of endeavor, and will radically change its geography by founding gigantic development projects. How can this be done?

On the face of it, this is an impossible mission. The land and her people are now staggering under the weight of the war effort and the security budgets. The tax burden is sometimes unbearably heavy. The national debt per capita is the highest in the world. The sums needed to close the social gaps within the population are tremendous. Our balance of payments is negative. The government and the treasury pursue the struggle on a day-to-day basis, attempting to prevent the entire structure from collapsing under the heavy weight it bears.

In this state of affairs, are not the objectives we have been speaking of but an idle mockery? Where are we to find the vast additional resources needed for immigration and absorption, for building the infrastructures needed for the novel fields of endeavor, for development projects on an international scale? Are we entitled to hitch our wagon to a star when it still slithers deep in economic mud?

The general answer to these questions—and they can only be answered in general fashion—is based on past experience of the Zionist enterprise and the State of Israel. It is that the bolder the objectives and the vision toward which we strive, the more strength and the more resources we find for their implementation. And contrariwise, to the extent that we have moderated and restrained our vision, we have been impoverished. Our people will perish for want of vision. We have found that when there has been no immigration, not only has the situation of the "old-timers" not improved, it has deteriorated. Without new development and new initiatives the present begins to crumble, and impasse and retreat set in.

In the light of past experience one may generalize and say that if Israel is hesitant about the future, she will not find the strength within herself even to sustain the present. A conventional, moderate Israel will not attract new resources from the two great sources we have been drawing on and whose assistance we have relied on all these years: the Jewish people and the countries of the world. Ever since we have been here the Jewish people has helped us with grants, loans, and investments on a scale unequaled anywhere in the world. We have found that the greater our distress and the more acute the danger to our existence, the greater the help we have received in the form of grants: but Jewish capital in the form of loans and investments has flowed to Israel only when the state has been in a surge of development and has had something to offer.

This is even truer of world assistance. German reparations were, of course, granted by way of some sort of restitution for our disaster, but loans and investment came only for the execution of new development plans. The greater, the more enchanting our objectives and our development plans, the greater will be the response of Jewry and the nations of the world. We must prove to our people and the world that we are speaking of a vision and that the vision is anchored in figures, facts, and real programs.

Let me illustrate this by describing how vast new resources can be mobilized for the development of two of the branches I have spoken of, medicine and education, and the development of the great Negev project known as the Arava Plan. The sum required for the development of the Arava is, roughly, ten billion dollars. This plan envisages the digging of a canal connecting the Red, Dead, and Mediterranean Seas and the construction of vast agro-industrial combines in that area. On tens of thousands of acres of controlled environment, we will be able to grow all kinds of food all through the year. This area will also produce chemical fertilizers and special metals.

Once the Arava Plan goes through the first stages of inspection and control by planning institutions of a superior international standard, the government of Israel can turn to some large financial institutions, both national and international (American, Japanese, German, British, Dutch, Belgian, etc.), and propose that together with her they should set up a multinational consortium for financing the plan. It is at present not difficult to mobilize huge sums around the world for great projects, assuming that the plans are good. Paradoxically, the corollary is that since the world does not have many great attractive and well-founded development plans, a potential reserve of unexploited multinational capital is formed, seeking channels of action. Multinational capital of this kind will not come to us because of our afflictions, our troubles, or our poverty. On the contrary, all these will only frighten it off. It will come if we submit plans capable of profiting both ourselves and the economy of the world.

The basic investments required for the development of the medicine and education branches are also beyond Israel's scope, since billions of dollars' worth of investment are involved. But these plans, too, are economic in the long range and will yield a profit.

I believe that it is possible for us to declare two new state development loan projects, in addition to the Israel Bonds program, which will continue to exist. The purpose of the one project will be to mobilize capital for founding medicine and health enterprises; the other will recruit capital for founding education and information enterprises.

Each of these projects, armed with a large, well-founded, and impressive master plan, will approach both world Jewry and the various countries' institutions for financing medicine (or education), and will invite them to invest in the founding of medical (or educational) centers in Israel on an international scale.

If these two capital-recruiting projects are established, and if they operate as dynamically and boldly as the UJA and the Israel Bonds, they will succeed in raising the sums required for the development of these two branches from the Jewish people and the countries of the world. The investors will regard it not as an act of charity but as a privilege to be able to take part in the setting up of modern branches of endeavor which have every prospect of becoming worthwhile and profitable.

In spite of our present severe economic situation and our tremendous current needs (which will continue to be covered by our own tax burden and the routine appeals, grants, loans, and American aid), the new plans and the new momentum can enable us to gain access to new reserves of capital and manpower, and harness them to the development of Israel.

CONCERNING RELIGION

Spiritual Values and Materialism

Those political, social, and economic Israeli goals that we have been discussing so far do not exist in a vacuum; they are related to abstract concepts and spiritual life. The Zionist enterprise in its entirety, its conception, gestation, birth, and growth, belongs to the realm of ideals, faith, vision, and hope.

Zionism is the most outstanding example in recent generations of the realization of an abstract and intellectual idea that germinated in books—Holy Scriptures and secular writings, books of philosophy, and stories of utopia. Out of the Zionist idea grew a national enterprise of great corporeal dynamism, of which the State of Israel is the crystallization.

We are only at the beginning of the path toward the realization of the great spiritual abstract hope that guided our ancestors. We cannot say that because we are here and our material existence is, as it were, assured, we need no longer pursue the spiritual goals of our enterprise. However, one of the stumbling blocks in the path of these goals is the present relationship between the secular and the religious elements in Israel.

The difficult future that lies ahead of the compromise between secular and religious viewpoints in Israel derives from the lack of tolerance displayed by the extremist element of the religious camp and from the system of "all or nothing," the attempt to claim more than has been granted, the politization and the materialism that have come to dominate religious life in Israel, and to no small extent in the Diaspora too. The root of this evil may lie in the unwillingness or inability of Jewish religious leaders to grapple with the spiritual problems of the Jew as man, in the Diaspora and in Israel, in a state of his own. This inability arises from a process that religion cannot deny and before which it stands helpless: the secularization of Jewish life both in the Diaspora and in Israel, and the inability of most Jews to live, at the end of the twentieth century, by the laws of the halakha, in spite of the love of tradition that characterizes most of them and the hope that many cherish in their hearts for a religious revival among the youth.

Most Israeli Jews are not religious in the orthodox sense, nor do they meet the test of observing practical religious commandments. Neither do most Jewish youth in Israel want to be put to the test of keeping the 613 commandments. Only a small minority keep all the practical commandments, and among them are a tiny minority who regard themselves alone as being truly religious, while the others seem to them to be out-and-out heretics.

If we are to judge by the yardstick of the keeping of practical commandments, then the great majority of Jewish youth in the United States are not religious, and although some of them are seeking the way back to Judaism, they do not intend to submit themselves to the yoke of the 613 commandments. The reawakening among the Jewish youth in the Soviet Union is also basically a national rather than a religious experience (in the sense of acceptance of the yoke of the commandments), without in any way detracting from the value of the marvelously heroic spirit that centers around the synagogues. The same applies to Jewry in Western Europe and other countries of the Diaspora.

What is the religious leadership doing in the face of this reality, and what can it do? Or perhaps this question should be preceded by another: Does the Jewish religion have a leadership? A leadership not in the narrow, institutionalized and political sense of the word, but religious thinkers who are desirous and capable of coming to grips with the problems of the Jewish people in the present, and its fate in the future? Are there religious leaders who are prepared to understand, to bring closer and to open the gates of religious experience to Jews who are not able, or not prepared, to pass through the needle's eye of a rigid halakha?

I find no difficulty in loving the Jewish religion, its great men, its struggle for its faith, its tradition and its customs, its great moral principles. But does all this make me religious in the sense intended by the leaders of the Jewish religion today? The answer is no. It is not enough that I believe in a supreme God, or that I experience religious rapture when I stand before Him; it is not enough that I identify with the monotheistic godhead, as first revealed in its pure essence in the Jewish religion, and

that this concept appears to me to be the truest and the purest
of all religions; it is not enough that I honor the Jewish tradition
and customs, and that I live them in my own way--all this is not
enough, and in the eyes of the religious officialdom I am nothing
but a secularist. And why? Because I do not want to take upon
myself the yoke of all the commandments, because I cannot live
by all the laws of the halakha, and because I do not want to
educate my children by the rules of the *Shulhan Arukh,* based
on the Law of Moses. Although expanded, very intelligently and
with great pliancy throughout the ages, this Law was congealed
a few centuries ago by mere mortals like myself, who transformed it into a rigid, binding, and all-embracing system.

In the eyes of the religious halakha I am thus an out-and-out
secularist. The Jewish religion is thereby barred to me. But I
feel that I am capable of receiving a Jewish religious experience, except that it would be of a most personal nature and not
necessarily one that has its source in the halakha. In the eyes of
contemporary Jewish religious leadership I am a Jew: born of a
Jewish mother, and therefore unchallengeably a Jew—but a
secular Jew in all respects.

Esotericism or Admissiveness

Contemporary Jewish Orthodoxy's established leadership
stands guard over the walls of the halakha, lest religious Jewry
be infiltrated by Jews like myself, or lest many more of its own
members throw off the yoke as being too heavy, break away,
and leave it an empty vessel. The religious leadership in Israel
and the Jewish world of today, by its esotericism and extremism,
is losing a great opportunity to stretch forth its hand to Jews,
especially Jewish youth, who are seeking a path to religious
experience, to principles of morality, and to ancestral tradition,
but are unable to pass through the fine-meshed and partly rusty
filter of the halakha in their search for religious revival.

The problem is one that touches upon the roots of our lives

as Jews in Israel and is far from being merely a philosophical one. Religious leaders in Israel, most of whom are wise and intelligent men, know in their heart of hearts that in the 1970s a modern and highly developed state cannot live in accordance with Jewish halakha. If a miracle were to happen and all the Jews of Israel were to become observant, then religious leaders would quickly have to hand down new and more pliable rulings on many matters to which the halakha contains no answer so that the state could continue to exist. Halakhic scholars would themselves have to create a new oral law, adapted to the society which would have to live by it.

Since this miracle is not likely to come about, and since the state will probably be a secular one in the future too, the very important question arises as to why religious Jewry cannot find within itself the strength to open its gates and admit the secular generation, or at least parts of it?

Unfortunately, the prospects of the Jewish religious establishment in Israel opening up and admitting of innovation are not bright. Most regrettably, a centripetal process is at work: the most extreme Orthodox are drawing into their orbit those sectors of the religious camp that ostensibly understand that they hold the key which will either open or close the gates of the Jewish religion in Israel to those who would like to pass through.

The religious revival that the leaders of the religious camp in Israel are anticipating will never arrive unless the gates are unlocked from the inside. There may be youth outside the religious camp that want and are prepared to reach out through the intermediary of religion toward the deep experience and tradition they lack, but cannot reach through a road pitted with the bans and prohibitions of the rigid halakha as it exists today. The majority will be deterred and will not even try to open the gates; those who do arrive (and they will be few in number) are liable themselves to be swept by that same centripetal force into militant religious extremism. There may be a seedbed for a religious revival among Israeli youth, but its fate is in the hands of the religious factions themselves; it will not happen of itself, and will not come about in any conventional manner.

Israel is not and cannot become a religious state or a halakhic state. The great majority of secular Jews living in it feel themselves to be Jews in every respect in the state as it exists today. The continuation of the partnership between religious people and secularists, and the continuance of the modus vivendi which with great difficulty has managed to survive until now, depends, as in every partnership, on both sides working together to maintain it.

I believe that most of the secular Jews in Israel want to go on with this partnership and that at present not many of them want to run up the flag of militant atheism. They want to carry on with the partnership, and not just because of the threatened rift that is liable to occur within the people, as the religious camp puts it, if such a partnership should break down. This threat contains a grain of truth, but it cannot serve the religious sector as a truncheon. The secular Jews want to go on with the partnership mainly because many of them feel that they lack religious experiences and Jewish tradition. But preparedness for this is conditional upon understanding and tolerance on the part of the leaders of the religious camp. There will not be an unconditional partnership. Even before religious admissiveness arrives, if it arrives, the Orthodox must understand that the secularists, too, have certain sine qua nons. We agree, many of us understandingly and willingly, that part of our personal lives will be entrusted into the hands of the halakha and its executors. We accept that the halakha should govern the focal stages of crisis and transition in our lives: birth, marriage, divorce, conversion, and death. For each of these we avail ourselves of the good offices of rabbis and the Rabbinate, without undertaking to live, either before or after the transition, as Orthodox Jews, by the letter of the halakha. The situation is a tolerable one. If the rabbis have the wisdom to endow these transition ceremonies with a dignified and pleasing form, most of the secularists will even be happy to take this yoke upon themselves.

The days are gone when Jews on principle did not want to circumcise their sons, enter the covenant of marriage through "the canopy and sanctification," or be buried according to the Law of Moses. Many rabbis have, in fact, taken a number of steps to impart a dignified character to these ceremonies. But most Jews in Israel cannot reconcile themselves to the thought that their preparedness to resort to the religious establishment for these purposes should be converted into a trap and a noose for certain individuals and for exceptional cases.

Most Jews, like other people, are born, marry, produce offspring, sometimes divorce, and also die, without halakhic problems. But a minority experiences terrible difficulties. The number of these exceptions in our generation is relatively large. Problems of conversion, mixed marriages, uncircumcised children, bastards, marriage between a kohen (man of the priestly branch) and a divorced woman, levirate marriage, deserted wives, and so forth have been difficult and bitter in every generation, but are very much more so in our generation, in which the afflictions of persecution, apostasy, wars, and holocaust have smitten our people. As a result of its being dispersed through all five continents, part of our people has been subjected to the lures of assimilation and another part has lived in societies which have forcibly prevented it from living a Jewish life and observing religious commandments, or even circumcising its children, conducting its marriages in accordance with the Laws of Moses and of Israel, or being buried with the customary religious rites.

In our generation and in our society, desirous as it is of gathering together all its lost lambs and all its "black sheep," we cannot be ruled by the rigid disciples of the House of Shamai, who will embitter the lives of these "odd men out" and make life in Israel a hell for them or, worse still, a sort of prolonged purgatory in which their souls will be doomed to wander.

We have discovered in recent years that high-handed treatment of these exceptional cases has aroused mounting waves of disapprobation and wrath among most of the population. If the lenient Bet Hillel school gains the upper hand within the religious camp and its leadership, it must find solutions that will be acceptable to modern minds and will also meet religious requirements. If the religious leadership has the wisdom to handle issues with leniency rather than severity, partnership with it may be able to continue for a further protracted period. But if the pedants come to predominate, there is going to be a very critical reaction on the part of the secularist public. There is going to be a heightened demand for the separation of church and state, for legislation and the establishment of secular procedures to enable people to live full lives as Jews in Israel who might otherwise not be allowed to. There will be a more vociferous demand for the introduction of civil marriage for those Jews who are precluded from establishing a family. Tension between religious and secular camps will heighten, and the schism that will rend the people will be a painful and everlasting cause of sorrow and regret.

We all want Jewish immigration to Israel to increase. In the countries of the Diaspora, especially in the United States, there are Jews who belong to the Reform or Conservative movements. In their own way they live a Jewish life, they pray in their own words, they are born, circumcised, get married, divorce, and die as Jews. It would not occur to them that when they arrive in Israel, Orthodox Jewry will inform them that they are not "proper" Jews, that their marriages and divorces are not valid, that they must tread a long, sad road in order to adapt themselves to the laws and customs of Orthodox Judaism. Surely it is unthinkable that these Jews, who are more religious than most of the Jewish population of Israel, will find that they cannot continue to live the Jewish life they want in the tradition of their fathers. Surely it is unthinkable that a secular Jew, living in Israel, who never visits a synagogue, does not keep a single practical commandment, who is an outright heretic and a militant atheist, should be considered a fit Jew, whereas a Reform Jew, who prays to the God of Israel in his own way, who keeps the commandments in his own way, and lives Jewish religious experience in his own way, should not.

The Jewish religious leadership in Israel must grapple with the problem of the existence of different religious streams in the Diaspora, and find, as their Orthodox brothers have in the United States, a common way of life with them in Israel.

The Jewish people is too small and too stricken to put up with a situation in which a small or large part of it, immigrating to Israel, finds itself boycotted, or its road to immigration piled high with difficulties and obstacles. The fate of a million Reform Jews and their children's immigration to Israel is not a matter to be sealed by the Orthodox. The disciples of Bet Hillel among religious circles in Israel can and must find among themselves the understanding and tolerance needed for a settlement. If some arrangement is not found for the immigration of members of the non-Orthodox movements which the secular camp will find acceptable, the result will be a deep crisis and a rift within the people.

Most regrettably, the religious leadership in Israel is investing most of its strength and resources in ceaseless friction within its own ranks, in the struggle to retain and enlarge positions of political power, and in the argument as to who is the more religious—in which the extremists always have the upper hand.

The leadership concerns itself far too little with the great problems now facing the Jewish religion: how to win people's hearts not by using a truncheon but by showing our youth its great precepts, morality, and values, how to struggle with the problems of Jewish society in the present and the future.

The Jewish religious leadership well knows, or ought to know, what the challenges presented by the scientific, technological, and biological revolution are in this generation and the next. It should seek and find answers to the problems that clamor for solution. What will be the stand of the Jewish religion on the great new problems of medicine: the implanting of various organs, the organ banks, and so forth?

It is not enough when confronted with every such problem to say, "No! This is forbidden!" or "We have a ready answer in the halakha" or to ignore these problems as if they did not exist. This would be a mere flight from reality, which in the final analysis will sever the Jewish religion from life processes.

Take, for example, the issue of the Sabbath, the Jewish day of rest. Now advancing upon us is not only the problem of the day of rest, but of the week that includes two days of rest, and in the future perhaps even three. What does the Jewish religion have to say to all this? Is the Sabbath alone sacrosanct, and are the other days of the week no concern of religion? Is it also no concern of the Jewish religion what its adherents will do with two extra days of rest?

The problems of recreation and leisure in the future are to no small extent also spiritual and intellectual problems. A religion that will not now take cognizance of these issues will do itself untold damage, because in the very near future it will stand powerless and have no answers to offer.

These are only two examples of the entire range of problems of the Jewish people and the people in its state, which will have significant repercussions in the field of the spirit and morality. Religion must also grapple with problems of peace and war, use of nonconventional weapons, environmental pollution, and, emphatically, problems of social justice and equality. Each of these problems also has a spiritual aspect. The Jewish religion cannot ignore this and say, "It's none of our business," or "The halakha does not provide an answer."

For historic reasons, the secular public in Israel has reconciled itself to the nonseparation of church and state. If religious leaders proceed on the lines of Bet Hillel, the existing situation will be able to continue for some time. But in the long run the glory of the Jewish religion will not derive from its interference in the life of the state and the state's secular affairs; nor is it likely that the modern State of Israel will countenance such interference.

I believe that today the Jewish religion, now exempted from the need to concern itself with the people's physical preservation, from the need to encircle it with ever-higher walls, the religion that gave the world pure monotheism, the day of rest, the precepts of "Love thy neighbor as thyself" and "Love the stranger that is within thy gates," is now more than ever capable of self-renewal and of coming to grips with problems that entail maximum tolerance. Abraham our forefather, Moses our teacher, exponents of the oral law, were in their time great innovators, and they tried to find solutions to the issues of their day. The religious leadership of today must also muster the courage to do its share—to innovate, to resolve problems, to draw up a *Guide to the Perplexed* for the twentieth and twenty-first centuries.

EPILOGUE

For ten days I had passed, as a reserve officer, among armored, infantry, and artillery units on the front lines. My job, part of an Israeli army educational program, was to tell the soldiers about the rescue of Jews from the various exiles.

One morning I traveled out to a stronghold in Jebel-Rus, or Har-Dov, overlooking the "Fatahland." I was accompanied by Brigadier Yitschak Arad, at that time the chief education officer. For two days the area had been lashed by torrential rains. We joined a column of vehicles—jeeps and half-tracks—making its way toward the mountain. Visibility was almost nil. We were received by the commanding officer of a renowned reserve unit that was manning the stronghold.

After a tour of the rain- and hail-whipped positions, the C.O. rounded up a few dozen soldiers in the cold and musty central bunker to hear my address. The soldiers, muffled in greatcoats and windbreakers of all sorts and shades, sat on wooden benches warming their hands on kettles and steaming cups of tea.

I brought up memories of the past: of meetings with the

Libyan Jewish exile in World War II, the "illegal immigration" from Europe and the Middle East after the war, the rescue of the Jews of Port Said in the Sinai Campaign, and our activities among the Jews of the Soviet Union. I had the feeling that in spite of the cold that chilled one to the marrow, and in spite of their fatigue after a night's guard duty, the soldiers were listening to what I had to say, they were with me. The talk ended.

I asked, "Any questions?"

A soldier who had been standing at the edge of the bunker advanced toward me. With some excitement he asked, "Do you know me?"

I took a close look at him. A soldier like any other. Average height, sturdy, strong build, about thirty years of age, a shock of lovely black hair, spectacles.

"No, I don't think I know you," I answered hesitantly.

"My name is Shmuel Carmona. In 1956 you brought me and my family to Israel from Port Said. I was a boy. I remember you in the uniform of a French paratrooper. I'm a nuclear physicist at Beersheba University. My father was a peddler in Port Said. . . ."

THE DOCTORS, SPRING 1972

Home from a long trip, I was advised to go to the hospital for a general check-up. "After all," I was told, "you've done plenty of mileage in your day and it would be worth letting some experts have a look at the engine, the generator, the dynamo, the fuel pump, the headlights, and the rest of it." I took the advice and had myself admitted for a week into a surgical ward at the Rambam Hospital, Bat-Galim, Haifa.

A generation ago, at the beginning of World War II, I started my army life in an artillery base a stone's throw from this hospital, and the young soldiers used to spend many a free hour in the company of the pretty nurses. I had now fallen once more into the hands of kindhearted nurses—Simha, Ahuva, Tami—

who bore so unbelievably close a resemblance to those of a generation before that they might have been their daughters.

The doctors asserted their proprietary rights over my body. They auscultated me by ear and by stethoscope. They photographed me up and down, back and front. I did likewise. I observed them with the eyes of one who has had a great deal to do with people in general and Jews in particular, the eyes of an amateur sociologist.

At first glance this was a ward like any other, in a hospital like any other. But a second and third glance discerned a marvelous molecular structure specific to Israel.

Head of the department, over which he ruled with a staff of pleasantness, was Professor David Barzilai, a native of Haifa, graduate of the Reali School, infantryman of the Jewish Brigade, a graduate of the first class of the Jerusalem Medical School.

His team included:

Dr. Yehuda Plevnik, a native of Argentina, a graduate of a medical school in Buenos Aires, a product of the Hashomer Hatzair youth movement, immigrant to Israel in 1958, and since then a member of Kibbutz Ramat Hashofet on Mount Ephraim.

Dr. Elitzur Hazani, a native of Kfar Yavetz, a graduate of the Jerusalem Medical School, for many years a field medic in the paratroopers, now a specialist in medical electronic research and in charge of the hospital's electronic microscope. His wife, Dr. Annie Hazani, née Abramovitz, was born in Bucharest, Romania.

Dr. Yoram Kantor, a native-born Israeli, a graduate of the Reali School, a former member of Kibbutz Hatzerim in the Negev, a graduate of the Jerusalem Medical School.

Dr. Jacques Sivillia, a native of Bulgaria who graduated in Sofia, an immigrant to Israel in 1952. In addition to his hospital job he also works at the clinic for the seamen of ships docking a Haifa port.

Dr. Maxim Schoenfeld, born in Haifa, a graduate of the Reali School, a graduate of a medical school in Switzerland, a doctor in the Northern Command. He was leaving for the United States for a period of advanced study in space medicine, so as to be qualified to teach this subject at the Haifa Medical School.

Dr. Yaakov Nahmias, a native-born Israeli, a graduate of the Reali School, scion of an eminent rabbinical family in Lebanon, formerly a doctor at the Air Force Technical School.

Dr. Regina Schwarzberg, born in Paraguay, a graduate of a medical school in Asunción, an immigrant to Israel in 1970.

Dr. Emil Khouri, born in the Arab village of Thouraan outside Nazareth, scion of a famous Greek Catholic family, a graduate of the Jerusalem Medical School.

Dr. Jackie Horner, native of South Africa who graduated in Capetown, a member of Kibbutz Dahlia, married to a daughter of the kibbutz. He also works as a doctor in the Druze village of Daliyat-Al-Carmel.

Dr. Zeev Kanupov, native of the USSR, a graduate of the Leningrad Medical School, a specialist in the treatment of children with pulmonary diseases, an immigrant to Israel in 1971.

Dr. Juan Rivera, a native of Argentina, a student at the Buenos Aires Medical School, an immigrant to Israel in 1971.

Dr. Tristan Trudart, a native of Chile, a graduate of the Santiago Medical School, a product of a Zionist home who studied Hebrew in his youth, an immigrant to Israel in 1971.

TANIA'S AUNTS, SUMMER 1970

When we served at the Israeli Embassy in the Soviet Union about a decade ago, we did not get to see the aunts of my wife, Tania. They lived in Kovna, which was completely barred to foreigners, including diplomats. We did not want to get them into trouble and bring them under suspicion by meeting them anywhere else.

Now they had come to Israel. Fania, an old lady, supported

Stasia, who tottered on her wooden legs down the ramp of the El Al plane that brought them from Vienna to Lod.

Fania, née Levinson, had been married to Chaim, of the Zvi family, brother of Moshe, Tania's father. Chaim was a qualified pharmacist, and their clean and polished pharmacy in Kovna, former capital of Lithuania, was known as the "green pharmacy." They had an only daughter, Leah'le, a sweet, laughing, black-eyed girl.

Stasia, Fania's younger sister, was the neighborhood beauty: very white-skinned, slim, light-footed. She attended the Russian gymnasium in Kovna, and her spoken Russian was as musical as the bells of the troika. All this was before the flood—in 1939, before the ax descended.

Chaim Zvi the pharmacist was killed by the Gestapo in one of the first actions. A short while later three-year-old Leah'le was taken away and sent to die with thousands more Jewish children. Widowed and bereaved, Fania, together with Stasia, drained their cups of affliction to the dregs in the ghettos and the camps. The Germans used to set their Alsatians on Stasia, to tear her white arms. In the cruel winter of 1944 she tried to escape from the camp to the lines of the advancing Russians. Her strength gave out and she lay half frozen in the icy fields. The Red army soldiers who found her transferred her to a field clinic, where both her legs were amputated.

After the war Fania and Stasia met in Kovna, and clung to one another again. No one else remained to them in God's world. Fania worked as a librarian in the municipal library, while Stasia received a welfare allowance.

In the course of time they learned that Tania, a remnant of the Zvi family had been saved from the holocaust and had arrived in Israel, and that a few other living coals snatched from the fire—also relatives—had managed to reach Israel.

They began to dream of immigrating to Israel. For years Fania dragged her sick legs and Stasia her artificial limbs from one office to another. Finally they arrived. They live in a little flat in the suburbs, trying to learn Hebrew from *Elef Milim,* a popular Hebrew grammar. Stasia had the greater success in her studies, because the older Fania undertook to make the rounds of the shops, the absorption offices, the Jewish Agency, and the Welfare Ministry. Peering through rose-tinted spectacles they now see Israel as a lovely land: "What good neighbors! . . . Such kind shopkeepers! . . . What a wonderful climate! . . ."

Fania has grown old and is not as strong as she was. Stasia now moves more nimbly. After preliminary tests the doctors put her in the Orthopedic Department, where they changed the old-fashioned, unwieldly, heavy artificial limbs that had warped and were causing her pain. The doctor, the young sabra who cared for her with love and devotion, told her with a doctor's special brand of mischievous humor, "Stasia, we shall fix you some lovely, graceful legs—the legs of a hart. . . ."